VOLCANOES

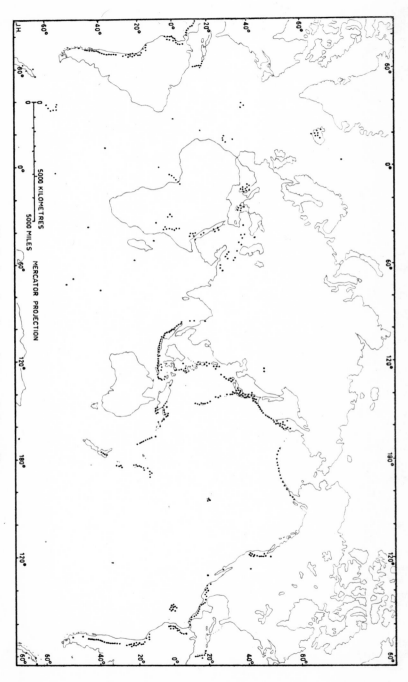

Distribution of active volcanoes of the world

An Introduction to Systematic Geomorphology

VOLUME SIX

VOLCANOES

CLIFF OLLIER

THE MIT PRESS

Cambridge, Massachusetts and London, England

SBN 262 15011 5 (Hard Cover)
Library of Congress Catalog Card no. 79-103009

Printed in Australia

INTRODUCTION TO THE SERIES

This series is conceived as a systematic geomorphology at university level. It will have a role also in high school education and it is hoped the books will appeal as well to many in the community at large who find an interest in the why and where of the natural scenery around them.

The point of view adopted by the authors is that the central themes of geomorphology are the characterisation, origin, and evolution of landforms. The study of processes that make landscapes is properly a part of geomorphology, but within the present framework process will be dealt with only in so far as it elucidates the nature and history of the landforms under discussion. Certain other fields such as submarine geomorphology and a survey of general principles and methods are also not covered in the volumes as yet planned. Some knowledge of the elements of geology is presumed.

Four volumes will approach landforms as parts of systems in which the interacting processes are almost completely motored by solar energy. In humid climates (Volume One) rivers dominate the systems. Fluvial action, operating differently in some ways, is largely responsible for the landscapes of deserts and savanas also (Volume Two), though winds can become preponderant in some deserts. In cold climates, snow, glacier ice, and ground ice come to the fore in morphogenesis (Volume Three). On coasts (Volume Four), waves, currents, and wind are the prime agents in the complex of processes fashioning the edge of the land.

Three further volumes will consider the parts played passively by the attributes of the earth's crust and actively by processes deriving energy from its interior. Under structural landforms (Volume Five), features immediately consequent on earth movements and those resulting from tectonic and lithologic guidance of denudation are considered. Landforms directly the product of volcanic activity and those created by erosion working on volcanic materials are sufficiently distinctive to warrant separate treatment

(Volume Six). Though karst is undoubtedly delimited lithologically, it is fashioned by a special combination of processes centred on solution so that the seventh volume partakes also of the character of the first group of volumes.

J. N. Jennings
General Editor

PREFACE

This book gives an account of volcanoes, their activity, and especially their landforms. It is written for high school and university students, and general readers interested in volcanoes and scenery.

Cotton's book of 1944 is the only previous book concerned mainly with volcanoes as landforms, and a very small proportion of the published articles on volcanoes deal with geomorphology. For this reason I have had to fall back on my own experience of Australian examples for many illustrations of volcanic geomorphology. However, it has been necessary to find examples from all over the world to illustrate the diversity of volcanoes so that the Australian bias is not too great, and I hope that the new examples will provide an interesting change for those readers familiar with the often-described classical volcanoes.

Volcanic terminology is not as precise as might be hoped. I have tried to use terms and definitions in the way I believe they are commonly used by geologists and geomorphologists. Definitions may be found by using the index, and for some terms varying usage is discussed, but this book is not meant to be authoritative on terminology. For more advanced work the standard glossaries of geological terms (listed in the bibliography) may be consulted.

The metric system is used throughout the book, and this has necessitated conversion of a wide range of units—fathoms, chains, cubic miles, knots, miles per hour, cubic yards per second, acres, and many others. Many of the figures given will therefore be approximations, but I hope that what may be lost in accuracy will be gained in ease of comprehension.

The chapters in this book are all interrelated, but it is not necessary to read them in sequence. Catalogues and lists are necessary in any textbook but they do not make entertaining reading, so most of Chapter I and parts of several other chapters may be read through quickly and used mainly for reference.

I am most grateful to the many people who have helped in the production of this book. Professor G. Imbo, Dr P. Gasperini, and Dr A. Rapallo showed me many Italian volcanoes. Professor M. Schwarzbach and Dr H. Noll introduced me to the Eifel region of Germany. Messrs E. F. Lloyd, M. J. Selby, J. Healy, and B. N. Thompson provided valuable information on New Zealand. On New Guinea volcanoes I have had the help of Dr D. H. Blake, Dr M. J. F. Brown, Dr G. D'Addario, Mr W. Manser, Mr B. P. Ruxton, and Dr G. A. M. Taylor. In East Africa I visited many volcanoes in company with Mr J. F. Harrop. These and many other people helped by joining in fieldwork, by discussion, by providing examples, photographs, or figures, or in the donkey work of writing.

I would like to thank Mr J. N. Jennings, general editor of this series, for his always helpful criticisms of the manuscript and his assistance in producing the book, and Mr John Heyward who drafted the maps and diagrams.

C.O.

Port Moresby
January 1969

CONTENTS

FIGURES

PLATES

I

VOLCANIC ROCKS

Volcanoes differ from other landforms because they are built up of liquid ejected from deep below the earth's crust which cools to form new rock. In this book we shall be concerned mainly with the landforms produced by volcanoes and their subsequent erosion, but we shall see time after time that the landforms are controlled to a large extent by the kind of volcanic rock involved. The correlation between rock type and landform is indeed so great that it is impossible to understand volcanic physiography without some knowledge of volcanic rocks, and so this chapter presents a simple outline of volcanic petrology and introduces the rock terms used later in the book.

Igneous rocks are those that have cooled from a molten state, and the ones produced by volcanoes are often referred to loosely as 'volcanics'. The molten parent material is called magma which becomes lava when it erupts at the earth's surface. Magma and lava are not quite synonymous because gases (the volatile constituents) dissolved in the magma tend to be lost from the lava, and Bordet (1965) has defined magma as volcanic material before separation into solid, liquid, and gas phases. The term lava is also applied to the rock formed when liquid lava cools.

Magmas (and lavas) are of variable chemical composition, the most important variation being in the amount of silica present. Magmas with 66 per cent or more are called acid, and give rise to acid lavas and acid rocks. Intermediate rocks have 66-52 per cent silica. Rocks with 52-45 per cent silica are called basic rocks. Ultrabasic rocks have less than 45 per cent silica.

When a magma cools it crystallises and a number of different minerals are formed.

Quartz, a mineral made of silicon dioxide, is commonly present in acid and some intermediate rocks. The total amount of silica in

1

a rock is not necessarily reflected in the amount of quartz present, and rocks with quartz contents as different as 0 and 35 per cent may have the same total amount of silica.

The feldspars, which are complex alumino-silicates, are an important mineral group. The *plagioclase* feldspars are a continuous series of minerals varying in composition between two end members —*albite*, the sodium feldspar and *anorthite*, the calcium feldspar. The variation is shown in the table below.

Percentage of albite

100%	90%	70%	50%	30%	10%	0%
Albite	Oligoclase	Andesine	Labradorite	Bytownite	Anorthite	

| 0% | 10% | 30% | 50% | 70% | 90% | 100% |

Percentage of anorthite

Oligoclase and *andesine* are common in intermediate lavas, *labradorite* is common in basalts. Potassium-rich feldspars include *orthoclase* and *microcline*. A variety of orthoclase called sanidine is the dominant potash feldspar in volcanic rocks.

Corresponding to the feldspars, but with less silica in the mineral structure, are the *feldspathoids*. These are not found in acid rocks. *Nepheline* is the sodium feldspathoid, and *leucite* is the potassium one.

The *mica* group of minerals are also alumino-silicates. The two main minerals in the mica group are *muscovite* which is potassium rich, and *biotite* which contains magnesium and iron as well as potassium in its crystal structure.

The *ferromagnesian* minerals are rich in iron and magnesium and include *biotite, pyroxenes, amphiboles,* and *olivine. Augite* is the commonest pyroxene and *enstatite* and *hypersthene* are fairly common. *Hornblende* is the commonest amphibole. *Olivine* has less silica than pyroxenes or amphiboles, and only occurs in basic and ultrabasic rocks. The opaque minerals *magnetite* (Fe_3O_4) and *ilmenite* ($FeTiO_3$) occur in small quantities in volcanic rocks. Figure 1 shows the proportions of minerals in common igneous rocks.

1 (Top) Eruption in Hale-
maumau, Hawaii, 1967; a
lava lake. There were 12
fountains that sent lava
spurting to heights of
80 m (Hawaii Visitors
Bureau).

2 (Left) Strombolian erup-
tion, Ngauruhoe, New
Zealand, 1954 (D. R.
Gregg)

3 Vesuvian eruption of Mt Mayon, Luzon, Philippines, in April 1968.
Mayon, one of the world's most perfect cones, rises to a height of
2421 m above a nearly level plain, but is dwarfed by the huge
eruption cloud. Note also the nuées on the left flank. (Courtesy
of the U.S. Air Force and the Smithsonian Institution Center for
Short-Lived Phenomena.)

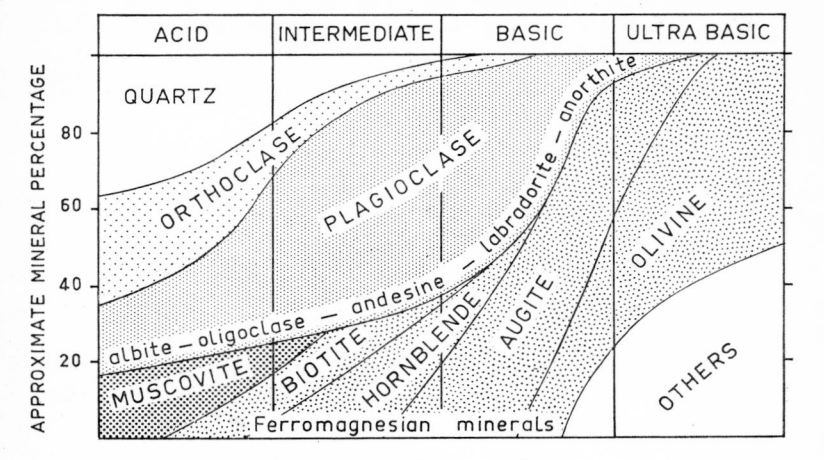

1 Mineral content of common volcanic rocks

If magma is chilled very rapidly there may be no time for crystallisation of minerals, and a glass is formed. With slightly slower crystallisation a few minerals will form in a glassy matrix. The next stage of slower cooling gives rise to fine-grained igneous rock (grains less than 1 mm). Slow cooling, especially when magma is not erupted but cools deep in the earth, gives rise to medium-grained rocks (grains 1 mm to 5 mm), and very slow cooling, deep in a magma chamber, gives rise to coarse-grained rocks (grains over 5 mm). Large crystals set in a fine matrix are called phenocrysts, and rocks with many phenocrysts are said to be porphyritic.

The mineral composition and grain size provide the basis for a simple classification of igneous rocks which is shown diagrammatically in the table below.

	ACID	INTERMEDIATE	BASIC	ULTRABASIC
Coarse-grained	Granite Granodiorite	Syenite Diorite	Gabbro	Peridotite
Medium-grained	Microgranite	Porphyry	Dolerite	Monchiquite
Fine-grained	Rhyolite Dacite	Trachyte Andesite	Basalt	Limburgite
Glass	Obsidian Pitchstone Pumice	Pitchstone	Tachylite	

With lavas we are mainly concerned with fine-grained rock, of which basalt and andesite are of major importance. Most 'rhyolite' is in fact ignimbritic, and not simply derived by cooling of liquid lava, as will be explained in Chapter VII.

Amongst the intermediate rocks, the feldspar type is used as the basis for distinguishing different varieties. Andesite and diorite have potash feldspar making up less than one-third of the total feldspar content. In trachytes and syenites potash feldspar makes up over two-thirds of the total feldspar content. Between these two groups, but not shown on the diagram, are trachyandesites and monzonites.

Basalt may be divided into several varieties including olivine basalt, which contains olivine and is common in oceanic volcanoes such as those of Hawaii, and tholeiitic basalt, which generally has little or no olivine and may even have quartz in the groundmass. The Deccan basalts of India and the basalts of the Snake River volcanic province, U.S.A., are tholeiitic. Deep submarine eruptions often produce a kind of basalt rich in sodium known as spilite. This often takes the form of pillow lava and is frequently associated with serpentinite and chert.

Dolerite (called diabase in American literature) is the commonest intrusive igneous rock associated with volcanoes. Coarse-grained rocks are of little direct importance in vulcanology, being formed deep below the earth's surface, but they are of course related to eruptive igneous rocks.

The rock types discussed so far are the fairly common ones, but there are many other, rarer types. One that may be mentioned is carbonatite, an igneous rock composed mainly of carbonate minerals and containing little or no silica. Carbonatites are mostly found in intrusive igneous rocks associated with ring complexes, but may be erupted as pyroclastics or as lavas (Dawson, 1964). In 1960 Oldoinyo Lengai, Tanzania, erupted a soda-rich carbonatite lava, virtually free from silica, which simulated in detail the features of normal lava flows, and took both pahoehoe and aa forms (Dawson, 1962).

Violent explosions may so break up erupting lava that it comes to rest as fragmental rocks rather than as more or less massive lava. Such fragmental rocks include volcanic ash, scoria, pumice, pala-gonite (an altered basaltic ash), and others, which are collectively known as pyroclastic rocks, or simply as pyroclastics. These are described further in Chapters VI and VII.

FORMATION OF IGNEOUS ROCK VARIETIES

Differentiation

There are a number of mechanisms by which an originally uniform magma may be differentiated into fractions having different composition. The simplest mechanism is gravity separation of heavy minerals. Suppose a basalt magma starts to crystallise. The first mineral grains to crystallise will be olivine, and as these mineral grains are denser than the melt they will sink, producing an olivine-enriched magma at the base of the magma chamber and a more acid, olivine-depleted magma at the top. The material at the top of the chamber is virtually a fresh non-crystalline magma of different composition from the original, and will itself then continue to crystallise. Under favourable circumstances a variety of differentiates may be erupted at the surface from a single magma chamber giving rise to a series of related (comagmatic) rocks. The area in which such related rocks occur is called a petrographic province.

Assimilation

Magma reacts with the rocks that make up the wall and roof of the magma chamber. The rocks may be merely altered by heat (thermal metamorphism), subjected to chemical alteration, or even totally dissolved and assimilated by the magma. Assimilation of sandstone, for example, adds silica to the magma, making it more acid; feldspathoids would be converted to feldspars, olivine to pyroxene. Assimilation of dolomite or limestone by a trachytic magma could produce a leucite-bearing magma. This has been suggested as a possible origin of the leucitic rocks of the Mediterranean.

Anatexis

Complete melting of formerly solid rocks of the earth's crust to form a new magma is called anatexis. Anatexis would normally produce acid magmas.

Volcanic rock suites

Although neighbouring volcanoes may produce different lavas it has become clear that many areas are characterised by assemblages of related rocks known collectively as suites. Suites are characteristic of petrographic provinces in which certain rocks are frequently associated, and others are absent.

There are three main suites:

1. Calc-alkaline suite. These rocks are relatively rich in calcium, and are also relatively acid rocks. Rhyolites and andesites are included in this suite. The calc-alkaline suite is found in the volcanoes of island arcs and the Pacific borders of North and South America. Since these areas are associated with mountain building, this suite is sometimes called the 'orogenic' suite. In the older geographical terminology this was called the 'Pacific Suite'.

2. Alkaline suite. These are basic rocks, relatively rich in alkalis (especially sodium) ranging from nepheline-bearing rocks to olivine-basalt. In the geographical terminology they are also known as rocks of the 'Atlantic Suite', an unhelpful term since they are the dominant rocks of the central Pacific, as well as occurring in the Atlantic. This suite is also known as the 'non-orogenic' suite.

3. Potassic suite. These are basic to intermediate rocks, relatively rich in alkalis (especially potassium), ranging from leucite-bearing rocks to olivine basalt. This suite is also known as the 'Mediterranean Suite', and indeed such rocks are characteristic of the Mediterranean volcanoes.

To indulge in great over-simplification, we can regard the alkaline suite as derived by differentiation of primary basalt magma (sima); the potassic suite as derived by assimilation of limestones, marls, and other sedimentary rocks by differentiates of primary basalt magma; and the calc-alkaline suite as being formed by the melting of crustal rocks to form a magma (anatexis), followed by assimilation and differentiation.

This chapter gives only an elementary and incomplete account of volcanic rocks. For a fuller and more accurate account of rocks and their classification reference should be made to standard books on petrology, such as that by Williams, Turner, and Gilbert (1954).

II

VOLCANIC ERUPTIONS

Volcanic eruptions may be classified in many ways, based on their activity, their relationships through time, their spatial relationships, or their violence.

ACTIVE, EXTINCT AND DORMANT VOLCANOES

These categories divide volcanoes into one of the most familiar classifications, and one that is of importance to people living in the vicinity of a volcano. Active volcanoes can be easily recognised, but distinction between dormant and extinct is difficult and sometimes dangerous. Vesuvius had long been thought extinct, until the great eruption of A.D. 79 proved it had been only dormant. Many volcanoes of the world are presumed to be extinct, with varying degrees of risk. The younger the volcano, the more risky it is to pronounce it extinct. There are no active volcanoes in Australia, though the youngest known volcano, Mt Gambier in South Australia, apparently erupted only 1400 years ago (Blackburn, 1966).

Continuity of eruption

Tsuya and Morimoto (1963) have classified the active volcanoes of Japan into two main groups:

(a) Those that erupt every few years, usually from a persistently open crater.

(b) Dormant ones that erupt once in several scores of years or less frequently. These tend to have closed craters and to erupt from new craters that are more or less unrelated to earlier craters.

Such a classification could be extended to other areas.

7

Volcanoes in almost permanent eruption include Stromboli, continuous since Homer's day; Masaya and Amatitlon in Nicaragua; Sangay in Ecuador; and Kilauea in Hawaii. Izalco in El Salvador has been almost continuous since it first appeared in 1770, and was long known as 'The Lighthouse of the Pacific', but eruption ceased in 1957.

CENTRAL ERUPTION, FISSURE ERUPTION, AND AREAL ERUPTION

Volcanic eruptions may be divided into those that issue from a central pipe or vent, known as central eruptions; those that issue from cracks or fissures, called fissure eruptions; and eruptions scattered over wide areas, areal eruptions. This classification can be difficult to apply at times, for an eruption may start along a fissure but later erupt from a number of separate centres. A lot of centres all in line are clearly associated with a fissure at deeper levels. On the other hand a large central type volcano may erupt many numerous parasitic centres along a fissure on its flank, as commonly happens on Mt Etna, Italy. Another good example comes from Chile. Two days after the great earthquake of May 1960, a lateral fissure eruption occurred on the northwest flank of Puyehue volcano. After initial pumice ejection, dacitic lava poured from twenty-eight craters aligned along a new fissure 14 km long. There was no activity in the central crater.

Thus the distinction between central and fissure eruption depends partly on the scale and stage which interest the observer, but nevertheless the distinction has some merit. Some very high volcanoes such as Cotopaxi in Ecuador (about 3000 m above its base) and Muhavura, Uganda (2500 m above base) appear to have erupted entirely from one central crater, while many Icelandic volcanoes obviously erupted from fissures. The Laki (Iceland) eruption of 1783 came from a fissure about 32 km long; Hekla, the best known Iceland volcano, is clearly built over a fissure for it is a ridge rather than a cone, and has a series of craters along its crest. Fissure eruptions are most often associated with basalt.

Areal volcanism (also known as polyorifice volcanism) is characterised by the absence of any tendency for eruption centres to be localised at definite points for any length of time (Karapetian, 1964). The individual volcanic structures tend to be of small size, seldom attaining a height over 450 m. Scoria and lava cones, domes and maars are the dominant volcanic types, and strato-volcanoes are absent or very rare. The volcanic regions of Auvergne, Armenia, Mexico, and Victoria are examples of areal volcanic fields. Individual volcanoes are short-lived, ranging from the forty-five days from initiation to extinction of Muhobili, Congo, to perhaps twelve years. The spatial distribution of the volcanoes is irregular in general, but there may be some clustering and occasional linear groups. The petrographic composition within an areal field remains fairly constant.

Karapetian (1964) believes that areal fields gravitate towards tectonic trenches or to zones of deep faults, which allow lava to penetrate into intermediate chambers. This is in contrast to polygenic central or fissure volcanoes, which stand directly on deep faults.

CLASSIFICATION BY THE TYPE OF PRODUCT

A classification of volcanic activity based on the type of products has been offered by Gèze (1964). The basic subdivision is based on the proportions of the gas, liquid, and solid components, which can be represented on a triangular diagram as shown in Fig. 2. The four basic triangles represent the domains of four basic kinds of volcanic activity, and each triangle is subdivided into smaller triangles by Gèze. The course of volcanic activity that changes through time can be plotted on this sort of triangular diagram.

VIOLENCE OF VOLCANIC ERUPTIONS

Volcanic activity is commonly classified by its violence, which in turn is usually closely related to rock type, the course of eruptive activity and the resulting landforms. In general we may distinguish between lava eruptions, generally associated with basic and intermediate magmas, and pumice eruptions, usually associated with acid magmas.

The percentage of the fragmentary material in the total volcanic material produced can be used as a measure of explosiveness, and if calculated for a volcanic area can be used as an explosion index (E), useful for comparing one volcanic region with others. Some examples are shown in the table on p. 11; data are from

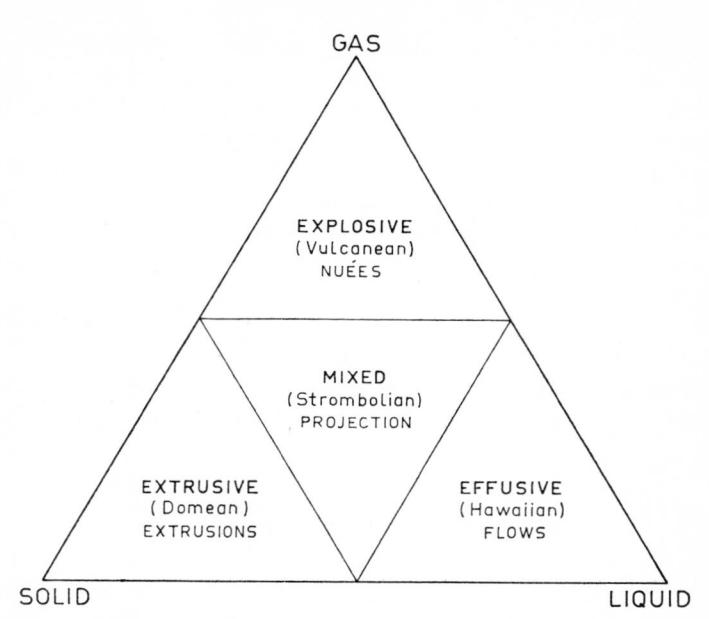

2 *Classification of eruptions by Gèze. The proportions of gas, liquid, and solids ejected correlates with type of eruption.*

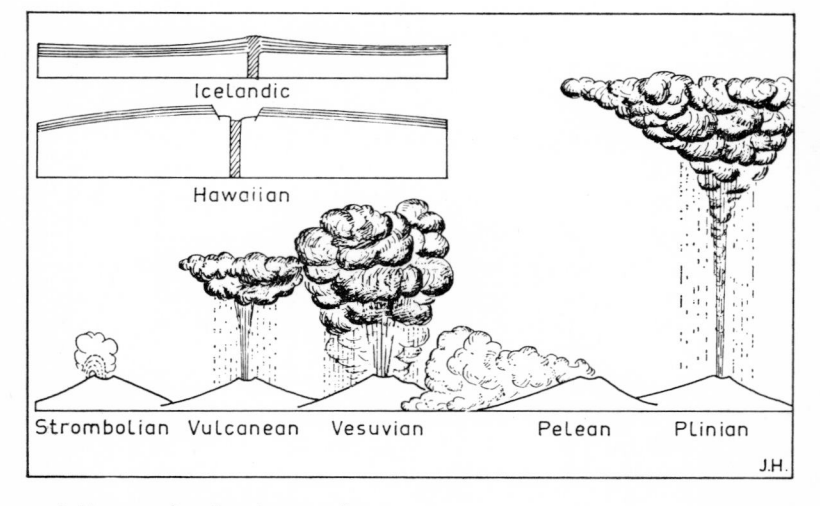

3 *Types of volcanic eruption*

Rittmann (1962) except the Victorian figure from Ollier and Joyce (1964).

Area	Approximate E (%)
Indonesian island arc	99
Solomon Islands—New Hebrides	95
New Guinea—New Britain	90
Southern Italy	41
Iceland	39
Central Pacific Ocean	3
Volcanic plains of Victoria	1

Degrees of eruptive violence are commonly named after type volcanoes or regions that exemplify particular kinds of activity. Some of these types are listed below, and shown diagrammatically in Fig. 3.

LAVA ERUPTIONS

Icelandic

In this type of activity fissure eruption is dominant and persistent. Vast floods of basaltic lava are quietly erupted, the lava flowing almost as easily as water and building wide horizontal lava plains. At the end of eruption a string of small cones may be built along the fissure.

Repeated Icelandic eruptions on a grand scale give rise to the great basalt plateaus and provinces such as the Columbia Plateau, the Snake River Basalts, and the Deccan. The only really vast outpouring in historic times is that of Laki, Iceland, in 1783.

Hawaiian

Basaltic magma is erupted as in the Icelandic type, but central activity is more pronounced. Fire fountains of lava spray at times and build small scoria mounds, but pyroclastics are very much subordinate to lava flows (Pl. 1).

Eruption often starts along fissures, making a 'curtain of fire' of frothing lava that may be several kilometres long, but in a matter of hours or days most of the fissure seals up and eruption continues through separate points. Small cones built in this way are of minor importance, and it is the piling up of many lava flows that builds up most of the Hawaiian type of volcanic landform.

Strombolian (*from Stromboli, Italy*)

This is a more explosive type of eruption than the Hawaiian (Pl. 2) and a higher proportion of fragmental or pyroclastic rocks is produced though the magma is still basaltic. Activity may be rhythmic or continuous, and fragments of incandescent lava that cool into scoria are thrown out of the crater. The type volcano, Stromboli, has a nearly continuous succession of minor eruptions a few minutes or a few hours apart. Occasionally lava may be poured from the crater, so volcanic deposits consist of alternating lava and pyroclastics. Strombolian eruption is commonly marked by a white cloud of steam emitted from the crater.

PYROCLASTIC ERUPTIONS

Vulcanian (*from Vulcano, Italy*)

Vulcanian eruption occurs where there are relatively viscous lavas which solidify rapidly. Explosions are violent and wreck earlier volcanic structures. A lot of volcanic ash is produced, and Vulcanian eruption is characterised by dark 'cauliflower' clouds. Many volcanic eruptions start in this way when a blocked vent has to be cleared. If no lava is discharged during an eruption and the fragmental ejecta are made up entirely of old rock fragments, the activity is said to be of Ultra-Vulcanian type. Activity of similar appearance at the end of a complex eruption may be termed Pseudo-Vulcanian. The pino (pine tree) is the name sometimes given to the black mushroom cloud produced by Vulcanian eruption.

Vesuvian (*from Vesuvius, Italy*)

This is a more violent type of Vulcanian or Strombolian eruption, in which a cloud of ash is thrown to a great height and scatters ash over a wide area (Pl. 3). The great cloud is incandescent and luminous at night.

Plinian

Even more extreme in violence than the Vesuvian eruption is the Plinian, which produces a cloud several kilometres high. It is named after the scholar Pliny who died while investigating the Plinian eruption of Vesuvius in A.D. 79. The amount of ash produced is not great by mountain-building standards, but sufficient to bury a town such as Pompeii.

Pliny described two characteristic features of the eruptive type named after him, namely the 'flashes of fire as vivid as lightning, and darkness more profound than night'. He also described 'a thick dark vapour just behind us [which] rolled along the ground like a torrent and followed us'. This rather suggests the base surge described later in this chapter.

Pelean (*from Mont Pelée, Martinique*)

This is a general name for very violent eruptions and explosion of very viscous magma. Large quantities of pumice are erupted very rapidly. The magma is intermediate to acidic, and nuées ardentes (glowing clouds of ash, see Chapter VII) are characteristic (Pl. 5). Pelean eruptions may be subdivided into a number of types, including the following:

(a) Pelean (*sensu stricto*). Ash clouds erupt laterally.

(b) St Vincent (or La Soufrière). Vertically directed ash clouds rather than the lateral ones of Pelée.

(c) Merapi. Ash clouds are blown laterally from the flanks of a cumulo-dome.

(d) Katmai. Eruption of pumice from fissures. (Actually it is not certain that the Katmai eruption, or any other, emitted pumice from fissures.)

To express the dimensions of the Katmai eruption of 1912, Griggs (1921) worked out what the effects would have been if it had taken place in New York instead of remote Alaska. New York itself would have been totally devastated, Philadelphia would have received one foot of ash, and ash would have reached Washington and Buffalo. The explosion would have been heard in St Louis and Atlanta, and fumes would have reached Denver and Jamaica. Approximating these dimensions to Australia, an eruption in Canberra would have deposited ash in Melbourne and Sydney, and the sound and fumes may have reached New Zealand.

Krakatoan (*from Krakatoa, Indonesia*)

The most violent volcanic eruption in recent times was that of Krakatoa in 1883.

Krakatoa was an island off Java. On 20 May 1883, noises of explosions were produced that could be heard 150 km away. On 26 August a Vesuvian stage set in, and eruption climaxed with four colossal 'Krakatoan' explosions on 27 August which were heard over about 7 per cent of the earth's surface, and at Rodriguez Island, 4750 km distant, the sound was reported as like the distant roar of heavy guns. A wave 17 m high on the open sea was set up, and 36,000 people were killed. The island was destroyed.

The eruption of Santorini near Crete about 1400 B.C. appears to have been of the same type as Krakatoa and even more violent. It seems to have been responsible for the disappearance of the Minoan civilisation, and it is possible that the disappearance of the island gave rise to the legend of Atlantis (Ninkovich and Heezen, 1965).

SPECIAL FEATURES OF ERUPTIONS

Phreatic and gas-blast explosions

The adjective 'phreatic' refers to groundwater of surface origin in the zone of saturation. 'Phreatic explosion' usually refers to violent explosion caused when ascending magma meets groundwater and rapidly produces great quantities of steam. The idea is frequently invoked to account for maars (Chapter IV) which in many areas are found in those places with abundant groundwater (near sea level, on river gravels, etc.) and thus favourable for phreatic eruption, while on nearby sites with little or no groundwater, eruptions are quietly effusive or make simple scoria cones. Stearns and Macdonald (1946) restrict 'phreatic' eruption to those instances in which the ejecta contain no igneous rock, and use 'phreato-magmatic' for those eruptions with igneous rock included in the ejecta.

Unfortunately the term 'phreatic eruption' has been used for eruptions other than those caused by the meeting of magma and groundwater.

The 1962 eruption of Mt Yaké, Japan, formed a fissure 700 m long from which issued milky, muddy hot water. Morimoto and Ossaka (1964) called this a low temperature phreatic eruption.

Rittmann (1962) explains the Bandaisan eruption of 1888 as being caused by the superheating of groundwater by juvenile gases ascending from depth, and he calls this phreatic eruption.

He also uses the term for another mechanism that produced some diatremes in Egypt. In Oligocene to Miocene times sills were intruded which heated up groundwater in porous sandstone beds beneath a caprock of impervious clay. High pressure steam was produced, which bored its way to the surface where it formed explosion craters. The craters contain no igneous material as the sill was largely solidified and only supplied heat.

These and other eruptions which produced no new lava whatsoever are probably best described as gas-blast explosions.

The base surge

The base surge is not a separate kind of eruption, but is a phenomenon associated with various kinds of vertical explosion (Moore, 1967). A base surge is a ring-shaped basal cloud that sweeps outward as a density flow from the base of a vertical explosion column. The initial velocity is commonly greater than 50 m per second, and it can carry clastic material for many kilometres. Ash, mud, lapilli, and blocks can all be transported. Trees, houses, and other obstacles may be knocked down by the surge, or sandblasted on the side facing the volcano, and the blast side may also be coated by layers of ejecta. The base surge may deposit material beyond the range of ejecta that simply fall through the air. Near the source of the eruption it can erode channels, and can deposit material with dune-bedding. In the 1965 eruption of Taal, Philippines, the base surge obliterated all trees within 1 km and sandblasted objects up to 8 km away. Wood neither burns nor chars, and it is possible that the temperature in a basal surge is less than 100°C.

The base surge has been reported from many recent shallow, submarine, and phreatic eruptions, including Anak Krakatoa, Indonesia, 1928, Myojin Reef, Japan, 1952, Barcena, Mexico, 1952, and Surtsey, Iceland, 1963.

SEQUENCES IN VOLCANIC ERUPTION

Many volcanoes have patterns in their eruption depending on their regularity, periodicity, and sequence.

The simplest type is continued eruption. Stromboli is the finest example, as it has been erupting more or less continuously since ancient times and has exhibited several thousand years of virtually uninterrupted but seldom violent eruption. Izalco in El Salvador was similar to Stromboli for over a hundred years, but in 1957 eruption ceased. It will probably resume when sufficient pressure has built up to reactivate it.

Many scoria cones are built as late stage eruptions on lava plains, but in the Parícutin type, also exemplified by Jorullo (both of these are in Mexico), there is first a building up of a large scoria cone, followed by the emission of large quantities of basalt from the base of the cone. It seems that the lava is too heavy to reach the summit, and finds an easier route near the base of the volcano.

Etna and Vesuvius appear to show typical patterns, described in Chapter XII, with cycles of activity and a typical sequence of events within any given cycle. In Hawaii no cyclic behaviour has yet been proved, but there does appear to be a fairly predictable sequence within any one eruption.

Hekla, Iceland, is another volcano that seems to have a repeated pattern in its eruptions. There have been fourteen eruptions since the settlement of Iceland, the first in 1104 and the latest in 1947. Tephrochronological studies (Thorarinsson, 1967) show that each eruption starts with a Plinian eruption of silica-rich ash, which lasts for only a few hours, and is followed by production of large amounts of basic lava and ash. The silica content of the initial ash is related to the length of the interval between eruptions, during which differentiation occurs.

Volcanoes classified as pumice-producing commonly alternate explosive activity with the production of domes and other bodies of viscous lava, which are often destroyed during the following explosive phases.

In the Central Volcanic Region of the North Island of New Zealand there is possibly a protracted sequence of eruption with pumice first, followed by the extrusion of rhyolite domes. In the Taupo area there are no domes, so it may be that the eruptive cycle is not complete. Possibly an even later event is caldera collapse and extrusion of basalt around the rim.

In contrast to those volcanoes that have a fairly constant, though rhythmically variable, type of eruption, there are some volcanoes that merely show a succession of widely different types of volcanic action.

Usu volcano, Japan, may be taken as an example (Ōba, 1966). Usu formed in early Holocene times on the wall of an older caldera. A strato-volcano was built of basalt, mafic andesite, and scoria. Violent explosion then destroyed the cone, pyroclastic flows occurred, and a crater 1·5 km in diameter was produced. After quiescence for 1500-2000 years, eruption started again, but this time completely different in petrology and style. Dacite plug domes were extruded in almost solid form, with striae along their sides, accompanied by explosive eruptions of pumice and ash. Ōba believes all the lavas could be derived from a tholeiitic parent magma by fractional crystallisation, without any assimilation of wall rock.

Various types of eruption may even occur simultaneously as at the new volcano Surtsey, off southern Iceland, which resulted from repeated submarine and subaerial fissure eruption of basaltic ash and spatter beginning on 14 November 1963. At one stage there were phreatic and Strombolian eruptions from vents within 15 m of each other in the same crater.

LATE STAGE VOLCANIC ACTIVITY

In the dying stages of vulcanicity no lava is produced, but eruption continues with the production of water, gases, and sublimates.

Hot springs usually occur in downfaulted areas, where there are suitable geological conditions for the circulation of ground-water and where heat can be provided by hot volcanic rocks. The water emitted by hot springs is usually of meteoric origin, that is derived from rain, and only a very minor part is likely to be derived from magma. Evidence for this comes from the fact that in many volcanic areas, including New Zealand, the hot springs and geysers are much more active some time after heavy rain (when the ground-water has been recharged) than after a prolonged dry spell.

Geysers are jets of hot water that are periodically spurted into the air (Pl. 6). The name comes from the Great Geysir in the Geysir region of Iceland, which has been inactive, except when artificially stimulated, since 1918. The highest geyser recorded was Waimangu in the Tarawera region of New Zealand in 1901, when the spray reached heights of 500 m. Old Faithful, a geyser in Yellowstone Park, U.S.A., commonly reaches 60 m, and is further notable for its regularity, erupting approximately every 63 minutes. Geyser water usually contains much dissolved silica which is deposited in a mound around the orifice of the geyser as sinter or geyserite. These mounds and terraces can attain the size of distinct landforms.

Not all hot springs produce geysers, and there are many areas where hot water appears in quiet pools. The thermal springs of the world have been catalogued by Waring, Blankenship, and Bentall (1965).

Mud volcanoes are simply dirty hot springs. The mud is sometimes brightly coloured, giving rise to interesting displays like the 'Paint Pots' of U.S.A.

Fumaroles are vents that emit steam or gas, as are solfatara, named after Solfatara near Naples, Italy. There is a tendency to use the term fumarole for high temperature emissions (200-1000°C.) and solfatara for low temperature emissions (below 200°C.).

Mofettes are openings exhaling carbon dioxide and water only. The heavy carbon dioxide tends to collect in hollows or on low ground, where it can be dangerous. Hence the sinister names of two examples, Death Gulch in Arizona, U.S.A., and Death Valley in Java.

THE BIRTH OF NEW VOLCANOES

Most volcanic activity takes place on well-established volcanoes, but the actual first eruptions of completely new volcanoes have occasionally been observed.

Monte Nuovo erupted about 10 km from Naples in 1538. After preliminary tremors a depression appeared from which water issued. Later the ground swelled and a fissure opened, through which incandescent material could be seen. Then rocks, pumice, and mud were thrown high in the air. The most violent activity occurred on the first two days and in eight days the eruption was over. Monte Nuovo is an entirely pyroclastic cone, about 150 m high and rather less than 1 km in diameter.

A new volcano started in Chinyoro, Teneriffe, on 18 November 1909. Observers were only 100 m away when the first eruption threw bushes, rock, and soil 80 m into the air. The eruption went on to erupt more lava than ash, and lasted 10 days.

The most thoroughly observed, documented, and well known of all new volcanoes is Parícutin in Mexico, 320 km west of Mexico City.

In a cornfield there was a small hole that had existed for many years, and an old inhabitant recalled that even fifty years earlier the hole emitted noises and a pleasant warmth. On 5 February 1943 a series of tremors commenced which increased in number and intensity until on 19 February there were about three hundred. At about 4.00 p.m. on the 20th, witnesses noticed a fissure extending through it, at first only half a metre deep. The fissure then started to erupt smoke or fine grey dust, accompanied by a continuous hissing noise and 'sparks'. Nearby trees began to burn. By 5.00 p.m. a thin column of smoke rose from the hole, and a little later a hole

4 Ruapehu, New Zealand, in action. The crater lake has been displaced by a tholoid (N.Z. Geological Survey). Compare with quiescent state in Plate 35.

5 (Top) Nuée ardente, Manam, New Guinea, 8 a.m.,
17 March 1960 (G. A. M.
Taylor)

6 (Left) Waikiti Geyser,
Whakarewarewa n e a r
Rotorua, New Zealand,
with water erupting ap-
proximately 10 m. Sinter
deposits in foreground
(E. F. Lloyd).

at the end of the fissure, only half a metre across at first, emitted red hot stones and smoke. By 8.00 a.m. the next morning a cone about 10 m high had formed, and by midday was 30 to 50 m high. The first lava issued on the second day. At the end of the first week the cone was 140 m high, eruption was increasingly violent, and the noise could be heard 350 km away.

In mid-April lava issued from the southwestern base of the cone, and on 10 June a section of the upper part of the cone collapsed. Lava flowed for a while from the lower part of the break; this was the only time that lava flowed from the crater. All other lava flows came from sources or *bocas* at or near the base. In October a parasitic vent opened at the base of the cone, and grew over a hundred metres within a few weeks. A lava flow then issued from its base, and carried a wide section of the cone with it. This breached cone was eventually buried by a succession of lava flows.

At the end of the first year Parícutin reached 325 m, and growth then became slower. When eruption ceased in 1952 the cone was 410 m above the original cornfield.

III

TYPES OF VOLCANO

In popular imagination volcanoes are always symmetrical cones like Fujiyama, but in reality volcanoes vary widely in shape, size, and composition.

As a first classification we shall consider the common forms of volcano associated with basic lava, acid lava, scoria eruption, mixed eruption, and finally some types of volcano recognised by features other than the type of material erupted.

BASIC LAVA VOLCANOES

Basic lavas are characteristically very fluid, so spread easily and give rise typically to volcanoes of low gradient (Fig. 4).

Lava shields

A succession of wide sheets of volcanic rock, built by repeated outpourings of basaltic lava, can pile up to produce huge 'shields' with gentle slopes (less than 7°) and convex outlines. The Hawaiian islands are the classic example. Mauna Loa, the largest island, rises 10,000 m above its sea-floor base, which is 100 km wide, and projects over 4000 m above the sea. Shields of this size are made up of a number of separate volcanoes; for instance Kilauea and Hualalai are mere flank volcanoes on Mauna Loa. Volcanic masses such as the island of Hawaii, formed by the overlapping of a group of shield volcanoes, may be termed volcanic shield-clusters.

Parasitic cones, flank eruptions, and fissure eruptions are commonly associated with shield volcanoes. 'Shield volcano' is a less exact term that usually refers to a lava shield, but may be used for a large strato-volcano or volcanic complex, such as the Tweed shield volcano of northern New South Wales.

20

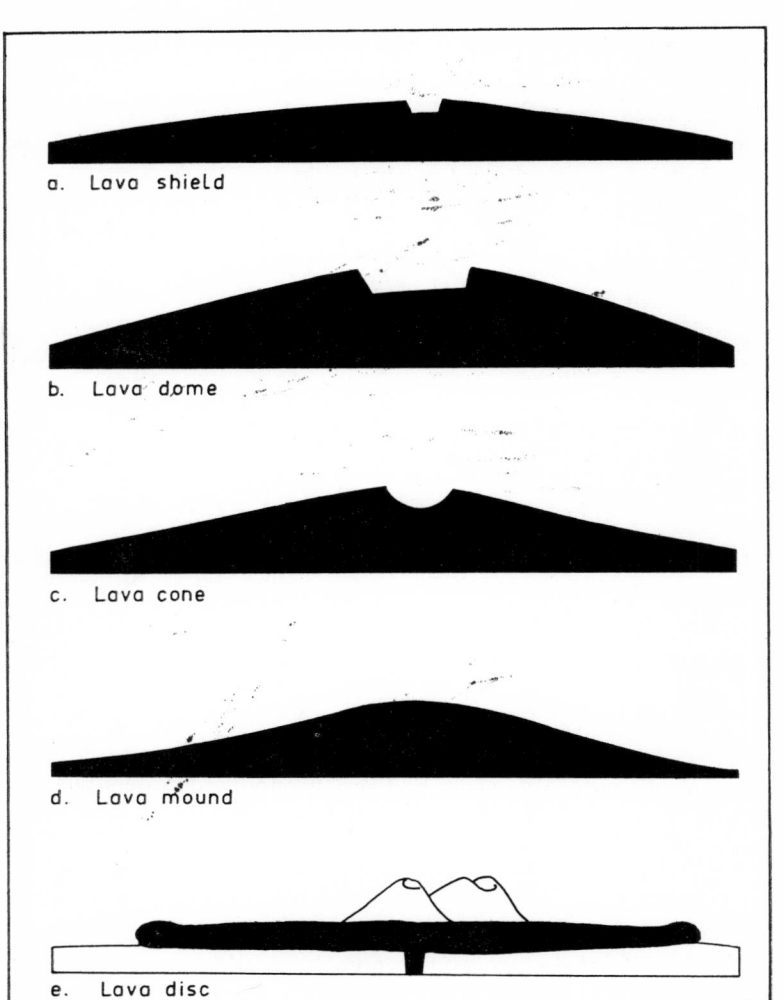

a. Lava shield

b. Lava dome

c. Lava cone

d. Lava mound

e. Lava disc

JH

4 Diagrammatic representation of basaltic volcano types (not to scale)

Lava dome

A smaller-scale volcano that erupts liquid lava may produce a convex dome rather than a shield. Any of the individual peaks on Hawaii, such as Mauna Kea, may be regarded as lava domes. The distinction between size used here is not standard practice and many authors use shield and dome interchangeably.

Lava cones

Central eruption on a still smaller scale may give rise to simple straight-sided cones built of successive lava flows, such as Mt Hamilton, Victoria. These usually have flanks of low angle (7° or less), but some examples are much steeper.

Beerenberg on the Arctic island of Jan Mayen, for example, consists of a broad basalt lava dome some 15-24 km in diameter at sea level, on the crest of which is a lava cone with steep 45° slopes, some 5 km in diameter and 750 m high (Fitch, 1964). In the Victorian volcanic province a final stage of scoria eruption often obliterates lava cones formed earlier. In Iceland a rim of scoria round the crater is characteristic.

The Kolotta Dyngja, a typical Icelandic volcano, rises to a height of 460 m with an average slope of 7°, approaching 8° towards the summit. The volcano has a diameter of 5 km and the crater a diameter of 550 m. A ring of scoria about 15 m high surrounds the crater, and has slopes of up to 30°.

Lava mounds

Some basaltic volcanoes have no sign of a crater, but are gently sloping mounds, such as Mt Cotterill, Victoria. Harveys Knob is a craterless basalt mound near Gayndah, about 290 km northwest of Brisbane (Stevens, 1962).

These extinct volcanoes may owe their shape partly to erosion, although they probably never had very pronounced craters but had lava welling right to the brim before solidification. Such volcanoes, distinguished from cones by their lack of crater, may be termed lava mounds by analogy with scoria mounds.

Lava disc

In Victoria there are a few anomalous volcanoes which have been described as lava discs (Ollier, 1967a). They are made of basalt, and display jointing perpendicular to the lava skin on both the upper surface and the sides. The smallest one, Lawaluk, has the form of a steep-edged, flat-topped disc of basalt. Mondilibi is probably of the same type, and the main lava sheet within the ring barrier of Mt Porndon appears to be a similar feature though larger (3 km in diameter). These hills appear to be made by eruption of single flows that develop a tough skin and spread out from the centre without breaking the skin, in the manner of a water-filled balloon collapsing into a disc.

ACID LAVA VOLCANOES

Acid igneous rocks are generally very viscous, and if they do not explode their lack of flow gives rise to a number of distinctive landforms (Fig. 5).

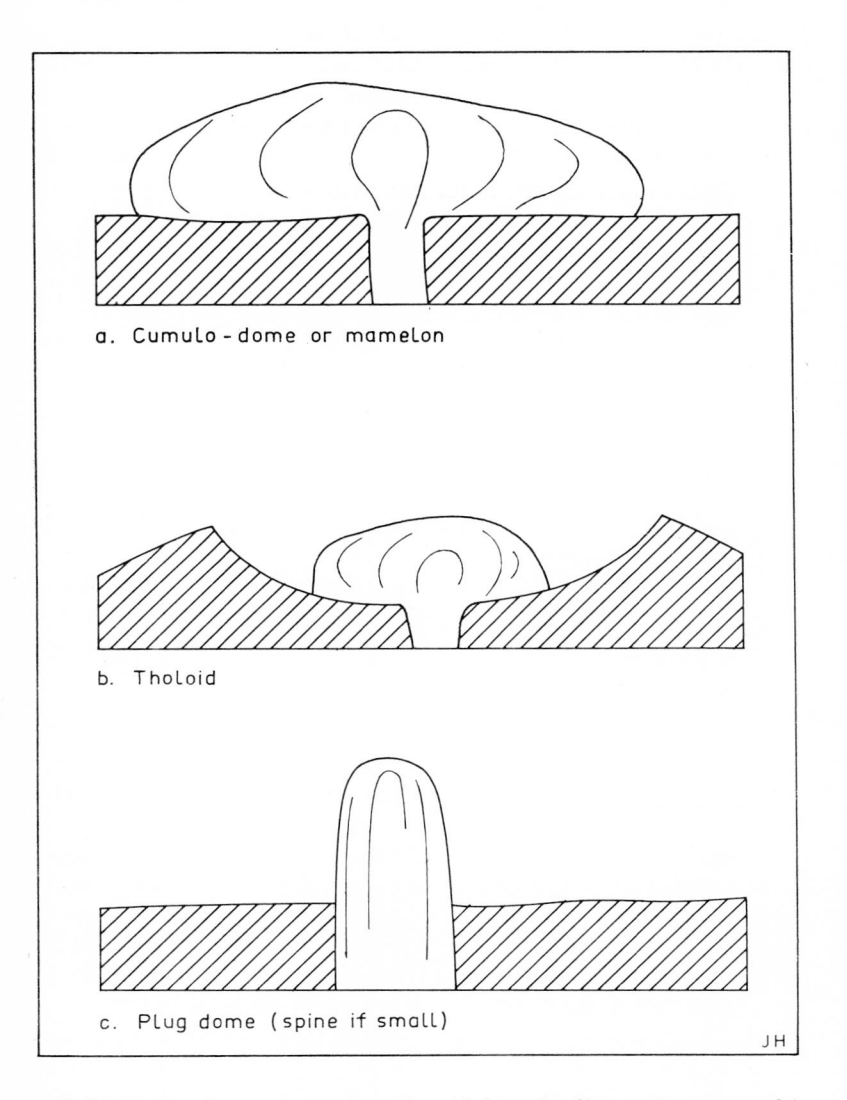

a. Cumulo-dome or mamelon

b. Tholoid

c. Plug dome (spine if small)

JH

5 Diagrammatic representation of acid lava landforms (not to scale)

Cumulo-domes

When viscous lava is extruded, it sags and spreads into convex dome-like bodies called cumulo-domes. These may be almost independent, or may be associated with and partly intrusive into previously deposited pyroclastics.

The main part of Lassen Peak, California, is a large-scale example, rising 800 m above pyroclastics and having a diameter of 2·5 km. In the Mullaley district of New South Wales there are two simple cumulo-volcanoes with the form of domes and three similar structures that are breached by trachyte (Wilshire and Standard, 1963). Mt Macedon, Hanging Rock, and Brocks Monument, Victoria, are examples of fairly small cumulo-domes.

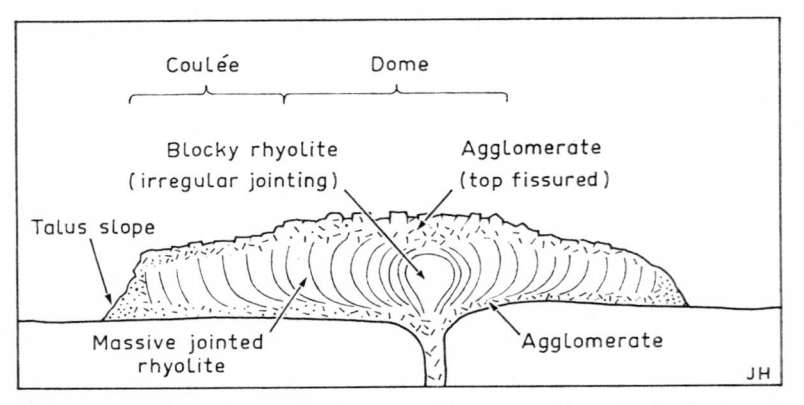

6 Cross-section of cumulo-dome at Tarawera, New Zealand

In the Central Volcanic Region of the North Island of New Zealand there are many rhyolite domes, akin to cumulo-domes, but with more mobile flows or coulées on their flanks (Pl. 7). These appear to erupt in the late stage of a volcanic cycle after vast ignimbrite flows and caldera formation.

Sometimes several cumulo-domes may coalesce. Tauhara volcano, New Zealand, is a multiple volcano of late Pleistocene age consisting of five coalescing dacite cumulo-domes. Internal flow structures suggest that each dome was formed from lava continuously extruded, but each had a separate vent (Lewis, 1968).

The Tarawera Rift explosion of 1886 exposed excellent sections through a number of domes, enabling a better interpretation of internal structure than is usually possible. There is well-developed circular jointing at the centre of domes, becoming vertical towards the edge and in the coulées. The tops of both domes and coulées are very irregular due to fissuring. These features are illustrated in Fig. 6.

The puys or volcanic hills of the Puy-de-Dôme landscape of Auvergne are typically scoria cones with craters, but some, such as the craterless Grand Sarcoui, are trachytic cumulo-domes, and the term puy is occasionally and unfortunately used to mean cumulo-dome.

Mamelons

The term mamelon is often used as synonymous with cumulo-dome, but Cotton (1944) suggests that the term be reserved for those domes built up by the eruption of successive flows of trachytic material, in contrast to the true cumulo-dome, which expands from within. Mamelons, like cumulo-domes, have no crater.

Tholoids

The term tholoid refers to cumulo-domes or mamelons when they occur in the crater of a larger volcano. They may be hundreds of metres high and in diameter. They are often covered with rubble and may be mistaken for nested cones, but they have no crater. The formation of a tholoid in a crater does not necessarily mark the end of activity, for they may be repeatedly built and shattered during the growth of large volcanoes. There is a well-marked tholoid in the crater of Mt Egmont, New Zealand.

Plug domes

In its most viscous form, the magma extruded from a vent may be so rigid that it moves up like a piston, producing a roughly cylindrical body known as a plug dome. The landform is also known as a piton. In American usage plug dome may refer to what are here called cumulo-domes. In New Zealand, Mt Edgecumbe is an andesite volcano that was apparently extruded through a jagged orifice, for it has grooves on the side and top that are not due to erosion, but are giant scratches.

The Pitons of Carbet, Martinique, are thought to be plug domes, and Merapi, Indonesia, is an active volcano which builds successive plug domes that are explosively destroyed.

Plug domes can grow rapidly, but during growth they are shattered by explosions and broken by uneven growth, and the accumulation of broken spines and extrusion ridges causes many plug

domes to be covered by a jumble of debris, which make a scree-like
deposit around the flanks with rocks piled up at their angle of rest.

Spines

Whereas plug domes are large bodies of nearly mountain size,
smaller-scale extrusion of very rigid lava, through chinks in the
cracked skin of plug domes or cumulo-domes, gives rise to ridges
and spines. The spine of Mont Pelée, Martinique, which was produced after the catastrophic eruption of 1902, reached a height of
over 300 m, but was rapidly eroded. At one stage it grew 13 m in a

7 *Two views of the spine of Mont Pelée. Left: from the east, after
a photograph by Lacroix; right: from the south, after a drawing by
Cotton (1944). The eastern side is convex, grooved, and slickensided,
while the western side is broken and ragged.*

day. Spines are frequently irregular in shape, and are not extruded
uniformly as cylindrical pillars. The two views of the Mont Pelée
spine (Fig. 7) show this. A spine on Santa Maria, Guatemala, that
grew between 1922 and 1925, reached a maximum size of 500 m high
and 1300 m across the base.

PYROCLASTIC VOLCANOES

When explosively produced fragments of lava fall around a volcanic
vent they build up a heap of debris, the slope of which depends on the
angle of rest of the fragments concerned. Fine particles have lower

slopes than coarse ones, and as the coarser fragments tend to
accumulate near the vent, beautiful concave slopes are formed,
like those of Fujiyama (Japan) and Mt Egmont (New Zealand)
(Pl. 8).

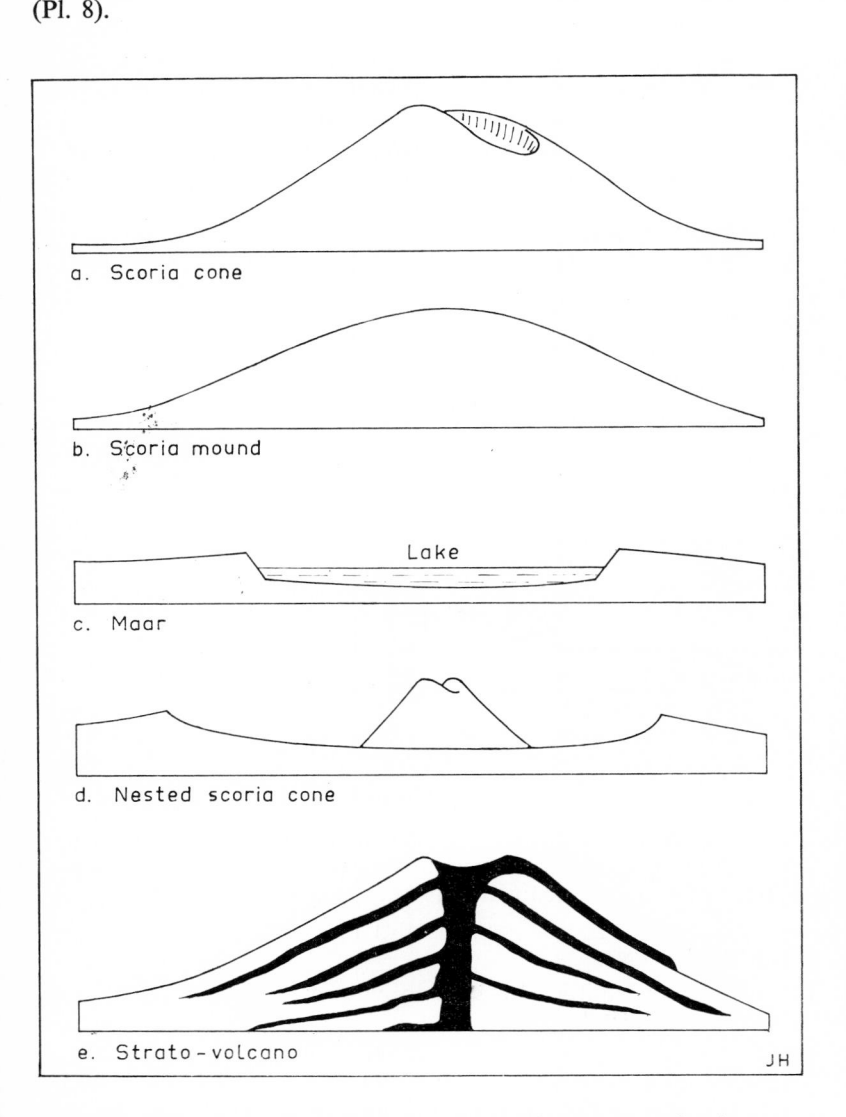

*8 Diagrammatic representation of dominantly scoria volcanic types
(not to scale)*

Scoria cone

The ideal scoria cone is single, steep, with straight or gently concave sides, and with a crater at the top. Mt Elephant, Victoria, 240 m high, is a good example (Pl. 9). The even height of the crater rim often causes scoria cones to appear flat-topped when viewed from a distance.

Scoria cones may be built very rapidly. Monte Nuovo near Naples, Italy, was built to a height of 130 m in a single eruption lasting a few days in 1538. Barcena, on the island of San Benedicto, Mexico, built a cone of 300 m in twelve days in 1952.

In the last stages of eruption basaltic magma tends to build up scoria cones. Thus in Victoria there are far more scoria cones than other types of volcano, though the province as a whole is dominated by flows of basic lava.

Scoria mound

Some scoria volcanoes have no apparent crater and may be termed scoria mounds to distinguish them from normal scoria cones. The Anakies, Victoria, are examples.

Nested scoria cones

Scoria cones are frequently produced as the last phase of an eruption on the site of larger volcanoes of other type. When they are in the centre of a large crater or caldera they are called nested cones. The V-sectioned trough between the inner cone and the crater wall is called a fosse.

Littoral cones

When aa lava reaches the sea it explodes and the ejecta pile up to form a cone up to 100 m high and 1 km in diameter. There is often a double hill, one hill built on each side of the lava stream (Wentworth and Macdonald, 1953).

Maars (tuff rings)

Maars are landforms caused by volcanic explosion and consist of a crater which extends below general ground level and is considerably wider than deep, and a surrounding rim constructed of material ejected from the crater. The rim consists of pyroclastic material, either igneous or comminuted bedrock, and is often markedly asymmetrical, with greater deposition on the downwind side of the crater. The rim deposit is also asymmetrical in cross-section, with a steep side towards the crater, and a gentle slope (commonly 4° or less) away from the crater, parallel to the bedding of the pyroclastics. The craters have a diameter often about 1 km and the rims are commonly less than 50 m high, although they may reach 100 m.

Maars are usually associated with basaltic igneous activity, but andesitic maars are known in Chile, and those of Basotu, Tanzania, are produced by carbonatite eruptions (Downie and Wilkinson, 1962). Maars are discussed in detail in Chapter IV.

MIXED ERUPTION VOLCANOES

In many volcanoes there is a mixture of lava and fragmental deposits.

Strato-volcanoes

Many of the world's great volcanoes, such as Vesuvius, Fujiyama, Egmont, and many others, are strato-volcanoes, with both lava flows and pyroclastic deposits. Many of these have erupted over a long period, and indeed the strato-volcano is the commonest form developed by long-lived central volcanoes. The cones become gullied by erosion and lava flows commonly follow such gullies. New gullies then form on the edges of flows, and so on. Scoria cones are built around the top of the volcano and pyroclastic flow and fall deposits may have a wide distribution on the flanks. Ngauruhoe, New Zealand, is a typical strato-volcano, almost perfectly conical and about 1000 m high (Pl. 10). The slopes are about 30° steep and the crater is about 400 m across. The highest point on the rim is to the east, possibly because of the prevailing westerly wind. Young aa lava flows have reached the base on all sides except the east.

Some strato-volcanoes are isolated, but many occur in groups. In McMurdo Sound, Antarctica, for instance, the large young strato-volcanoes, Mts Erebus (altitude 3700 m), Bird, Terra Nova, and Terror coalesce to form Ross Island.

Hekla, Iceland, is intermediate in many respects between a typical Icelandic shield volcano and a strato-volcano such as Vesuvius. It has been built by repeated eruptions from a fissure, often with several craters active at the same time.

Intra-glacial volcanoes

Intra-glacial volcanoes are those that formed from eruptions beneath a thick ice sheet. Such volcanoes have several phases of growth.

1. Volcanic heat causes a melt-water vault to form within the ice, within which pillow lavas pile up around the vent. Eventually the roof collapses and activity takes place in an intra-glacial lake.

2. As the pile of lava reaches the water surface, explosive activity replaces effusive activity, and tuff deposits mantle the pillow lavas.

3. When the volcano builds above water level, lava flows are produced. These flow into the surrounding lake, where they are brecciated, and a flow-foot breccia is deposited. This is made up of breccia, pillows, and ash (mixed hyaloclastics), deposited as cross-bedded sediments with a dip of about 30°.

4. If the volcanic mass grows large enough, there will be a mass of pillow lava, flow-foot breccia, and pyroclastics overlain by normal lava. Since the lava is fluid it builds a low-angle sheet or shield which is virtually a caprock over the underlying hyaloclastics. These processes produce two main kinds of volcano.

Tablemountains (Tuyas)

This is the name given to a particular kind of volcanic mountain in Iceland; examples include Hrutfell, Kjalfell, and Skridufell (Kjartansson, 1966). Tablemountains are isolated plateaux roughly circular in plan, with gently convex tops and abrupt sides. They are built in the manner described above of a mixture of pillow lava and hyaloclastics (locally known as móberg in Iceland) but capped by basalt lava flows. During the whole process the material was moulded within the walls of ice, more or less into the present shape.

Occasionally the process was only partially operative, as at Leggjabrjotur. This is a shield volcano except on its southern side, where it has an abrupt scarp of 300 m formed where lava was ponded against a thick ice margin.

The 'tuyas' of British Columbia, Canada, appear to be similar to the Icelandic tablemountains (Mathews, 1947).

Ridges

Another kind of Icelandic volcano, formed in association with tablemountains, is known as a ridge (Kjartansson, 1966). Ridges are ridge-shaped, serrated mountains, built up by fissure eruption of móberg under a thick cover of ice. The volcanic products were not sufficient to reach the surface of the ice at the time of eruption.

MISCELLANEOUS VOLCANOES

Composite volcanoes

This term in a strict sense refers to those volcanoes which have a mixture of lava and scoria forms, but not in a simple layered sequence. Mt Rouse, Victoria, is an example, with an elongate crater in a scoria hill and with a smaller and more distinct crater with a basalt rim on the south. The composite Mt Porndon, Victoria, has a large basalt disc with a diameter of about 3 km, in the centre of which are a number of scoria cones and mounds. Staughtons Hill, Victoria, consists of a maar, a scoria cone, and a basalt-rimmed separate crater. Most composite hills appear to consist of individual hills which are genetically related, but it is possible that some, such as Staughtons Hill, are due to accidental superimposition of unrelated eruption points of different ages.

Parasitic cones (also called adventive cones and secondary cones)

When a volcano becomes very high, very great pressure is required for the rising lava to reach the summit crater. It is sometimes possible for the lava to find an easier route to the surface, and erupt on the flanks of the main volcano. Once such an eruption has taken place, the solidified lava in the conduit plugs that outlet, and in succeeding eruption another opening must be made. In this manner a large volcano comes to have many small parasitic cones on its flanks. Mt Etna, Sicily, with over two hundred parasitic cones and over eight hundred small mounds of lava known as boccas, is the finest example. Here each new series of eruptions occurs along a rift, and succeeding new cones appear higher and higher up the fissure until it is sealed. A volcano may have a single parasitic cone, such as Fanthams Peak on Mt Egmont, New Zealand.

It must be noted that volcanoes do not inevitably produce parasitic cones when their column of lava becomes very high. Cotopaxi (Ecuador), for instance, attains a height of 5897 m and 3000 m above its base; it is the second highest active volcano in the world after Guallatiri in Chile, 6060 m high and 2000 m above its base, yet its volcanic activity is confined to the summit crater where lava flows and pyroclastics are produced. Flank eruptions are unknown on Cotopaxi.

Multiple cones

In some areas, as, for instance, on the volcanic plains of Victoria, a number of scoria cones are built very close together. The general mechanism appears to be the same as for parasitic cones, that is the first cone blocks the vent, and the second one occurs on a new vent close by. The difference here is that no cones grow to any great size, and all the separate cones tend to be of about the same size; that is there is no main volcano with parasites, but a series of equal volcanoes. These may be called multiple cones.

Seamounts and guyots

Thousands of submarine mountains or seamounts are known from all oceans, but especially from the Pacific (Menard, 1964). These are of volcanic origin and many, distinguished by a flat and horizontal top, are known as guyots.

They are large mountains, rising up to 400 m above their bases, and their flat tops commonly lie at a depth between 1000 m and 2000 m. A guyot south of Eniwetok atoll in the Marshall Islands is 55 km across the base and 14 km across the plateau; one to the north of Eniwetok is 55 km across the top and 95 km wide at its base. There is no regularity in the levels of guyot tops. Standard (1961) described three guyots from the Tasman Sea, the Taupo, Bargoo, and Derwent Hunter, with platform depths of 130 m, 250 m, and 270 m respectively.

Guyots frequently occur in groups, especially on swells on the ocean floor, though they are also common on deep ocean floors. One guyot is known from the Aleutian trench in the Gulf of Alaska, at a depth of 2500 m. Many guyots have now been dredged and photographed. There is no doubt that they are basaltic and they often have thin veneers of Cretaceous or Tertiary fossiliferous sediment on the tops and slopes.

Guyots represent a late stage in the development of oceanic volcanoes, which erupt, are planated at sea level, and then sink beneath the sea too fast for coral growth to keep pace.

The speed with which erosion can reduce a volcano to a flat-topped shoal is demonstrated by many examples given in Chapter X.

When a volcano erupts, the weight of the volcanic pile adds a load concentrated on a small area of the earth's crust already weakened by withdrawal of magma from beneath it. The mechanism for subsidence of guyots is probably the overloading of the ocean floor caused by the weight of the volcanoes themselves. Some guyots even have an annular depression around their base, supporting the sinking hypothesis.

Cryptovolcanoes and meteor craters

Cryptovolcanoes are roughly circular holes or rims, sometimes with highly disturbed strata, where a volcanic origin is postulated, but where no igneous rock can be found. Such structures may be due to eruption of gas only, or may be surface expressions of volcanic pipes that did not quite reach the surface. Mt Abbott is an example in Western Australia (Prider, 1960) and Gosses Bluff in central Australia may be a cryptovolcanic structure, although at present an origin by impact is favoured (Cook, 1968). Bucher (1933) has described examples from the United States.

Meteorite craters have a superficial similarity to volcanoes. The best known of all, Meteor Crater, Arizona, is a rimmed basin 170 m deep and 1200 m wide. At Henbury in central Australia there are thirteen craters with inconspicuous rims, the largest of which is 200 m by 110 m, and the circular Wolf Creek crater of Western Australia is 840 m across and 50 m deep.

When a meteor strikes the earth it explodes, and it is the explosion rather than the impact that forms the crater. Meteoritic iron is seldom found inside the crater, but is scattered outside the rim by the explosion. Other indications of meteoritic origin are the presence of fused bedrock fragments, and the development of outward dipping rocks in the rim and imbricate structures in the bedrock due to impact.

IV

CRATERS AND CALDERAS

Depressions on volcanoes are usually known as craters or calderas (Pls. 11-14). These are formed in a number of ways and have many variations of form, some of which have been given specific names.

CRATERS IN SCORIA CONES

The simplest craters are the depressions usually found at the top of scoria cones. These are generally 1 km or less in diameter, and seldom exceed 2 km. They are thus different in scale from calderas, described later, which are often over 5 km in diameter.

Summit craters mark the vent from which pyroclastics were ejected, and around which scoria was heaped to build the cone. Craters vary in depth, and in general the wider the crater the deeper it will be. The particle size of the pyroclastics largely controls the angle of the inner slope, and the crater may not exhibit its greatest depth because of later fill by lava, eroded debris, or by pyroclastics which were emitted with insufficient energy to leave the crater or in such a way that they fell directly back into the crater. When the crater rim is of even height the volcano often has the appearance of a truncated, flat-topped cone when seen from the side.

Many craters are breached, however. That is to say they have a low gap on part of their rim, which may be caused in a number of ways. The eruption may be directed laterally by an inclined or partly blocked vent. If a strong wind blows during eruption it may cause preferential accumulation on the downwind side and an apparent breach on the upwind side. A lava flow may be erupted from the crater and erode a channel through the pyroclastics making a true breach. The breach may be due to an overspilling lava flow, as for example Cerro El Ciguatepe, Nicaragua (McBirney and Williams, 1965). Alternatively a Parícutin-type flow may erupt

34

7 (Top) Whakapapaterenga rhyolite dome (foreground) and Tutukau rhyolite dome beyond, New Zealand (E. F. Lloyd)

8 (Bottom) A large strato-volcano: Mt Egmont, New Zealand (National Publicity, New Zealand)

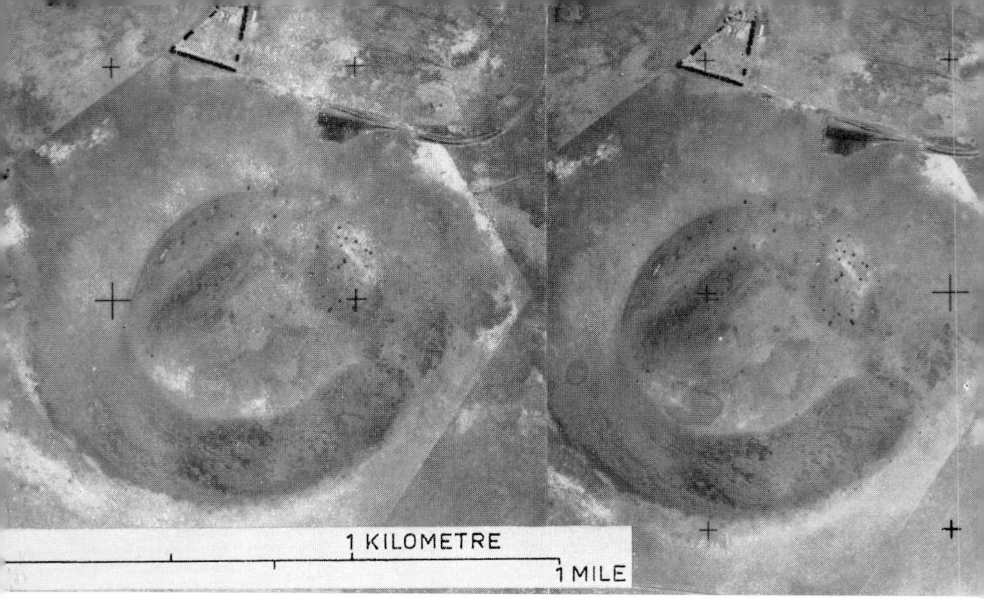

9 (Top) Mt Elephant, Victoria: stereo-pair of a scoria cone (Crown copyright. Courtesy of the Director of National Mapping, Department of National Development, Canberra)

10 (Bottom) Ngauruhoe, New Zealand: flank of a strato-volcano showing lava flows

from the base of the scoria cone, causing collapse of the overlying pyroclastics and thus a breach of the crater rim. The breach of Mt Elephant (Pl. 9) may be of this type. Breaching may be caused by land-sliding during eruption, as was actually observed at Parícutin on 10 June 1943.

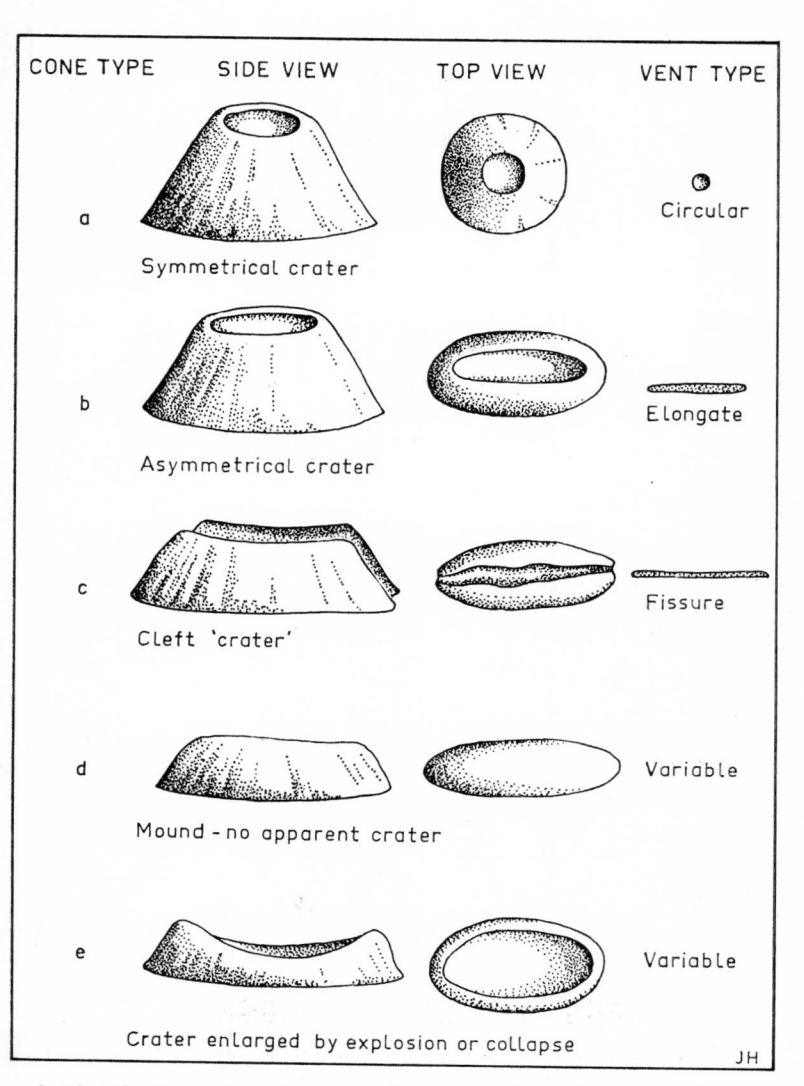

9 *Classification of scoria cones by crater shape (after Breed, 1964)*

The shape of the crater may be used to classify scoria cones into the various kinds shown in Fig. 9.

Craters are normally a few times wider than the pipes beneath them. Exceptionally violent explosions may produce much wider

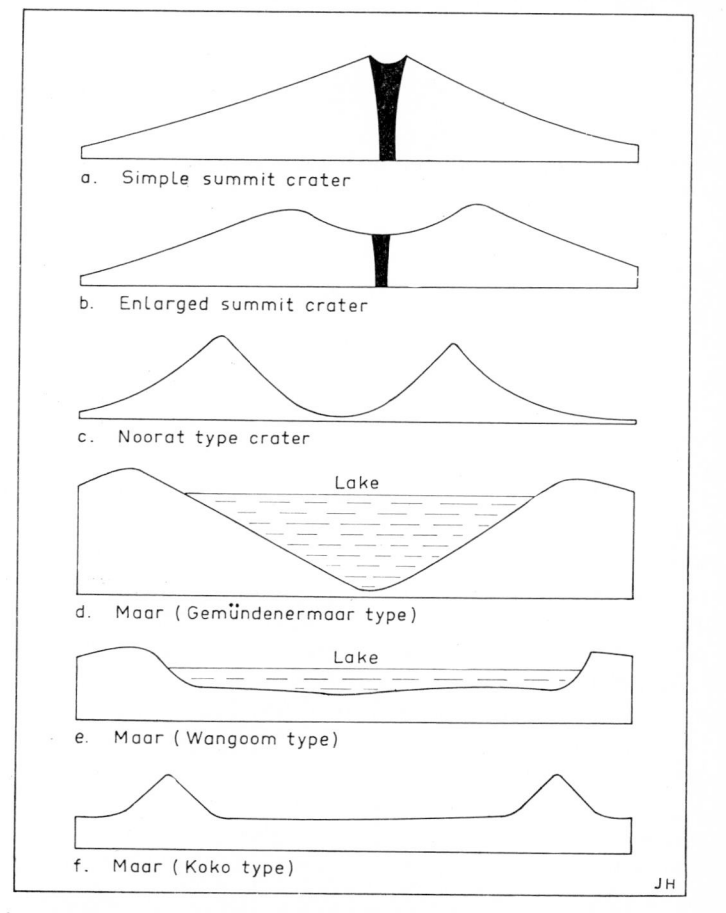

10 Diagrammatic representation of kinds of crater: (a) simple summit crater. The crater is not very much wider than the conduit. (b) Enlarged summit crater. The crater has a diameter several times larger than that of the conduit. (c) Noorat type crater. The bottom of the crater reaches about the same level as the general ground level outside the volcano. (d) Maar (Gemündenermaar type). By Holmes's terminology this would be an 'explosion vent' type of ring crater. (e) Maar (Wangoom type). By Holmes's terminology this would be a 'fluidisation crater' type of ring crater. (f) Maar (Koko type).

craters, such as maars. The diameter of craters may also increase by the caving-in of the walls. In this way the crater of Irazu, Costa Rica, increased from 200 m to 525 m during the eruption of 1963-5.

The relative depth of the crater to the surrounding cone can also be of significance. In the majority of scoria cones, the crater is a comparatively small feature on the large cone. In what has been termed the 'Noorat' type (Ollier, 1967b) the crater is as deep as the volcano is high; in other words the volcano consists almost entirely of a ring of scoria around a vent and there has been very little accumulation over the vent itself. If the crater is actually below the general ground level then the volcano is usually of maar type.

Maars

Maars are landforms caused by volcanic explosion and consist of a crater which extends below general ground level and is considerably wider than deep, and a surrounding rim constructed of material ejected from the crater. The word comes from the German *Maar*, a name given to numerous lakes in craters of this type in the Eifel district of Germany. The rims of maars are characteristically low, the slopes are generally low, about 4° being characteristic, and the diameter of maars is usually between 500 m and 1 km, though Tower Hill (Victoria) is 3 km in diameter. There is, however, a distinct difference between the size of the largest maars and that of calderas which are normally 5 km or more in diameter.

A very frequent suggestion in connection with maars is that they are formed by phreatic explosion due to the violent reaction of ascending magma and groundwater. In most areas with maars this is very feasible. In Hawaii (Stearns, 1935) and on Ambrym, New Hebrides (Stephenson *et al.*, 1967), there are pyroclastic cones of apparently phreatic origin near sea level with coral limestone fragments in the ejecta, suggesting possible reaction of ascending magma with water in a coral reef. Volcanoes on higher ground in both areas have normal scoria cones, and presumably did not erupt phreatically. Similarly in the Auckland area of New Zealand the volcanoes near sea level have a form that suggests phreatic eruption, while those on higher ground are normal scoria cones (Searle, 1964). In the Mud Lake area of Idaho there are five possible maars on the gravel fan of the Snake River which is saturated with groundwater; elsewhere in the region, where groundwater is negligible, quiet fissure eruptions occurred (Stearns, 1926). The maars of

Victoria usually occur over porous limestone which would have
provided ideal conditions for phreatic explosions.

Maars with nested scoria cones (the Zuni type) may be explained
satisfactorily on the phreatic hypothesis by supposing that the first
ascending magma hits groundwater and explodes violently, using
up the groundwater and drying the ground. If emission of lava continues, it cannot explode violently as there is no longer any groundwater, and so erupts as a lava flow or more commonly as a scoria
cone.

However, there are some areas of maars, including the type area
of the Eifel district, where conditions seem unfavourable for phreatic
eruption.

Holmes (1965, p. 313) divides ring craters (here called maars)
into explosion vents and fluidisation craters. The former are said
to give rise to small funnel-shaped craters and coarse angular
debris, and the latter have wide shallow craters with nearly flat
floors and low rims of distinctive material due to fluidisation. In
fact this regular association of form and type of ejecta is not
generally found.

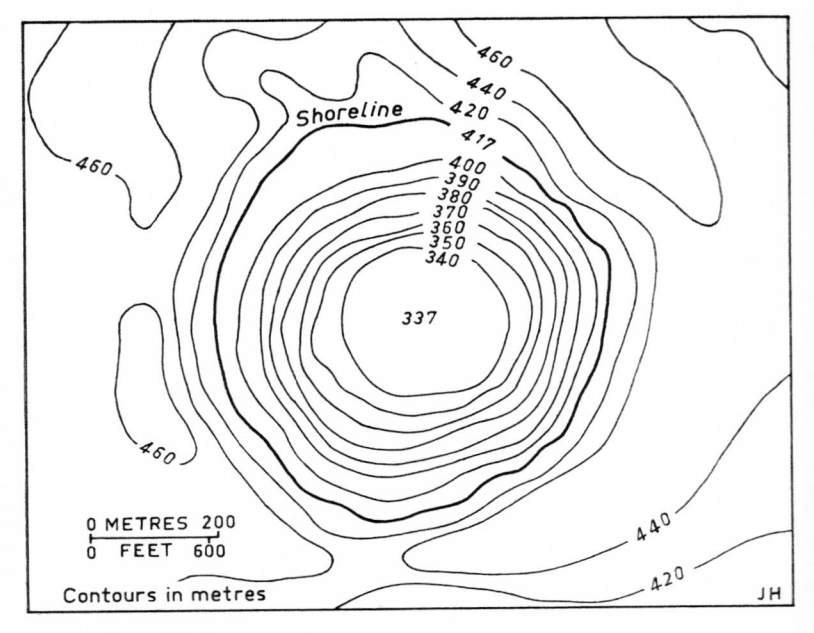

11 Plan of Pulvermaar

Maars may be classified by means of their approximation to the following type examples (Ollier, 1967):

1. Pulvermaar (Fig. 11; Pl. 12)—a simple, circular maar. This is the commonest type, and includes both flat-floored maars such as Wangoom (Victoria) and funnel-shaped maars like Gemündenermaar (Germany).

2. Zuni—a maar with a scoria cone or cones inside on the same centre of eruption. The nested cone may be very small or large enough to almost bury the maar, as at Mt Wellington, Auckland.

3. Koko—a maar with steep walls both inside and outside the crater, and thus a sharp crest.

4. Red Rock—the sort of landform that results when several maars are so closely spaced that the typical circular form cannot be developed.

CRATERS IN LAVA VOLCANOES

In lava volcanoes no mound is built up around the vent as in scoria cones, but the lava volcano builds up by periodical overflows of the lava in the vent, which is then sometimes called a crater. This may be enlarged by the collapse of the crater walls. An even larger area

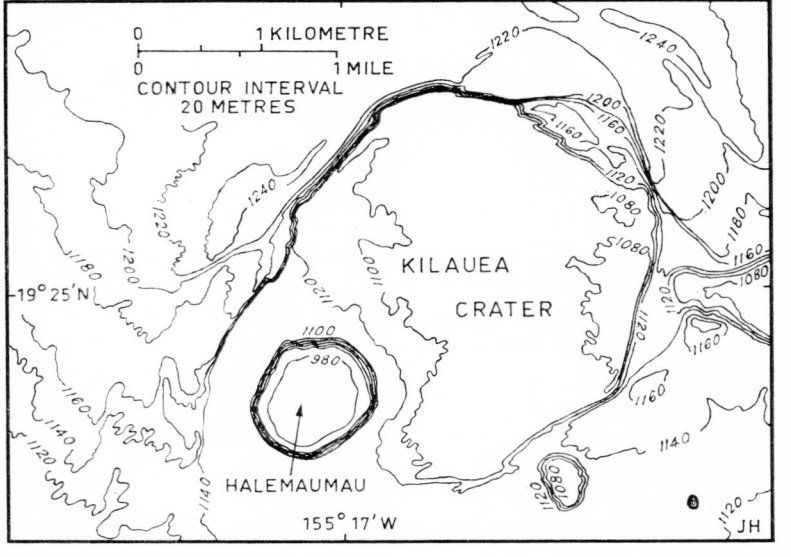

12 *Plan of Kilauea*

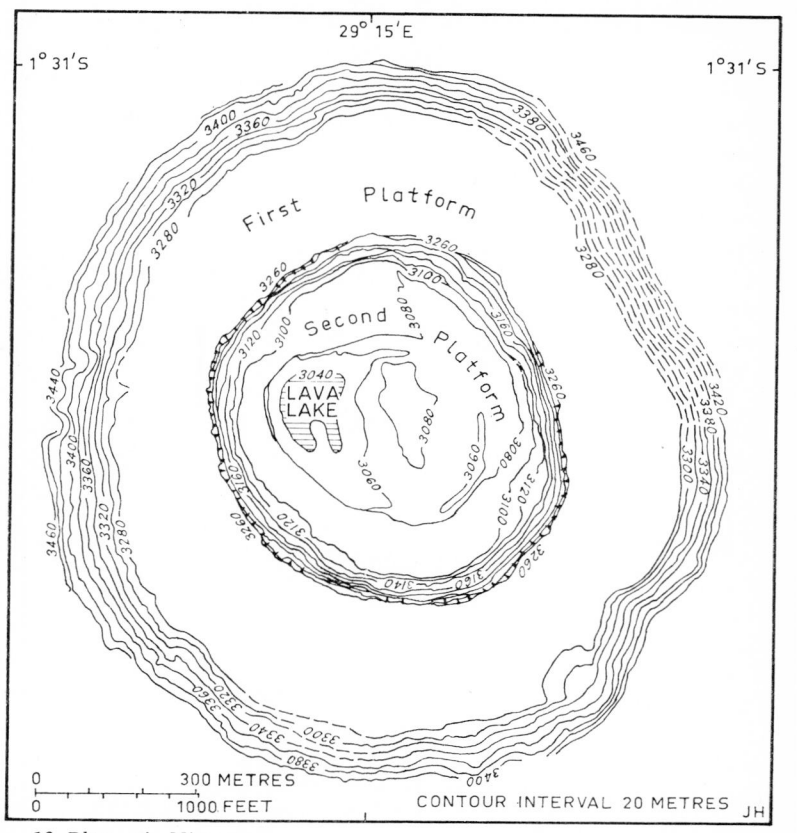

13 Plan of Niragongo

around the vent may also sink to form a caldera. Both the caldera and crater formed in this way have sometimes been called lava sinks, and this term is better than crater for the actual top of the vent, though the larger depression is more simply called a caldera. Mauna Loa has both types represented by Kilauea, the caldera, in the base of which is Halemaumau, the lava sink (Fig. 12). This was formerly continuously active, and was known by yet another term, a fire-pit. Niragongo in the Congo is another volcano, in this case a strato-volcano, exhibiting both a caldera and a lava sink, in which a lava lake is still active (Fig. 13).

Long records have been kept of the lava levels in the lava sinks of Hawaii. Lava is occasionally withdrawn to great depths; in 1924 Halemaumau sank 400 m and then exploded.

Pit craters

Pit craters reported from Hawaii (Wentworth and Macdonald, 1953) are circular or elliptical features sunk below a lava surface. They have never been full to the brim and there is no accumulated material surrounding them. They are collapse features on lava shields or domes, and in their nearly vertical walls the edges of horizontal lava flows are exposed. In some groups there is a tendency to alignment, suggesting a distribution following a fissure or a rift zone. At the largest size, pit craters merge topographically into lava sinks such as Halemaumau, but besides a size difference it seems that pit craters form rather rapidly and then become inactive, whereas lava sinks may remain active for very long periods.

Similar pit craters have been described from the recent lava volcanoes of the Chyulu Range, Kenya, including one 500 m across and 30 m deep (Saggerson, 1963).

Rifts

Very elongate craters are commonly known as rifts. The 1886 eruption of Tarawera, New Zealand, blew out a rift or line of elongated pits in a trench 15 km long, 100 to 400 m deep, and about 200 m wide (Pl. 14). The rift passes across the top of Mt Tarawera and continues to Lake Rotomahana, around which is a thick deposit of fragmented pre-existing rocks.

The term rift (Icelandic *gja*) is also applied to large open fissures that are found in Hawaii and Iceland. Some of these have emitted lava and scoria, but others appear to be simply tension cracks. The largest in Hawaii is the Great Crack, Kilauea, which is 13 km long, 12 m wide, and has a visible depth of 15 m (Wentworth and Macdonald, 1953). The Eldgja in Iceland is an exceptional rift that has been enlarged by explosion and is over 30 km long (Cotton, 1944). Most rifts are very much smaller.

Crater groups

In Iceland there are 'crater groups' consisting of hundreds or even thousands of craters in an area of about 50 km². The craters are 1-2 m high, and 2-3 m in diameter, ranging to over 30 m high and 300-400 m in diameter. The best-known crater group is the Skutustadir group south of Myvatn. The craters in these groups are all pseudocraters, formed by lava overflowing ground soaked in water. The water turned to steam and was explosively erupted through the lava. Crater groups appear to be especially common in

Iceland because of the combination of thin basalt flows, flat topography, and plentiful water.

IMPACT CRATERS

Eruption on Arenal Volcano, Costa Rica, in 1968 threw out numerous incandescent blocks. Most of these literally disintegrated when they hit the ground, but they left numerous large craters ranging up to 30 m in diameter, and craters up to 2 m in diameter were found as far away as 10 km from the volcano.

CALDERAS

Very large volcanic depressions, commonly over 5 km in diameter, are called calderas. The world's largest caldera is that of Aso, Japan, which measures 23 × 16 km. Ngorongoro, Tanzania, is 19 × 17 km and the caldera floor is 650 m below the rim.

At one time calderas were classified into explosive calderas, collapse calderas, and erosion calderas. The term erosion caldera has now been generally abandoned since it refers to a depression formed by completely different processes from the others and leads to confusion. It now seems doubtful if any true calderas are due to explosion, so the old classification is of little use and the word caldera will nowadays almost always refer to a volcanic depression caused largely by subsidence. There are a few large depressions in which the mode or origin is in doubt or dispute, like Tower Hill, Victoria, which has been interpreted as a caldera by some and as a maar by others.

Topographically many calderas are marked by distinct fault lines bounding subsided blocks, and the tops of fault blocks sometimes make topographic benches within the caldera rim.

One kind of caldera is the large, fault-bounded depression found on top of lava shields. The largest caldera in Hawaii is on the summit of Mauna Loa and is called Mokuaweoweo, and is approximately 6 km long, 3 km wide, and 200 m deep. Kilauea (Fig. 12) ranks next in size, but since it is much better known having the volcano observatory and tourist hotel on its rim, its name is used for this kind of caldera.

It was noticed at many volcanoes that after great eruptions large parts of the original mountains were missing and great calderas had appeared. In 1772 Papandayand (Indonesia) was reduced in height by 1300 m by a great Plinian eruption. In 1815 Tamboro (Indonesia) lost 1400 m of height and the eruption produced a caldera 12 km in diameter. It seemed fairly obvious that calderas were formed as huge explosion craters when the volcano 'blew its top'.

As an example, the eruption of Vesuvius near Naples, Italy, in A.D. 79 was often cited. The top of the old volcano was completely missing after the eruption, and in its place was a huge depression 2·5 km across, within which a new volcano, Vesuvius, had grown. The wreck of the old volcano was a ragged ring, the larger part of which is now Monte Somma. Somma has become a general term given to such relics of volcanoes, and somma caldera may be used as a term for the depression formed by this kind of eruption.

It seemed natural to suppose that the old mountain had been shattered into countless fragments during the eruption and scattered around the countryside. However, when the deposits of the eruption were examined it was found that they consisted almost entirely of new pyroclastic rock, and that fragments of the old volcano were present in only small quantities in the first deposits laid down. It therefore seemed that the volcano had not blown its top but had emitted vast quantities of lava until it emptied itself out, and the summit of the old volcano had then collapsed into the empty magma chamber.

The summit caldera of Ruapehu, New Zealand, about 3 km $\times$ 1·5 km, has likewise produced little lithic ejecta, and is thought to be due to subsidence like the somma caldera at Vesuvius (O'Shea, 1954).

Eruption and caldera collapse may be repeated many times on the one volcanic site, as in the case of the Somma-Vesuvius complex (Fig. 14).

A similar story of collapse was found in many other calderas, such as Krakatoa (Indonesia), Coseguina (Nicaragua), and Crater Lake (Oregon), on the site of the original Mt Mazama, where Williams (1941) has calculated that the volume lost is almost 70 km³, but ejecta from the volcano amount to only a third of this.

Figure 15 shows the stages in the development of this kind of caldera as envisaged by Williams (1941). The early stages of eruption discharge enormous quantities of pumice, much of which is expelled as pyroclastic flow deposits. Eruption continues to a stage where the upper part of the magma chamber is emptied and so there is no

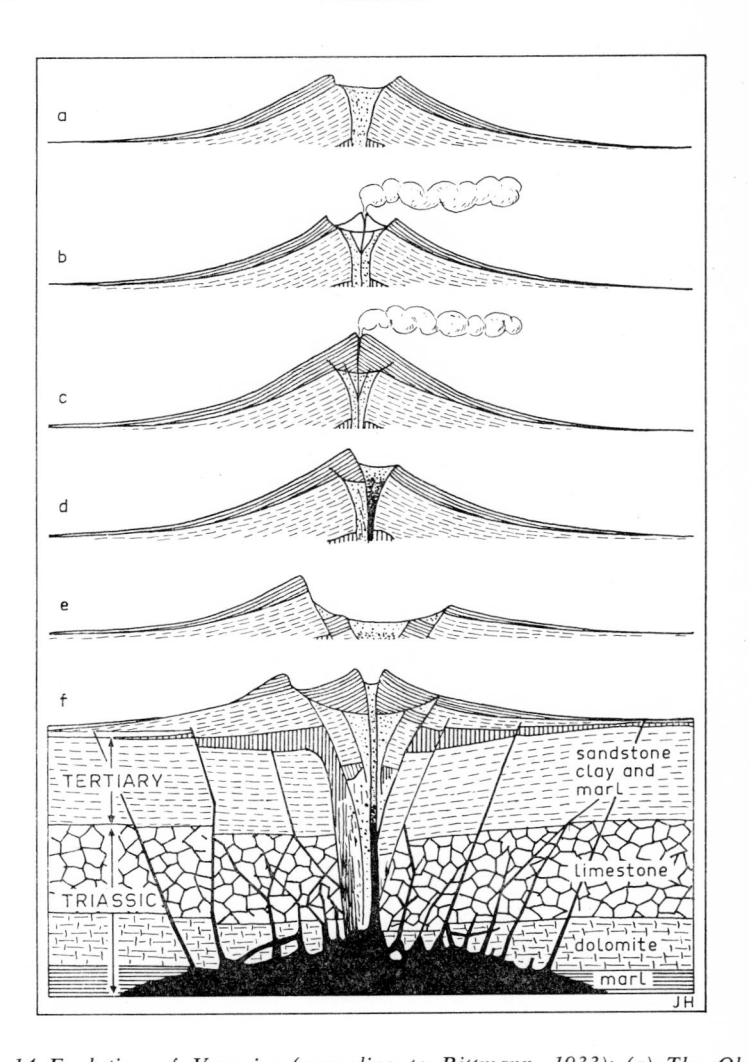

14 *Evolution of Vesuvius (according to Rittmann, 1933): (a) The Old*
Somma volcano, at the top of which a large caldera is formed.
(This volcano covers the Primitive Somma volcano, which is not
shown in the figure.) (b) A new volcano (Young Somma) begins
to grow in the caldera. (c) The Young Somma volcano has
reached its maximum height, covering the Old Somma volcano.
(d) On the top of Young Somma is a partially filled caldera
(around 800 B.C., described by Strabo). (e) The large caldera
formed at the great Plinian eruption of A.D. 79. (f) Vesuvius
has grown in the caldera, largely filling it.

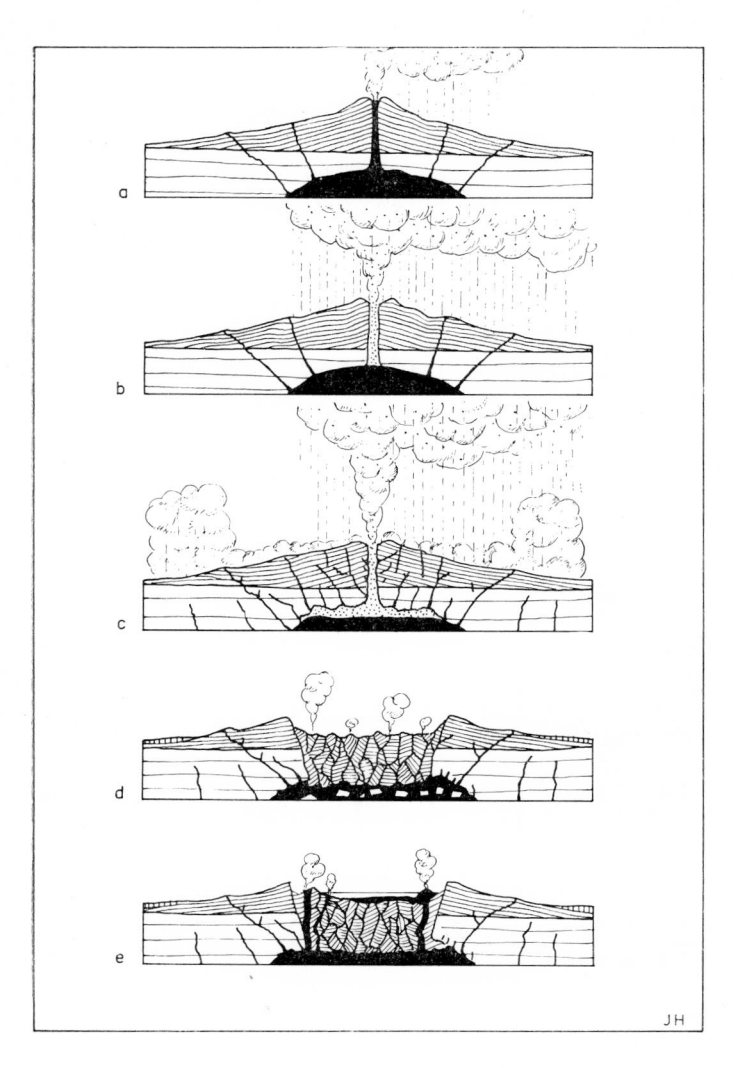

15 *Stages in the formation of a caldera (after Williams, 1941): (a) Mild explosions. Magma stands high in the conduit. (b) Increase in violence of activity. Magma sinks to the top of the magma chamber. (c) Activity climaxes in Plinian or Pelean eruptions. Magma sinks below the roof of the magma chamber, removing support. (d) Collapse of the cone into the magma chamber. (e) Renewed eruptions on the caldera floor, especially near the rim.*

longer any support for the top of the cone, which therefore collapses. The collapsed material is presumed to be broken up considerably, but most of the material engulfed disappears completely or is hidden under a cover of later volcanics.

This is the sort of mechanism that is thought to account for calderas such as Krakatoa, Crater Lake, and Santorini amongst others, and such calderas may be referred to as of Krakatoan type.

These calderas are similar in general mechanism of formation to those of the somma type, but differ in degree. Krakatoan calderas

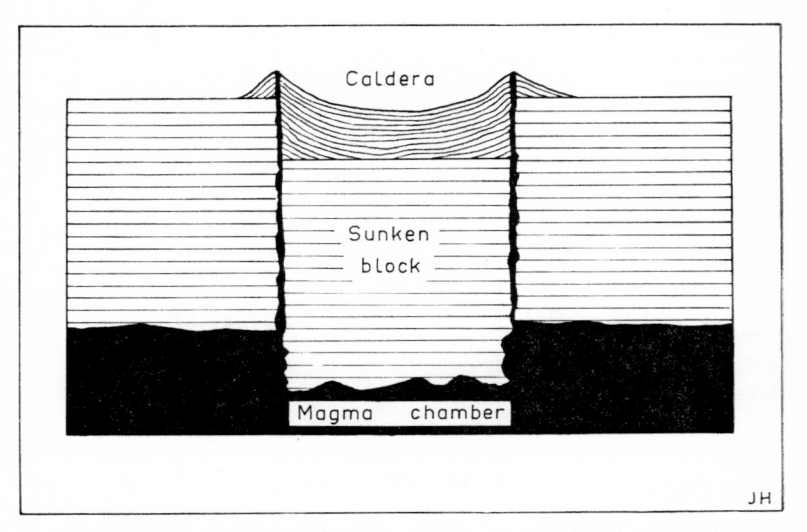

16 Cauldron subsidence, Glencoe type. A cylindrical mass of crust sinks into the magma chamber, forming a caldera at the surface. Ascending magma forms a ring dyke around the sunken block and erupts at the surface around the edge of the caldera, which becomes partially filled with lava.

are generally larger than somma calderas, they are associated with more violent eruptions, generally including pyroclastic flows, and the remnants of the old volcanoes are smaller than those around somma volcanoes.

Another mechanism for caldera making is shown in Fig. 16, in which a cylinder of material falls as a single unit, and is surrounded by a ring dyke of igneous rock. This mechanism is called cauldron subsidence, and gives rise to calderas known as the Glencoe type, after an example in Scotland.

Branch (1966) described cauldron subsidence areas of enormous size from north Queensland, including one of 120 km × 55 km, and he suggests a distinction between *cauldrons*, formed by collapse resulting from the subterranean withdrawal of magma from a deep magma chamber, and *calderas*, caused by collapse as a result of colossal eruptions of pumice derived from a high-level magma chamber.

A modern example of a Glencoe-type caldera may be the Askja cauldron in Iceland which has a rim of volcanoes pouring lava into the great subsidence hollow. Another example is Niuafo'ou near Tonga, where a complex of fissures forms a ring 5 km in diameter around a central caldera. The caldera of Ambrym, New Hebrides, appears to have subsided quietly and there is no evidence for any dramatic cataclysmic eruption accompanying caldera formation (Stephenson *et al.*, 1967). Silali caldera, in the Rift Valley of Kenya, is a Glencoe-type structure, 8 km × 5 km, the floor of which has subsided 300 m without any significant eruptivity, and there is negligible mantling of pumice associated with the caldera formation.

It thus appears that violent volcanic eruption is not normally associated with Glencoe-type subsidence, and the main distinction between Krakatoan and Glencoe types of calderas is that the former emits enormous quantities of pyroclastics, and the latter tends to be quietly effusive. The Glencoe type of caldera appears to be more often associated with basaltic provinces, and the Krakatoan with orogenic, acidic provinces. Nevertheless the two processes may be in some ways related. McCall (1963) has suggested that the Glencoe mechanism is the primary mechanism involved in the majority of subsidence calderas, and that the Krakatoan mechanism is in the nature of a special case, a complication of the Glencoe mechanism operating where volatiles are particularly abundant within the magma chamber at the time of subsidence. He believes that a complete gradation is possible between calderas showing only the effects associated with ring-fracture and the truly catastrophic Krakatoan calderas.

This proposed interrelationship of calderas is supported by the fact that different kinds of caldera may occasionally occur in close proximity or even on one site. For example, McCall and Bristow (1965) interpret Suswa volcano, Kenya, as having an earlier caldera of 100 km² of Glencoe type with Krakatoan elements, and an inner caldera of 18 km² of Glencoe type, on the edge of which is a small Kilauean caldera.

Several calderas appear to have been formed by lateral withdrawal of support. The Katmai eruption of 1912 occurred on the southern coast of the Alaskan peninsula. Mount Katmai lost 240 m from its top, and produced a caldera 5 km in diameter, and at first it was thought that this was the main source of the eruption. Later investigation showed that the main eruption produced an altogether new mountain, Novarupta. In sixty hours Novarupta and associated fissures ejected 30 km³ of rock; 150 km² of valley floor was covered

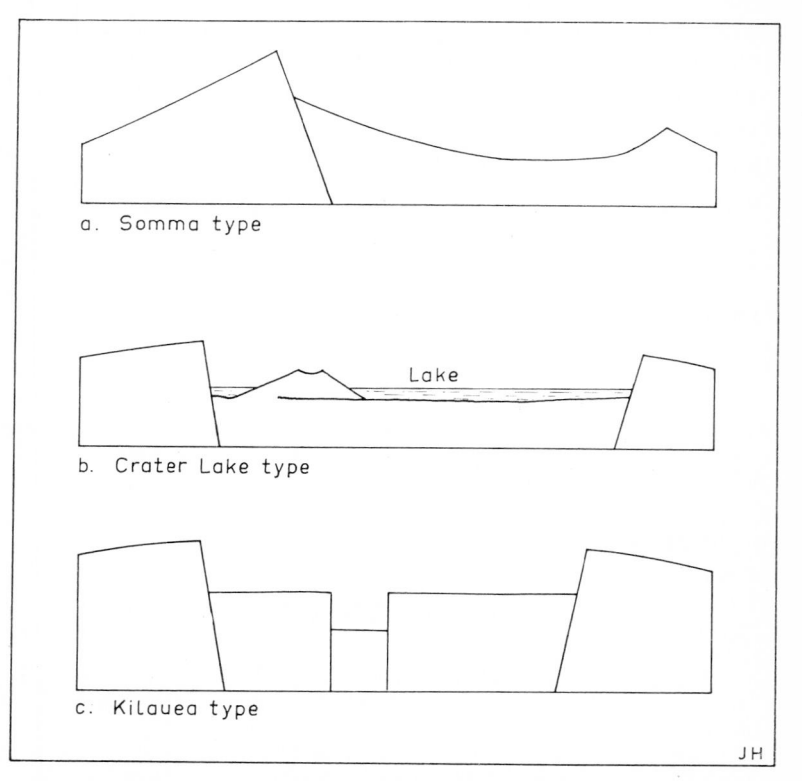

a. Somma type

Lake

b. Crater Lake type

c. Kilauea type

JH

17 Diagrammatic representation of some kinds of caldera: (a) Somma type. A considerable part of the steep cone is left behind, and may be overtopped by growth of later cones in the caldera. (b) Crater Lake type. Large calderas in which most of the original cone was destroyed. New scoria cones often grow in the caldera floor. (c) Kilauea type. Large calderas on the top of lava shields. One or more nearly level platforms are present within the caldera, and below the lowest platform is a steep-sided lava sink, about the same diameter as the conduit. A lava lake may be present on the floor of the lava sink.

by up to 200 m of ash flow deposits. It is remarkable that although the main eruption took place from Novarupta, it was Katmai, 8 km distant, that collapsed. The new vent tapped magma located under the old mountain. In a way Novarupta can be regarded as a distant parasitic cone, 8 km distant and 1500 m lower than Katmai, and probably connected by fissures. Groundwater buried by the pyroclastic flow deposits produced thousands of fumaroles that played for many years; this was the Valley of Ten Thousand Smokes.

Another example is the Atitlan basin in Guatemala, a cauldron subsidence caused principally by collapse resulting from subterranean withdrawal of magma (Williams, 1960).

To summarise (Fig. 17), calderas may be classified into the following four types:

Kilauean caldera: collapse of the top of a lava shield or dome

Somma caldera: collapse of the top of a volcanic cone, generally following Plinian eruption

Krakatoan caldera: collapse following Krakatoan eruption

Glencoe caldera: cauldron subsidence, accompanied by quietly effusive volcanic activity.

VOLCANO-TECTONIC DEPRESSIONS

Volcano-tectonic depressions as defined by van Bemmelen (1930) are depressions due to collapse of the roofs of magma chambers brought about by rapid eruptive evacuation of the magma. The type area for such depressions was the basin of Lake Toba, Indonesia, and the explanation was also applied to the Rotorua-Taupo depression in New Zealand. In the Lake Toba area, however, it has been shown that the depression already existed as a fault trough before the paroxysmal outburst that produced enormous quantities of ignimbrite. In New Zealand, too, the deformation of the Rotorua-Taupo area is largely tectonic and occurred before the eruptions of ignimbrite, though some major faults are younger than the earlier ignimbrite eruptions. The subsidence has taken place intermittently over a long period, and the evidence is inconsistent with a hypothesis of volcano-tectonic depression in the sense of development in a single major paroxysm by collapse of an arched roof (Cotton, 1962).

V

LAVA FLOWS

Liquid lava flows away from its point of eruption under the influence of gravity, partly impelled by further lava arriving behind it. Some lava is very liquid, some very viscous. Acid, rhyolitic lavas are the most viscous, and never flow freely. At most they give rise to bulbous, thick short flows or tongues, often known as coulées. Basic, basaltic lava can flow much more readily, though it may sometimes flow quite slowly. Intermediate lavas have intermediate properties.

The fastest lava flows can attain speeds of 100 m/sec., though 30 m/sec. is more common for a fast flow, and many flows grind along at barely perceptible rates.

Basaltic lavas retain their fluidity for a considerable time, and so can flow greater distances. The longest flow in Victoria is the Tyrendarra flow from Mt Eccles, 48 km long and in parts only 100 m wide. The Frambuni flow from Trolldaungja, Iceland, is 120 km long. Lava flows are usually several metres thick, rarely over 10 m, and Icelandic lava flows are commonly less than 1 m in thickness.

The greatest lava flow of historic times was the Laki flow of 1783 in Iceland; it erupted from the Lakagigar crater row which is 25 km long and has about 100 craters. The eruption lasted for seven months. Lava streams were up to 64 km long on the western side and 50 km long on the eastern side. The flow covered an area of 565 km² and had a volume estimated at 12-15 km³.

On level topography lava may spread widely to form extensive veneers of basalt on a pre-existing plain. The volcanic plains of western Victoria are a fine example of this kind of lava plain, covering an area of about 15,000 km². Some lava plains may be produced by extensive fissure eruptions, but the Victorian one was made by lava from central eruption points. Islands of old land that

11 (Top) Crater of Ngauruhoe showing subsidiary cone built during
1954 eruption, with formation of fosse (E. F. Lloyd)

12 (Bottom) A maar: Pulvermaar, Eifel, Germany

13 (Top) The crater of Rabalenekaia, New Guinea. High temperature and sulphurous emissions prevent vegetation growth around most of the edge of the crater.

14 (Left) Tarawera Rift, New Zealand

project through a 'sea' of surrounding lava flows are called 'steptoes'. Kipuka is the equivalent Hawaiian term.

On irregular topography basalt tends to flow down valleys, sometimes filling them and spilling over interfluves. Such flows disrupt the pre-existing drainage, displace rivers to new courses, and sometimes completely alter drainage patterns, as will be described in detail in Chapter IX. On the cones of strato-volcanoes flows also tend to follow gullies (Pl. 10).

The outpouring of lava in a region may sometimes be on so vast a scale that even the valleys of originally mountainous areas may be completely filled, and a lava plateau is produced. The Columbia River Plateau is one of the best known examples. These lavas are

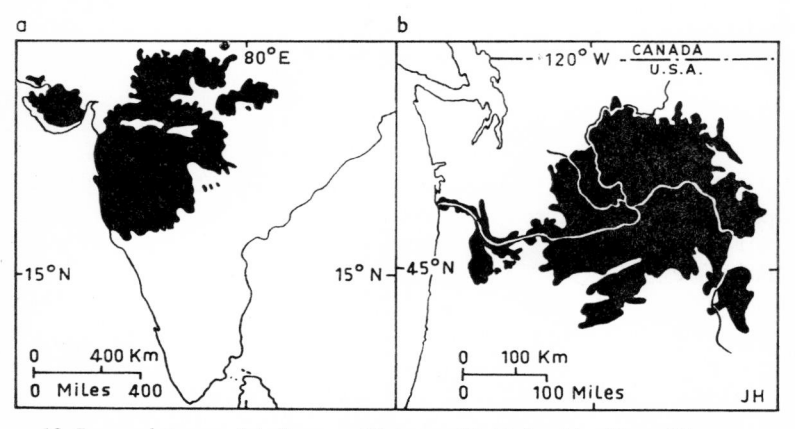

18 Lava plateaux: (a) Deccan Plateau; (b) Columbia River Plateau

mainly of Miocene age. The original topography had a relief of over 1500 m which was eventually all buried, and new valleys have been incised in the plateau up to 1500 m, deeper than the Grand Canyon of the Colorado. This great thickness of lava was attained by the piling up of hundreds of individual flows, averaging only 10 m with the largest only 120 m thick. The Columbia Plateau basalts average 1000 m thick and in places are over 1500 m. Besides this great thickness the plateau basalts covered a vast area, about 130,000 km². The Snake River basalts in southern Idaho, U.S.A., are Quaternary volcanics covering an area of 50,000 km². The Snake River and Columbia Plateau basalts are often described together as if they were parts of one province, but they are in fact quite different in location, age, and physiography.

Other major basalt plateaux are those of the Deccan of India, Eocene in age, with a present area of 500,000 km², but originally of a considerably greater area. The Deccan traps attain thicknesses up to 2000 m, and are made up of many flows varying in thickness from less than 1 m to about 60 m. The Parana plateau basalts of Brazil cover an area over 750,000 km²; the Karroo basalts of South Africa cover over 50,000 km² and were once probably as large as those of Brazil. Both are of Jurassic age.

Very many smaller regions of flood basalts are known, some of which are remnants of once much more extensive areas. Examples are the Tertiary lavas of northern Ireland and Scotland, and the Hunter Valley area of New South Wales, where Galloway (1967) has shown that Tertiary basalt once covered 15,500 km² at least, and possibly twice that area.

KINDS OF LAVA SURFACE

The basalt flows of Hawaii have been divided into two types depending on the nature of the flow.

Pahoehoe

Pahoehoe flows are the most liquid type of lava with little froth (Pls. 15 and 16). Cooling forms a very thin skin that may be dragged into folds by movement of the still mobile lava underneath. This produces varieties known as sharkskin, filamented, corded, ropy, entrail, festooned, elephant hide lava, and numerous other kinds.

Aa (pronounced ah ah)

Aa lava is blocky, frothy, and slow moving. The lava has a thick skin, broken into blocks that ride on the massive, pasty lava underneath. Such flows have the appearance of slowly advancing heaps of boulders (Pl. 17), and their movement is accompanied by loud grinding noises. Aa and blocky lava are often used synonymously, but Finch (1933) and Macdonald (1953) distinguish between aa, which is spinose and clinkery, and block lava which has the form of fairly smooth angular blocks.

The terms pahoehoe and aa have been adopted all over the world, but a few other terms have been used at times. Rittmann (1962) used 'slab lava' for that in which a skin several centimetres thick solidifies and then is broken by further movement so that the slabs are jumbled together. Another kind of slab lava has been described from Acicastello, Mt Etna (Italy) by Re (1963). These slabs are tens of metres thick, and made of pillow lava and hyaloclastics.

INTERNAL FEATURES OF LAVA FLOWS

Pillow lava

If lava flows into water or is erupted under water a special structure known as pillow lava is commonly formed (Fig. 19). The lava chills rapidly to form a glassy but plastic skin around still liquid lava, and rolls along in the manner of plastic bags full of

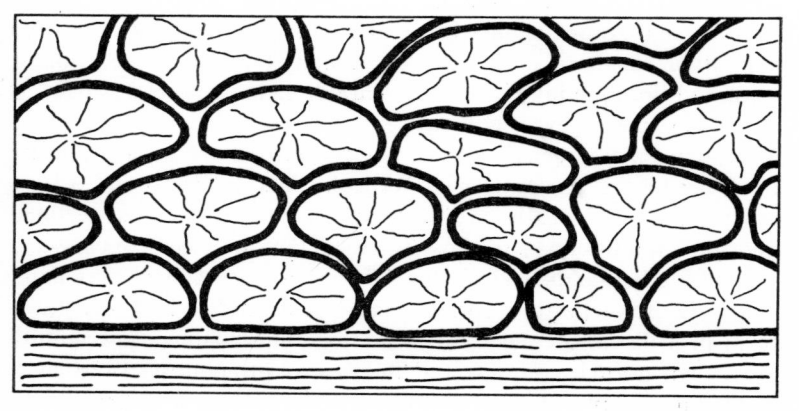

19 *Pillow lava in cross-section. Upper pillows sag into hollows between lower pillows. Each pillow has a glassy skin and radial cracks.*

liquid. The round or sausage-shaped bags are known as 'pillows', and are usually heaped one on another. They have rounded tops, but their base fits into the shape of the underlying surface. This feature, together with the glassy, tachylitic skin and radial cracks, makes pillows easy to distinguish from rounded basalt boulders produced by spheroidal weathering. Most pillow lava is formed in the sea, but some is formed in fresh water. Pillow lava is often associated with hyaloclastic deposits.

Layered lava

A cross-section of a lava flow may reveal lava in distinct layers, often associated with tubes or lava caves (Pl. 18). The 'layers' are usually a few decimetres to a metre thick, varying rapidly in thickness and not traceable for long distance. The partings between layers are cracks, sometimes crossed by strings of lava or lined by shark-tooth projections. This shows that liquid lava was present between solid or semi-solid lava at some stage, and it is thought that layered lava is formed when a flow is moving and solidifying at the same time, with movement by laminar flow.

A succession of thin flows could give a similar effect, but there would be a separate cooling crust on each layer; in layered lava flows there is only one real crust at the top of the flow.

Jointing

Cooling of a lava flow causes shrinkage, and this results in the formation of joints. These may be irregular in originally pasty masses, but attain geometric regularity in originally widespread, very fluid basalts. Centres of contraction develop in the cooling lava, and lines joining these centres are directions of greatest tensile stress, so cracks eventually appear perpendicular to such lines. When contraction centres are evenly spaced the cracks will join to form hexagons. The pattern of vertical joints divides the lava into columns, which ideally are vertical, hexagonal in cross-section, and broken into blocks by cross-fractures that are often concave-up, resembling ball-and-socket joints. The vertical joint faces may have distinctive scratches known as 'chisel-marks'. Joints in many flows form in a definite sequence with master joints first, mega-columns next, then normal columns and finally cross-fractures.

Columns may be tens of metres high, depending on the thickness of the original flow and its cooling history, and a few decimetres across. They are seldom perfectly hexagonal, but polygonal, and the columns are not always vertical. Columnar direction is controlled by the orientation of planes of equal tensile stress, which are normally parallel to the isotherms, which are in turn normally parallel to the flow surface. However, this parallelism is not always maintained, and complicated curved forms of columns can be produced. Curved columns make various patterns such as fans, chevrons, and basins, which are often given local names such as 'harps' or 'fans', while the vertical columns are most commonly known as 'organ pipes'.

In some flows a threefold division is recognised with a 'lower colonnade' with good vertical columns, a central 'entablature' which often contains various patterns of curved columns, and an upper layer that may be columnar, crudely columnar, devoid of columns or scoriaceous (Pl. 19).

Presumably the upper and lower parts of a flow with this three-fold division became immobile before shrinkage caused joint formation, but the central part took longer to cool, developed an irregular isotherm pattern (possibly associated with late movement of the lava), and so formed curved columns.

A horizontal surface eroded across columnar lava has the appearance of being paved with polygonal flagstones, and is known as a tesselated pavement. The Giant's Causeway in Ireland (Pl. 20) is perhaps the most famous example of columnar lava, but there are many examples in Australia.

Some lava flows develop a platy jointing in a roughly horizontal direction. In Victoria this seems to be confined to the older weathered lava, and may result from the weathering out of an obscure flow structure. Rittmann (1962) suggests that rapid cooling may produce some platy jointing.

Jointing in pyroclastic flow deposits is not nearly so regular as that of lava flows, and is sometimes said to have a rectangular rather than a hexagonal pattern. Sills frequently have very well developed hexagonal joints, very similar to those of lava flows. Carey (1958a) has described some joints from the sills of Tasmania that are almost at right angles, and suggests that they may possibly be due to epeirogeny rather than cooling.

SMALL-SCALE FEATURES OF LAVA FLOWS (Fig. 20)

Illustrations of many lava features may be found in Wentworth and Macdonald (1953) and Macdonald (1967).

Toes

The mechanism of lava flow by the successive formation and breaching of toes will be described on p. 62. The toes are convex lobes, often about 3 m high and tens of metres long.

Convex lava surface

In cross-section many flows have a convex surface, and the more viscous the lava the greater the convexity. Even the most fluid lavas cool fastest on the edges, where the solid sides present some obstacle to spreading and a convexity develops at the edge of the flow. This is important in locating lateral streams.

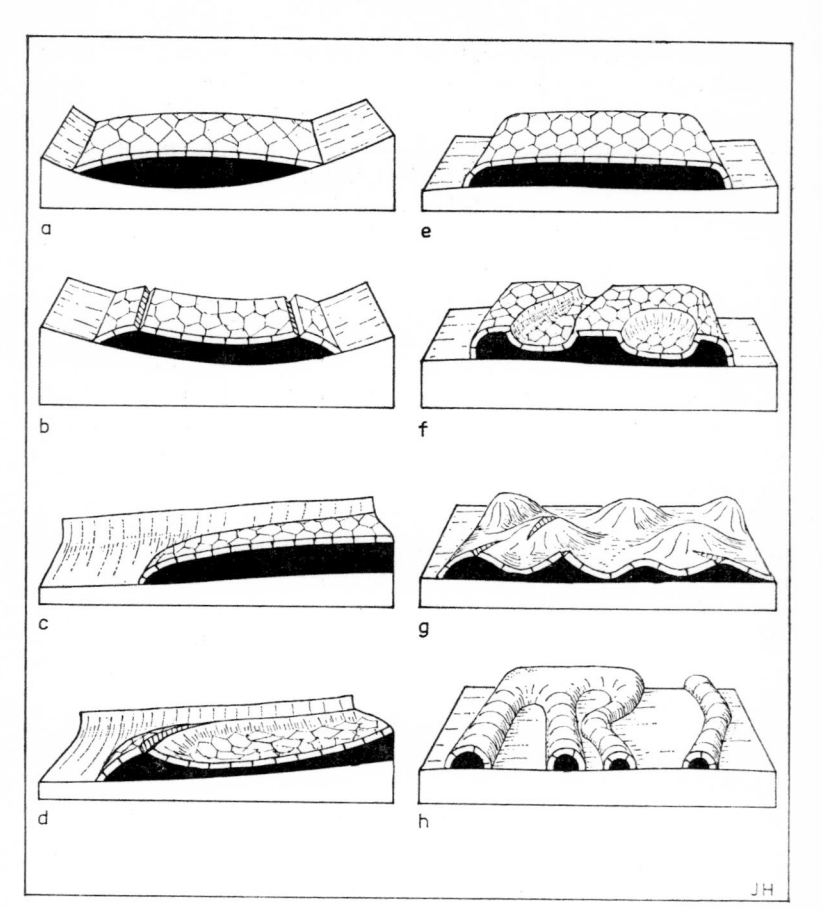

20 *Some features of lava flows: (a) Simple convex surface of valley flow. (b) Lateral ridges, formed by sagging of simple convex flow. (c) Toe, at front of lava flow. (d) Toe ridge, formed by sagging behind toe. (e) Broad, flat-topped lava flow. (f) Stony rises formed by collapse of broad lava flow, parts of which remain at accordant heights. (g) Stony rises formed by irregular collapse. (h) Stony rises formed of divided, narrow lobes.*

Lateral ridges (sometimes inaccurately called pressure ridges)

Suppose a flow has a convex top, and then the liquid in the centre is drained away. The crest will then sag, but the edges, solidifying faster because thinner, will be stronger than the centre and the collapse therefore stops some distance in from the edge. This collapse leaves two ridges, one on each side of the flow. The ridges are usually cracked at the top, and the broken edges reveal cross-sections of the original crust of the flow.

Toe ridges

Sagging of the main part of a flow may push lava into a stationary toe, so that it swells, the crust is pushed up and sometimes broken at the top in the same way as a lateral ridge (Fig. 20).

Side curtains

In a gutter carrying water and fallen leaves it may be seen that the leaves tend to be pushed to the side, and a clear channel of water flows in the centre. In the same way a lava flow may run fastest in the centre and heap solidified fragments of crust at the side. Topographically the effect of two ridges and a central depression is similar to the lateral ridge situation, but heaps of crust fragments should be exposed rather than a neat cross-section of a single crust. Boutakoff (1963) called such features side curtains, and says they are present along the Tyrendarra flow, Victoria, especially above bottlenecks in the valley.

Pressure ridges

Pressure ridges, also known as barriers, are elongate ridges of basalt pushed up by movement of the underlying lava. They are often in pairs, with a trough in between. They curve convex downstream, and are found most often some distance above bottlenecks where there is sufficient width for a pressure ridge to form, and sufficient differential flow between the centre and the edge of the flow to cause dragging.

Tumuli

Tumuli, also known as squeeze-ups, are humps on the surface of a generally flat lava flow (the singular is tumulus, the name coming from the Latin term for ancient burial mounds). They are often about 3 m high and usually unbreached, that is the lava crust runs continuously from flat areas right over the hump. However, if the curvature becomes too extreme the crest of the tumulus cracks. Tumuli are caused when pressure changes in the still liquid lava within a flow are localised at a point, or sometimes along a line, for some tumuli are rather elongated.

Lava blisters

Wentworth and Macdonald (1953) report lava blisters from Hawaii, consisting of shells a few centimetres thick around bubbles up to 1 m in diameter. So-called lava blisters in Victoria appear to be very exaggerated tumuli, though Skeats and James (1937) considered they were formed by gas bubbles generated beneath lava when it flowed over swampy ground. Ollier (1964a) showed that they are not hollow, and may take a variety of forms.

Steam bubbles

Boutakoff (1963) has found what he terms steam bubbles in the basalt along the coast west of Portland, Victoria. They are hemispherical or egg-shaped depressions, 10 to 15 m in diameter, surrounded by concentric joints. Boutakoff believes they are cavities left by steam and gas bubbles escaping from a viscous magma.

Spatter ramparts

Parallel ridges of welded spatter on each side of a fissure eruption are known as spatter ramparts.

Spatter cones

After the rampart stage described above, most of a fissure may seal, and agglutinated spatter may build up over a few points to make a spatter cone, sometimes called a cinder cone. Spatter cones differ from hornitos in being directly over a fissure, but some authors use the two synonymously.

Lava rings

These are walls of spatter, similar to spatter ramparts, but built up around the edge of a lava lake. Examples are given by Wentworth and Macdonald (1953).

Hornitos

Spatter may be erupted through a crack in the surface of a pahoehoe flow, and build up a small cone or spire of scoria and driblets. This is called a hornito or driblet cone. The term is usually restricted to small features perhaps 5 m high, and larger cones built in this way (that is not directly connected to any feeder pipe but deriving their lava within a flow) are called *adventitious cones.* Some of the smaller spatter cones to the south of Mt Eccles, Victoria, have been interpreted as adventitious cones (Ollier, 1964b). Hornitos commonly have an open pipe at the centre. Parasitic cones are sometimes called 'adventive' or 'adventitious' cones and should not be confused with the type of landform described here.

Rootless vents

Rootless vents are similar in some ways to hornitos, but are said to be produced when lava pours down earlier lava tunnels and reappears at the surface some distance away from the original source (Wentworth and Macdonald, 1953).

Open fissures

Where lava sheets issue from rift zones, there may be open cracks along the line of the fissure. These are generally fairly small features, a metre or so wide and a few tens of metres long, but they sometimes attain much larger size when they may be termed 'rifts'.

Squeeze-ups

These are somewhat similar to tumuli, but the crust has been cracked open and pasty lava has been squeezed through as a dyke-like auto-intrusion. Colton (1930) described squeeze-ups 2 km long and 20 m wide from Sunset Crater, Arizona. Nichols (1939) described bulbous squeeze-ups from New Mexico that spread slightly and are up to 5 m across. On aa flows, spines up to 30 m high are the equivalent of squeeze-ups.

Grooved lava

When semi-solid lava is extruded through a crack, as for instance in a squeeze-up, the edges may be scratched, slickensided, or grooved by projections on the solid lava at the edge of the crack. This is called grooved lava.

Shark-tooth projections

If two sheets of solidifying lava are pulled apart, liquid lava between the sheets may be drawn out into strands, as treacle in a sandwich may be pulled into strands if the two halves are pulled apart. The pointed projections thus formed have been termed shark-tooth projections, and are up to 25 cm long.

High-lava marks

When very liquid lava stands for some time at a certain level it cools around the edges, and if the lava is then drained away to a lower level, a narrow shelf of lava may mark its former position. This is known as a high-lava mark (and by the less accurate names slumpscarp and tidemark). Some high-lava marks in Victorian lava caves have curved downwards while still plastic, and have been called benches (Skeats and James, 1937). In Staircase Cave, Byaduk, Victoria, there is a whole series of high-lava marks.

Lava tree moulds

When trees are buried by lava, their shape is often preserved in the lava, though the wood may be completely burned away. The hollows so produced are called tree moulds, and may be so numerous as to play a major part in determining the porosity of the rock.

Stony rises

These are known as malpais in the United States, though the terms may not be entirely synonymous. Many widespread lava flows have a very irregular surface, though tending to a plain on a broad scale. Hummocks and depressions, ridges and blind channels, make a completely confused topography called 'stony rises' in Australia, with relief usually about 10 m. There appear to be several varieties. Some are made of a coalescing group of narrow flows emerging from the base of a broad lava sheet. Good examples are found on the south side of Lake Corangamite, Victoria. In this case the bases of the depressions, being an old plain, have accordant levels, but the height of the ridges is variable. Another kind of stony rises is produced by draining of lava from beneath the skin of a partly congealed plateau. The crust then sags into a series of irregular hollows and channels, but the ridges in between tend to be flat-topped and of accordant level. Sometimes the depressions are predominant, and only a few flat-topped hills remain. Mt Violet, Victoria, is a flat-topped hill of this kind.

Depressions

When lava is drained from beneath the crust of an extensive lava sheet, large closed depressions may be formed. There are two such depressions about 1 km wide and 50 m deep near Exford, Victoria.

Lava channels

Flows on Hawaii have been observed which run mainly along a central channel but occasionally overspill their banks and deposit thin layers of lava, in a manner analogous to the building of levees by rivers. When activity ceases there is a long sinuous channel bordered by banks about 10 m high. Such lava channels are found at

Mt Eccles, Victoria, where they are known as 'canals', and have been reported from Tristan da Cunha by Baker and Harris (1963). The formation of lava channels by levee building was actually observed on Lopevi, New Hebrides, in the 1963-5 eruption (Warden, 1967), and others were attributed to draining of molten lava from beneath a clinker cover.

Lava caves

Lava caves, also known as tubes, tunnels, and caverns, are caves inside lava flows, formed not by erosion but as primary features of the flow (Pl. 21). They are elongated in the direction of

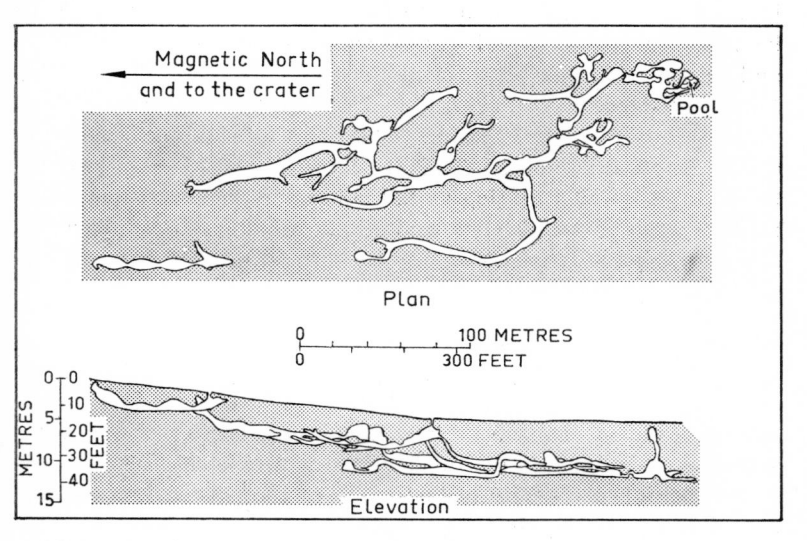

21 Mt Hamilton lava cave, Victoria: plan and elevation

lava flow, and may be up to several miles long. The longest continuous network of completely underground tunnel in Australia is that of Mt Hamilton, Victoria, with a total surveyed length of 950 m (Fig. 21). Some lava caves in Iceland, Hawaii, and Washington, U.S.A., are said to be many kilometres long, and some collapsed lava caves in Queensland can be traced on air photographs for several kilometres.

An active lava tunnel, 2 m high, was observed during the 1963-5 eruption of Lopevi, New Hebrides (Warden, 1967). Concentric 'skins' tended to break off the roof and walls, and the lava tunnel was seen to continue as a laval channel where the roof had collapsed. In many lava caves there is further collapse of the roof when the lava is cold, producing closed depressions, channels, and natural arches.

To express the matter simply, lava caves are formed by the withdrawal of still liquid lava from beneath a solid lava crust. Actually the mechanism is very much more complicated (see p. 63).

Lava stalactites and stalagmites

The lava lining of a cave may be liquefied, usually by hot gases filling the cave when the original contents are drained out. This liquid drips, and may solidify to form lava stalactites. These may be up to a metre long and may be smooth and shiny, or vesicular and rough. Lava that drips to the floor may form lava stalagmites. These are rarer than stalactites, and no good examples have been found in any of the Victorian lava caves, though some very good specimens occur in New Zealand lava caves. The lava usually appears to solidify somewhat during its fall, and many lava stalagmites are made of agglutinated driplets, and do not become smooth. In many caves dripping lava probably falls on to a still liquid floor, and is simply incorporated in it.

THE NATURE OF LAVA FLOW

Although the mechanism of lava flow seems fairly obvious, little work has been done on the fundamental nature of liquid flow close to the melting point, and in fact many of the peculiarities of lava flow are due to solidification and flow occurring together. An account of the physical behaviour of basalt flows and a comparison of the flow of lava and water is given by Wentworth (1954).

The surface of the flow naturally cools faster than inner parts, so a crust is repeatedly formed only to be broken by further movement. In some flows blocks may be carried over the toe of the flow and buried beneath advancing lava, so that the flow moves almost like a caterpillar track, and the massive interior of an aa flow may be both underlain and overlain by clinkery boulders. Alternatively, the top of a flow may cool over, and then suddenly rupture so that a new toe, or flow unit, is extruded on to the top of a flow through cracks in the surface, where it spreads out to form flow units. Flow units are the individual lobes of lava that pile up one on another during a single eruption. Each unit has an individual cooling crust. Flow units are typically lenticular bodies, up to about one kilometre long, 30 to 100 m wide, and about a metre to 6 m thick (Nichols, 1936).

Flows are deepest in the middle and so cool more slowly there. The centre is therefore more fluid than the edges, and remains mobile for longer. This gives rise to differential flow, fastest in the centre and slowest at the sides, which causes some of the small-scale features described earlier. Lava flows respond to topography, and flow fastest down the steepest slopes, although lava can flow on very low gradients. At cliffs there may be lava-falls analogous to water-falls. The more viscous lavas may override obstacles, but the fluid lavas flow around them, and may sometimes be diverted by quite small embankments. Some lavas flow and solidify in a complicated manner, giving rise to various features such as layered lava, lava caves, and stony rises. In this kind of flow the partly congealed lava appears to undergo laminar flow, with individual layers separated by partings and vesicles, and by still liquid lava. The rate of cooling of lava is often too slow for the laminae to be preserved, but in the regions where lava caves are present the layered lava is well displayed. When the layered lava first becomes separated into laminae something rather remarkable happens. The liquid lava becomes further segregated and comes to occupy cylindrical tubes running through the layered lava. The tubes are completely full of liquid which exerts a hydrostatic pressure, so the tunnels can change levels at times and flow upwards for short stretches. The mobile liquid lava eventually becomes concentrated into a few major cylindrical lava streams which are a continuing source of heat, and the hot liquid contents may even erode or melt some of the earlier layered lava. However, all these processes are contemporaneous; solidification and remelting, flow and pressure effects, are all working together. The result is a cylinder of liquid lava flowing through tubes cut in virtually solid layered lava. In confined valley flows there is likely to be just one main tube; in extensive spreading flows there may be a branching and anastomosing net-work of tubes (Ollier and Brown, 1965).

The lava may finally solidify in this form, and cross-sections of totally filled tubes are occasionally seen (Pl. 18). Alternatively the lava may be finally drained away from the tubes. If the roof is sufficiently strong a cave will be preserved. If not, the surface will sag down into the tubes, forming stony rises.

Repeated rupture and healing of the toe of a lava flow will cause constant changes in the hydrostatic pressure in the tubes, as will the amount of lava supplied at the source. In the tubes, pressure may cause bulbous swellings and dome formation. Changes may also affect the surface of the flow, creating tumuli, lava blisters, and squeeze-ups. Reduction in pressure leads to sagging, and the formation of lateral ridges.

The mechanism of lava flow is not always as complicated as that outlined above. Some viscous lavas flow as a pasty mass, moving slowly under a cover of blocky and scoriaceous debris. When such a flow comes to rest no layering will be present and when the flow cools it will be a solid, more or less uniform mass, except for cooling structures. Some pahoehoe lava moves almost as a pure liquid to a position of rest and then solidifies. Such very fluid lava will also come to rest as a homogeneous mass, except perhaps at the surface, and will solidify into an apparently uniform rock except for cooling structures.

The different types of lava flow are of some petrological significance. Slow-moving pasty flows would be expected to have a uniform petrology throughout. In those very fluid lavas that reach their position of rest as liquids and slowly cool, there may be vertical segregation of minerals and differentiation of slightly different rock types from bottom to top of a flow. This sort of differentiation cannot happen in layered lava, though there may be some difference between the early-formed layered lava and the later lava that cools within the tubes.

VI

PYROCLASTIC FALL DEPOSITS

Pyroclastic rocks are fragmentary rocks produced by volcanism. Magma contains considerable quantities of dissolved gases or volatiles. In some conditions the gas may be suddenly released, with the explosive production of many gas bubbles that can shatter the lava into countless fragments of rock, mineral fragments, and glass shards. These produce deposits known as pyroclastics. An account of the physics of vesiculation is given by McBirney (1963).

Most kinds of magma may produce pyroclastics, but the majority of pyroclastics are of acid and intermediate composition, for such magmas are more viscous than basic ones. Basaltic lava commonly erupts as a fluid and allows gentle release of volatiles.

Most pyroclastics are produced by the expansion of gas inherent in the parent magma, but gas may be produced by other means, as when an ascending magma hits a large body of groundwater and converts it into steam (a 'phreatic eruption'). In this case a considerable amount of lithic (bedrock) ash may be expected, as is often found in maars.

A lava flow that reaches the sea may be shattered by the explosive generation of steam. The pyroclastics that result are coarsely cross-bedded to form foreset-bedded breccias dipping about 25° outwards and so indicating the direction of flow.

Submarine eruptions may produce pyroclastics, but at depths of 2 km the hydrostatic pressure is greater than the critical pressure of water, and it is impossible for volatiles to be discharged explosively. Steam blast eruptions and eruptions of pumice from submarine volcanoes must therefore take place at a lesser depth.

The term palagonite has been applied to many glassy pyroclastic deposits, but the name hyaloclastite is now generally preferred (Cucuzza Silvestri, 1963) for the brecciated products of underwater eruption of lava. The name palagonite refers to altered basic glass and since some hyaloclastites are fresh the name is not suitable. 'Hyaloclastics' is used as a general term, in a similar way to 'pyroclastics' or 'volcanics'.

Lastly lava may be erupted beneath ice sheets, as in Iceland, where once again steam generation produces pyroclastic deposits. Móberg is the name given to the hyaloclastite deposits in the central graben of Iceland, which occasionally overspill on to the edges of the lava plateau.

There are two kinds of pyroclastic deposits: pyroclastic fall deposits dealt with in this chapter, and pyroclastic flow deposits which will be treated in the next chapter.

Pyroclastic fall deposits are made up of fragments that fell through the air after a volcanic eruption. 'Tephra' is a convenient name that has been suggested as a collective term for all volcanic matter that falls through the air. 'Ash fall deposit' is another term sometimes used, though such deposits may contain particles of sizes other than ash (see below).

In many volcanoes tephra is the main product. In the great eruption of Coseguina in 1835, for example, almost all the ejecta were ash, thrown high into the air and falling as showers; there were a few pyroclastic flows towards the end of activity but no lavas. The andesitic tephra was very finely divided; in most places only sand size particles are found, and even close to the vent there is nothing larger than gravel. The ash was produced by sudden 'ultra-vesiculation' (Williams, 1952).

Tephra may be produced rapidly. Thorarinsson (1956) has calculated that the 1947 eruption of Hekla released ash at 100,000 m^3 per second for the first half hour, production later falling to about 30,000 m^3 per second. The total volume of ash erupted was 220,000,000 m^3 of ash, equivalent to about 50,000,000 m^3 of rock.

The fragments produced in pyroclastic eruption vary in size between wide limits, and are classified by size into the following divisions:

Blocks and bombs	>32 mm
Lapilli	4-32 mm
Ash	<4 mm

Other terms such as sand, gravel, scoria, cinders, and dust are sometimes used as size indicators, and not all authorities use the same size limits as class boundaries. Fisher (1966) tabulates a number of modern classifications of particle sizes of pyroclastics.

15 (Top) *Pahoehoe. Ropy lava, Iceland (D. H. Blake)*
16 (Bottom) *Pahoehoe. Slab lava, Halemaumau, Hawaii (Hawaii Visitors Bureau).*

17 (Top) *Advancing aa lava tongue, lower slopes of Ngauruhoe (E. F. Lloyd)*

18 (Bottom) *Layered lava, with undrained lava tunnel, Byaduk, Victoria (M. C. Brown)*

The names 'ash' and 'cinders', like the more scholarly term 'igneous', suggest fire and combustion, and derive from early beliefs that volcanoes were indeed the burning mountains that their heat, flame, and smoke suggested. The modern use of ash and cinder has no such implication.

The action of strong wind on a fountain of very liquid lava may blow it into thin glass threads known as Pele's hair, Pele being the fire goddess of the Hawaiians. Pele's hair has been known to fall thickly in the streets of Hilo, Hawaii, and may be used by local birds to build their nests.

Volcanic bombs are commonly spindle-shaped with twisted 'tails' (Pl. 22). They often contain a core of basalt, country rock, or peridotite inside a wrapping of younger, often frothier, basalt.

22 *Formation of volcanic bombs from a ribbon of lava with projected inclusions. The terminal bomb is called uni-polar, the two-ended bombs are bi-polar.*

To some extent they may get their shape by spinning through the air, but most seem to be shaped by the hurling of solid pieces of rock through liquid in the throat of the volcano (Fig. 22), a process first described by Reck (1915).

Bombs may continue to expand after forming a first skin, which then cracks. The appearance of the split skin backed by frothy lava gives rise to the name 'breadcrust bomb'.

Most bombs vary from fist size to football size, but occasionally very much bigger ones are known. One on Mt Vulcano is said to be of 25 m³ and weighed 65 tonnes. Asamayama (Japan) is said to have thrown out a bomb or block in 1783 that measured 75 m x 40 m and formed a small island. In 1930 the usually moderate Stromboli threw blocks up to 30 tonnes for 3 km, and Cotopaxi is said to have thrown a 200-tonne block for 14 km.

Blocks are irregular in shape, more angular than bombs, and often made of pre-existing rock, either volcanic or country rock, thrown out by a volcanic explosion but not made of the magma produced during the same eruption.

A rock made of consolidated and cemented pyroclastics is known as agglomerate if coarse and tuff if fine. Tuffs are further distinguished as lithic tuff if most fragments consist of comminuted old rock, vitric tuff if most fragments are of glass, and crystal tuff if well-formed crystals predominate. Augite crystal tuffs are found on Vesuvius, Monte Rossi (a parasitic cone on Etna), and Muhavura (Uganda). Vesuvius also produces leucite tuffs, while Mt Erebus in Antarctica produces anorthoclase crystals in abundance, and Miyakijima in Japan produces anorthite.

The terms lithic, crystal, or vitric can be applied to the unconsolidated ash and lapilli.

Dark, vesicular lapilli and small bombs of basic composition may be known as scoria or cinders. In Australia the term lapilli is little used, and scoria takes its place.

Acid and intermediate volcanoes tend to produce pyroclastics with many closely-spaced bubbles making a rock foam that cools as pumice. This often has so much void space that the bulk density is less than that of water, so pumice floats. Continued expansion of gas bubbles can shatter ejecta into fragments of bubble walls, recognised under the microscope as curved splinters and fragments with concave edges. These shards are common in fine ash and tuff.

Although fragments produced in pyroclastic eruptions can vary greatly in shape, size, and weight, they tend to be somewhat sorted as they fall. The coarsest material accumulates as a cone around the vent. This is badly sorted and the space between large blocks and bombs is filled with finer material. With increasing distance from the cone the sorting becomes better, and the average grain size smaller. At some distance from the cone there is often an area which is well sorted but not too fine, and here there is a paucity of fine ash to make a 'matrix' so the deposit has much void space. This is important in holding groundwater, and affects the future course of erosion. Beyond this porous zone the ash is very fine, but makes only a thin deposit, getting thinner with distance from the cone. Plate 37 shows the typically asymmetrical distribution of ash around a volcano, due to the effect of wind on the finer particles.

Large bombs and blocks are little affected by wind and so may be dispersed all around a cone, even though the finer material is confined to one flank. This was observed in the 1947 eruption of Hekla (Iceland).

The finest volcanic dust is almost impalpable and travels to great height and for great distances. Dust from the eruption of Krakatoa in 1883 travelled right around the world, and produced very spectacular sunsets for several years.

During settling the coarse and heavy fragments fall quickest and the fine dust slowest, so that deposits from individual 'puffs' in an eruption may exhibit graded bedding, with coarse bombs or lapilli at the base and ash at the top (Pl. 23). If there is a strong horizontal wind at the time of deposition sorting may also result in aeolian cross-bedding (Pl. 24). This may be due to a simple meteorological wind, but since cross-bedding seems to be radially disposed around craters it may be due to the blast of the volcanic eruption itself. At one time the cross-bedded tuffs of Victoria (the Hampden Tuff near Lake Bullenmerri) were interpreted as re-sorted sedimentary deposits because it was thought that the cross-bedding indicated fluvial deposition. Marshall (1967) has shown that some sedimentary structures at Tower Hill, Victoria, are aeolian, and caused by a southwesterly wind.

Dune-building and cross-bedding can be produced by a base surge, as observed during the 1965 eruption of Taal volcano, Philippines (Moore *et al.*, 1966). The dunes are steeper on the blast side, and dune crests of successive beds are displaced away from the explosive crater. In the examples from Taal, the wavelength was up to 19 m. Base surge dunes would be disposed radially around the volcano, in contrast to dunes caused by meteoric wind which should have a preferred orientation corresponding to the prevailing wind direction.

Details of the eruptive and erosional history of a volcano may be recorded in some detail in pyroclastic deposits, as for instance in the products of the Irazu eruption of 1963-5 in Costa Rica (Murata, Dondol, and Saenz, 1966). In sections, rainy season deposits could be distinguished from those of the dry season by their well-developed stratification. A zone with three persistent pumice horizons represents the climactic period of eruption. A highly rilled surface records a cloudburst of 10 December 1963, and a rilled lag deposit records the strong winds of the 1964 dry season.

Pyroclastic deposits at some distance from the cone are generally draped over pre-existing topography as a sheet that follows all the old topography, but in general makes it more subdued. This is known as mantle bedding (Pl. 25). The topographic effect of an ash field has been likened to that of a blanket of loess. Around several East African volcanoes, including Kerimasi, Elgon, and Napak, there are beds of limestone that can be traced to the volcanoes and are often interbedded with ashes. These have generally been supposed to be lacustrine limestones, but Dawson (1964) suggests that they may be altered volcanic ash of carbonatite composition.

The welding together of fragments, very common in pyroclastic flow deposits, is generally absent in fall deposits, and welded scoria is found only in the immediate vicinity of vents, spatter cones, and hornitos.

TEPHROCHRONOLOGY

Some layers of tephra provide useful markers in stratigraphic correlation. For this purpose the ideal bed is distinctive in appearance and mineralogy, and is widespread. In any stratigraphic section where the layer is found it clearly separates those beds older than the ash from those younger. Where the ash lies over datable material, most commonly some charcoal that can be carbon dated, then an absolute age can be used in the correlation of sections and geological events. In New Zealand, for example, the Taupo rhyolite pumice overlies logs dated A.D. 130 and provides a marker between older and younger events. Determination of the refractive indices of phenocrysts and glass in ash falls whose stratigraphic position is known often enables correlation with distant ash layers to be effected. Chemical composition and mineralogical composition may also be used. The method is made difficult by reworking of ash, by alteration with increasing age, and by the strong resemblance that is sometimes found between ash from different vents. Nevertheless some ash layers prove to be useful markers.

In Iceland every eruption has left a layer of tephra, which in some instances covers the greater part of the country. Where not eroded by wind or water these layers make distinct horizons in soil profiles, and there may be up to a hundred layers in a single profile. Thorarinsson's tephrochronological studies show that most activity of Hekla, Iceland, has been cyclic for 8000-9000 years. There have been five cycles, each starting with a basic mixed eruption, followed by a period of a couple of centuries of quiescence, followed by a purely explosive rhyolitic eruption.

Ash falls are of great importance in the North Island of New Zealand, where Holocene and Late Pleistocene ashes cover about half the island. Deposits of sixteen separate showers have been recognised in the surface soils, and areas with over 3 inches (7·6 cm) of each ash have been mapped during soil surveys (Gibbs and Wells, 1966). The tuff and lapilli distributed by the Tarawera eruption of 1886 form a recognisable layer over an area of 10,000 km^2.

A summary of the many geomorphic purposes to which tephrochronology has been applied in New Zealand is provided by Pullar (1967). Ash layers can be used to determine rates of infilling of depositional basins. They are also useful markers for measuring the rate of alluvial fan building; for instance, the 80-year-old Tarawera Ash is buried by 30 cm of alluvium on the fans at Whakatane. Where an ash layer is complete, there has been virtually no erosion since the time of its deposition, so the preservation of ash layers on hillsides provides a basis for the study of the distribution of erosion. Dated tephra layers mantle old dunes and beach ridges at Whakatane, Gisborne and elsewhere, and are useful in indicating the position of the shoreline in past time and the rate of progradation of the coast. Pullar also describes, with examples, the application of tephrochronology to terrace correlation and chronology, archaeology, tectonics, and the study of sea level changes.

From the stratigraphic viewpoint, it is important to distinguish individual beds of short time range from larger units of tephra with a longer time range, but which may nevertheless prove useful in tephrochronology. Kaizuka (1965) has proposed the following categories:

1. Tephra bed or a fall unit: products of a single or continuous explosion (duration 10^{-2} years).

2. Tephra member or an eruptive cycle unit: products of single eruptive cycle unit (10-10^2 years).

3. Tephra formation: products of a polycyclic volcanic mass (10^3-10^4 years).

4. Tephra group: products of a volcanic belt (10^6-10^7 years).

VII

PYROCLASTIC FLOW DEPOSITS

A mixture of solid particles suspended in a gas can behave in many ways like a liquid, a principle used in industrial 'fluidisation' for the transport of such materials as cement and coal dust through pipes. Fluidisation can occur naturally in volcanic eruptions, when finely divided pyroclastics are suspended in volcanic gases. This natural fluidisation is in many ways more active than the industrial process, for the suspended particles are themselves emitting gases. The physical principles involved in fluidisation of ash flows are discussed in papers by Brown (1962) and McTaggart (1962). The fluidised ash moves like a fluid at very great speed even over very gentle slopes. Pyroclastic flow deposits are the results of deposition from such flows of hot fragmentary volcanic material made buoyant by hot gases.

Active pyroclastic flows have the appearance of rapidly projected clouds of dust. They are generally dark, but sometimes, especially at night, incandescent material may be seen and gives rise to the common name for such emissions—nuée ardente, generally translated as glowing cloud or glowing avalanche.

Many names have been used for the deposits that result from pyroclastic flows, including ignimbrite, ash flow deposit, welded tuff, tuff flow deposit, nuée ardente deposit, and many others.

Ignimbrite will be used here in the sense of Cook (1966). This is a rock unit term, and should not be used as a petrological term: several petrological types can give rise to ignimbrites though rhyolite and andesite predominate. Neither does the term imply any post-depositional alteration such as welding, though this may be present. Thus one pyroclastic flow gives rise to one ignimbrite, which may or may not be welded, and may be of any petrological type.

SIZE AND CLASSIFICATION OF PYROCLASTIC FLOW DEPOSITS

The length of flows and the area of deposition depend to some extent on pre-existing topography, but some examples will give an idea of the size of pyroclastic flow deposits.

Flows in the Valles Mountains, New Mexico, are traceable for over 30 km. Some from Mt Mazama, Oregon, went for 70 km. The Valles Mountain flows cover over 900 km². The Lake Toba, Sumatra, ignimbrites cover 25,000 km², and the Taupo-Rotorua ignimbrites of New Zealand have an area of 26,000 km².

The thicknesses of ignimbrites vary from a few metres to 300 m in the Valles Mountains, and up to 500 m in some Russian ignimbrites. The thickest individual ignimbrite sheet so far revealed by drilling in New Zealand is 135 m.

Calculated volumes of ignimbrite deposits are very great. The New Zealand field has an estimated volume of 8300 km³, the San Juan ignimbrites of Colorado 9500 km³, and the north Queensland ignimbrites 2800 km³. Individual calderas also produce large amounts of material, ranging up to the 90 km³ of Aira caldera, and the 80 km³ of Aso, both in Japan.

These vast volumes suggest that the magma chambers that produce them were originally close to the surface. This idea is supported by geophysical data, and by the discovery of old ignimbrites in the geological column which have been intruded by a related pluton, for example in the Georgetown area of north Queensland (Branch, 1966).

Ignimbrites may be erupted very quickly. The Katmai eruption produced 28 km³ in 60 hours, and it is estimated that the 2800 km³ of northern Queensland were produced in a few days (Branch, 1963). However, some ignimbrites, including those of New Zealand, may continue to be produced over a long period.

Yellowstone Park in the U.S.A. is an area of broad ignimbrite sheets produced in Eocene times, remarkably similar in many ways to the ignimbrite plateaux of the North Island of New Zealand. In the Lamar River area of Yellowstone Park some forest trees are preserved in an upright position, and there are the remains of twenty-seven distinct forests, one on top of another, each buried in its turn by pyroclastics.

Classification of pyroclastic flows

Aramaki (1961) recognised an important relationship between the size of an ignimbrite deposit and the viscosity of the magma.

He made a threefold classification of pyroclastic flows based on viscosity and volume. However, since the viscosity of old flows is difficult even to estimate quantitatively, this scheme was replaced by one using size of flow and the degree of vesiculation of the erupting magma, which is reflected in the bulk density of the products and is easily measured. Density of pyroclastic flow deposits ranges from about 0·5 to 2. It was also decided that earlier terms were not quite appropriate and so a simpler threefold classification was proposed (Aramaki and Yamasaki, 1963):

Dense pyroclastic flows	0·001-0·3 km³
Intermediate pyroclastic flows	0·05-1 km³
Vesicular pyroclastic flows	0·1-90 km³

This threefold division is also present, though with other names, in Murai's classification of 1961, which stresses the manner of eruption and has the following divisions:

Nuée ardente

Pelée type   e.g. Mont Pelée
(flow from the side of a dome)

Merapi type   e.g. Lamington, Merapi, Hi-
(flow from a collapsing dome)   bok

Lakurajima type   e.g. Lakurajima, Hambara
(flow from an open crater)

Intermediate type   e.g. Asama, Agatsuma

Ash flow

St Vincent type   e.g. St Vincent, Komagatake
(vertical eruption from a crater, with high ash column)

Krakatoa type   e.g. Krakatoa
(as St Vincent, but of greater magnitude)

Valley of Ten Thousand   e.g. Valley of Ten Thousand
Smokes type   Smokes
(magma discharged mainly through fissures)

ROCK TYPES IN PYROCLASTIC FLOW DEPOSITS

Many kinds of rock from basalts to rhyolites may give rise to pyro-clastic flows, but silicic rocks are by far the most important. Nuée ardente and Intermediate types of flow generally have silica per-centages from 55 to 65 per cent. Ash flow types are generally in the range 60-75 per cent silica. The bulk density of the rock also appears to be related to type of flow. Nuée ardente types have a bulk density greater than 1·2; St Vincent type flows are in the range 0·7-1·2; Krakatoa type ash flows are in the range 0·5-0·7.

Homogeneity of pyroclastic flows

Ash flows are remarkably homogeneous, because fluidisation causes intense mixing of material and there is little lateral or vertical variation (Pl. 27). This homogeneity is present regardless of the magnitude of the flow, and is very different from the variability generally found in all parts of pyroclastic fall deposits. In some volcanoes there is not even variation with time, and similar material may be found in deposits discharged at different times from the same volcano. The material erupted from Komagatake, Japan, in 1929 was exactly like that of the previous eruption.

However, some modern studies (e.g. Lipman, 1967) have shown a significant variation in chemistry and mineralogy from bottom to top of thick pyroclastic flow deposits. The changes in composition apparently reflect in inverse order a compositionally zoned magma chamber, more silica rich at the top.

Kuno *et al.* (1964) have provided interesting data on the homo-geneity of lithic and pumice content of pyroclastic flow in compari-son to variation in pyroclastic fall deposits. In a pumice flow eruption of Tawada caldera (North Honshu) the fragmental lithic material, but not the pumice, exhibited a systematic size variation with dis-tance from the crater. In a pumice fall eruption from the same caldera all erupted material showed systematic variation. In the flow erup-tion most energy was used in shattering country rock, whereas during the pumice fall the energy was involved in explosive ejection of material to great heights.

Welding

Although flow material may be originally homogeneous, great apparent changes are caused by welding and compaction. Because pyroclastic flows move with great rapidity the time for cooling is small, and so when they come to rest they retain a considerable amount of heat. Above a certain temperature the glass shards will adhere together, a process known as welding. Degrees of welding are marked by the amount of cohesion, deformation of shards, elimination of pore space, and even homogenisation of the glass. Those parts of ignimbrites that are most welded are often known as welded tuffs.

The degree of welding depends on the initial temperature of the magma, the quantity and composition of the volatiles, the chemical composition of the ash, the pressure of the superincumbent load, and the speed of cooling (itself affected by the thickness of the flow since ash is a good insulator). In some sheets the degree of welding varies over short distances, which later leads to differential erosion.

Ignimbrites are often zoned, especially if thick, the main zones being an unwelded layer at the base (where cooling was rapid), a welded zone in the middle, and an unwelded upper zone (Pl. 26). The welded zone has a fairly sharp boundary with the lower layer, but merges into the upper zone. Welding and compaction cause a change in the shape and colour of pumice fragments. Fresh pumice is white or grey, and it changes through shades of brown to dense black obsidian-like material in the strongly welded zones. Compaction flattening gives a foliate structure to welded tuff, and the compaction of pumice results in a relative increase in the content of crystals per unit volume which can be most striking in tuffs with an initially high crystal content.

Vapour squeezed out of the welded zone during compaction may react in the porous zones and give rise to the growth of crystals of feldspar and tridymite, a process known as vapour phase crystallisation. The welded zone may eventually devitrify to form aggregates of feldspar and cristobalite, resulting in a rock that closely resembles a lava flow.

Jointing and weathering may further enhance the differences between zones, and often give the impression that an ignimbrite is made up of many distinct flows and ashfall layers when in fact it is one rock unit.

Jointing

Columnar jointing is common in many welded tuffs, such as those of New Zealand, and the Brisbane tuffs, but joints seldom extend into the non-welded zones. Joint spacing varies from a few centimetres to over a metre, the closest joints being associated with the most intense welding. Like joint-columns in lava flows, the columns in welded tuffs are generally vertical but are occasionally fanned or curved. The joint pattern is irregular, tending to rectangular or square in plan rather than the roughly hexagonal jointing of lava flows.

The zone of maximum compaction often has horizontal platy jointing as well as vertical joints. This should not be confused with the platy structure developed by weathering of foliation planes in the zone of partial welding.

THE FLAT TOP OF PYROCLASTIC FLOW DEPOSITS

Because pyroclastic flows move almost like a liquid they can spread out over great distances as fairly thin sheets. They can move over very low gradients and even flow uphill for short distances; they fill in hollows, and flow around obstacles. When they settle they have a very flat top, however rugged the pre-existing scenery may have been. In this they are markedly different from pyroclastic fall deposits which are draped over the topography fairly evenly. The zones of welding and compaction are roughly parallel to the flat upper surface.

When an ignimbrite sheet is thin relative to the available relief of pre-existing topography, it will follow the old valleys and will inherit the drainage pattern. This kind of deposition simply makes the old valleys flat bottomed.

Thick multiple sheets on the other hand can obliterate pre-existing topography and produce extensive plateaux such as the Mamaku Plateau, New Zealand.

OTHER KINDS OF PYROCLASTIC FLOW DEPOSITS

Although ignimbrites are by far the dominant kind of pyroclastic flow deposit, two other kinds of deposit may be regarded as belonging to this category. Basic agglomerates are not definitely known to be flow deposits, but many of their features indicate that such a deposition is probable. Lahars are flows of pyroclastic material mobilised by water.

Basic agglomerates

Mt Elgon on the border of Kenya and Uganda is about 50 km across and over 3000 m above its base. It is built up of a large number of layers of volcanic agglomerate, each marking a separate eruption (Davies, 1956). After each eruption there was evidently a period of quiescence when soil was formed and trees grew, for fossil trees are found in the thin layer of ash that marks the start of each new eruption. They are invariably flattened. Despite the size of the pile that makes up Elgon, there is virtually no change in the petrology, which is basaltic, and little sorting of the agglomerate. This suggests that some kind of pyroclastic flow may be responsible.

Exactly the same conditions of deposition of agglomerate layers, ash layers, and moulds of fallen trees are found in the Sogeri Plateau near Port Moresby, Papua. There is no cone here and the source of the agglomerates has not yet been identified.

In both Elgon and the Sogeri Plateau the agglomerate tends to make flat-topped plateaux or steps, with well-developed vertical jointing giving rise to steep cliffs, often undercut at the base by erosion of the less resistant thin ash layer.

Lahars

Lahars are landslides or mudflows of volcanic material. They may be divided into hot mudflows of fresh ejecta mixed with water, and cold mudflows caused by the mixture of rain or surface water with a mass of unconsolidated and unstable ash. Most lahars are very mobile, travelling rapidly down valleys or hillsides and doing great damage in inhabited areas, though some cold mudflows can spread fairly slowly as rather stiff lobes. In the eruption of Vesuvius in A.D. 79 the town of Herculaneum was buried under 20 m of mud, which crushed houses and knocked down walls, but the absence of skeletons shows that people had time to get out of the way.

Displacement of a crater lake is very likely to cause lahars. One of the best known examples of this is Kelut, Indonesia, where the 1919 eruption displaced a crater lake estimated at 38,000,000 m^3 and killed 5500 people. Ruapehu, New Zealand, has also produced many lahars in the past that were probably started by displacement of the crater lake.

Lahars carry material for long distances; Cotton (1944) describes a boulder of about 37 tonnes transported 75 km by a lahar from Ruapehu. Lahar debris is deposited as large sheets of crudely bedded, ill-sorted sediment with occasional layers of cross-bedded sands (Pl. 28). Large boulders are scattered randomly in the deposit and give rise to the typical lahar landscape of moundfields with hundreds of hillocks from a few metres to several tens of metres high, each having a core of boulders.

The 1888 volcanic explosion of Bandaisan, Japan, was a very exceptional kind of eruption (see p. 14) in which a large part of the mountain, estimated at $1\cdot2$ km^3, was blasted away and descended as a huge avalanche or mudflow. A moundfield was formed that was similar in all respects to those produced by smaller lahars.

Galunggung, Indonesia, is an amphitheatre-shaped volcano and on a gentle plain below the breach are the Ten Thousand Hills of Tasik Malaha (actually fewer than 4000), ranging from 3 to 70 m high. This vast moundfield covers an area of about 250 km^2, but its estimated volume is only one-twentieth of the missing sector of the volcano.

VIII

INTRUSIVE IGNEOUS ROCKS

The magma that erupts in volcanoes originates deep in the earth's crust and reaches the surface through fissures and pipes. Igneous rocks that cool in the feeding channels or other weaknesses in the crustal rocks are called intrusive or hypabyssal rocks, and they occur in a few fairly well defined forms (Fig. 23).

Intrusive igneous rocks cool more slowly than effusive ones, so are more coarsely crystalline and the crystals can usually be seen with a hand lens. The commonest intrusive rock associated with volcanoes is dolerite.

The slow cooling of intrusive rocks often gives rise to well-developed jointing due to shrinkage. Columnar jointing is the commonest type, and the columns are usually vertical in sills and horizontal in dykes. Jointing is explained in Chapter V.

When erosion has removed upper portions of volcanoes and neighbouring rocks, the intrusive igneous bodies give rise to land-forms due to differential erosion.

VOLCANIC NECKS

These may be filled with solidified lava, or with tuff-breccia and agglomerate, depending on the nature of the original eruption and magma type. Volcanic necks may also be referred to as plugs. The term 'neck' suggests a lava column joining the head of the active volcano to the body of the magma chamber, but some necks may never reach the ground surface and never give rise to active volcanoes.

The numerous plugs of the Fitzroy Basin in Western Australia provide an interesting sequence where, by carefully comparing the rocks in many plugs, Prider (1960) concluded that they were sections at different levels in similar pipes. A typical plug is shown in Fig. 24 and examples of hills at different levels can be seen. Some

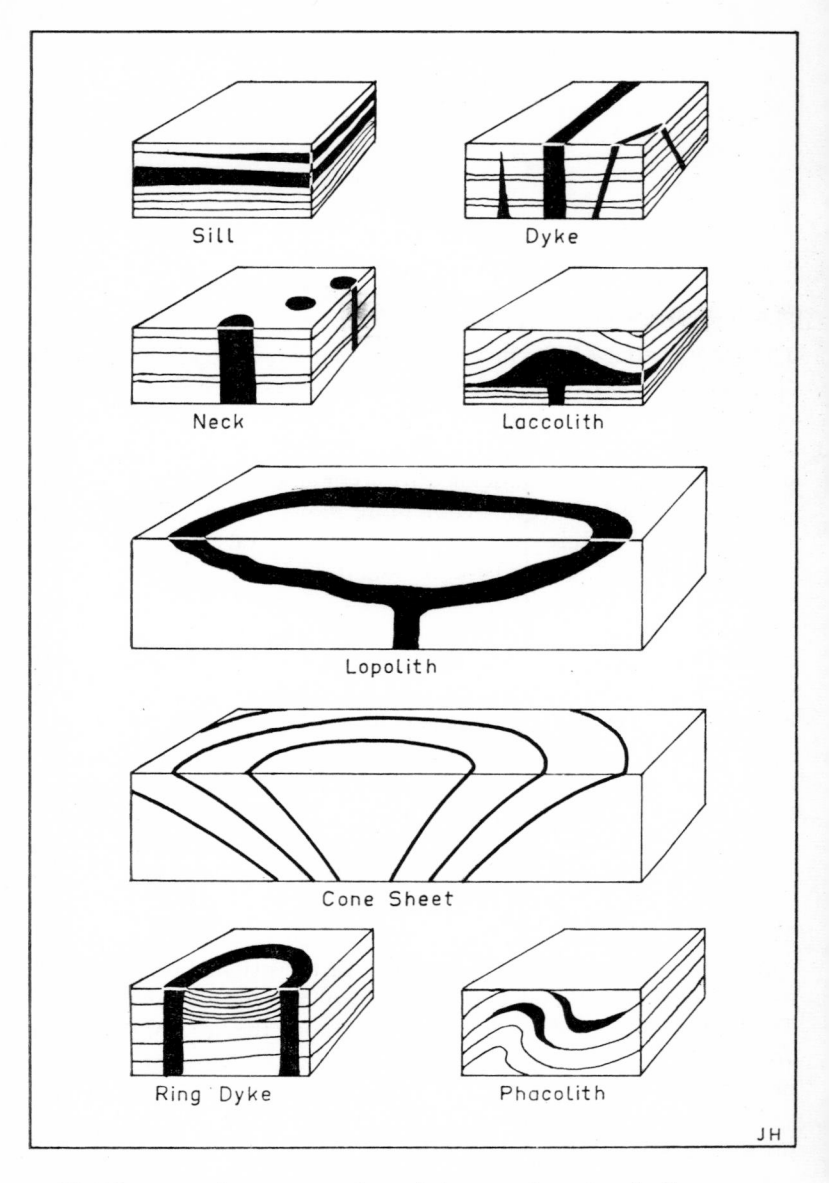

Sill

Dyke

Neck

Laccolith

Lopolith

Cone Sheet

Ring Dyke

Phacolith

JH

23 Diagrammatic representation of igneous intrusive bodies

19 (Top) *Lava flow at Narre Warren, Victoria, showing lower colonnade with vertical columns, a central entablature with curved columns, and an upper scoriaceous zone without columns (A. A. Baker)*

20 (Bottom) *The Giant's Causeway, Northern Ireland. Perfect hexagonal columns and a tesselated pavement in the foreground (Northern Ireland Tourist Board).*

21 (Top) *Inside a lava cave, Byaduk, Victoria (M. C. Brown)*

22 (Bottom) *Olivine cored bi-polar bomb, Mt Noorat, Victoria: length 1 metre (A. A. Baker)*

23 (Top) *Horizontally bedded scoria with bombs, Mt Noorat, Victoria (A. A. Baker)*

24 (Bottom) *Cross-bedded ash, Purrumbete, Victoria (E. B. Joyce)*

25 (Top) *Mantle bedding, Waiouru, New Zealand. An ash layer of uniform thickness overlies with angular unconformity eroded lahar deposits.*

26 (Left) *Unbedded, unwelded, and highly porous ignimbrite near Otamarakau, New Zealand*

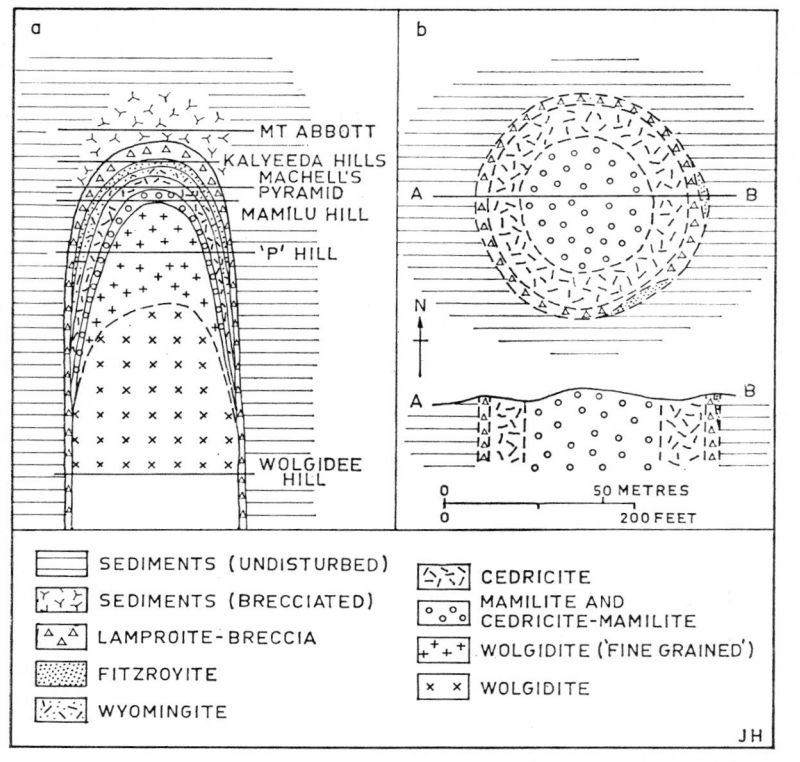

24 *Plugs of the Fitzroy area, Western Australia: (a) Vertical section of ideal plug, showing the level exposed in several actual plugs. (b) Plan and cross section of Mamilu (after Prider, 1960).*

pipes did not reach the surface, but may have had crypto-volcanic features above the pipe, as at Mt Abbott. Other pipes reached the surface and gave rise to surface volcanoes such as Mt North.

Two distinct joint patterns seem to occur in lava-filled volcanic necks. Where the conduit has been deeply eroded there is a rosette with horizontal columns radiating out from the axis, perpendicular to the walls. In others, such as the famous Devil's Tower, Wyoming, the columns make an inverted fan. This is an anomalous pattern that probably forms at a high level in the neck (Hunt, 1938; Spry, 1962).

Williams (1936) distinguished two types of volcanic necks (Fig. 25). The first, called the Hopi type (from the Hopi Buttes of New Mexico), is near the very top of the original volcanic pipe, and is virtually a

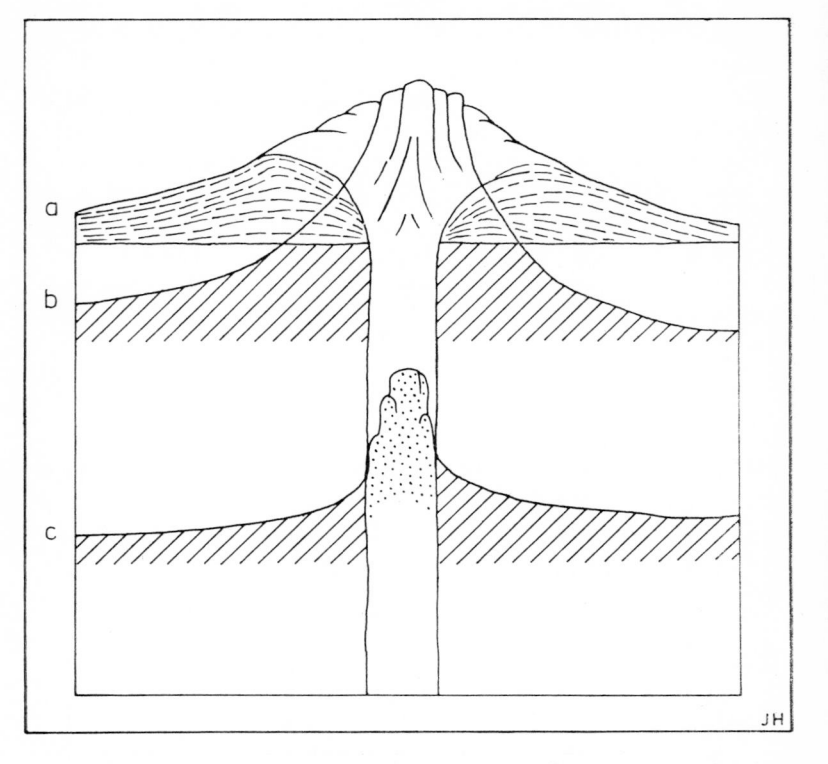

25 *Types of volcanic neck. The original volcano was at level a.*
A Hopi-type neck is produced by erosion to b, and erosion to c
produces a Navajo type neck.

crater fill. The columns of lava may rest upon inward dipping tuffs.
The second type, called the Navajo type, is formed by erosion to a
lower level, and is at a section far below the original ground surface.
Most necks are of the second type, but in younger volcanic areas
examples of Hopi necks can be found. Saddle Hill, Dunedin,
New Zealand, is a Pliocene volcano of Hopi type (Benson and
Turner, 1940).

Volcanic necks often rise abruptly from the surrounding country,
as in the Warrumbungles, New South Wales (Pl. 29) and the
Glasshouse Mountains of Queensland, where the necks rise for
hundreds of metres from the coastal plain, here floored by Mesozoic
sandstones. Beerwah, 550 m above sea level and about 430 m above
the surrounding country, is the highest. The peaks are mainly

trachytic, frequently columnar, and dykes of the same material radiate from some of them.

It is also possible for the volcanic rock in a pipe to weather faster than the surrounding rock, creating a hollow. In parts of New South Wales necks give rise to many remarkable amphitheatres bounded by sandstone cliffs more than a hundred metres high forming unbroken circular walls, except where streams leave them through clefts in their lower rims. Davis and Gospers Holes are two examples described by Carne (1908), and many examples nearer to Sydney are described by Adamson (1969), including that shown in Pl. 30.

DYKES

Most volcanic feeders are vertical fissures which give rise to vertical sheets of igneous rock called dykes. Sometimes a dyke splits up near the surface into a number of pipes. Some dykes are seen to thin out towards the surface, indicating that the lava is emplaced by wedging aside the bounding rocks.

Dykes vary in thickness from a few decimetres to hundreds of metres, but widths of 1 to 10 metres are commonest. In length they can be many kilometres long, or only a few metres. They commonly occur in swarms or in radiating patterns around a volcanic centre.

Parallel swarms of dykes are thought to be formed deep in the crust, while radial dykes (Fig. 26) and concentric fractures are produced in the upper layers around pipes or domes of rising lava. Even without erosion the radial pattern of feeders can sometimes be determined from the pattern of satellite or parasitic volcanoes. The giant basaltic volcano, Klutchevskoi, in Kamchatka, has twelve lines of vents 6 to 18 km long, radiating down the slopes from the summit crater, the number of vents along each line ranging from three to eleven.

Dykes give rise to wall-like ridges such as the Breadknife in the Warrumbungles (Pl. 31). More commonly dykes give more subdued ridges, and occasionally the rock of the dyke weathers faster than the surrounding rock, forming a trench or depression that will often be followed by a watercourse. The island of Arran, Scotland, provides examples of three relationships between dyke and landform: in the north dykes give rise to trenches in high-grade metamorphic rocks; in the south they form walls in weak sedimentary rock, except where the margins of the dyke have been baked to an

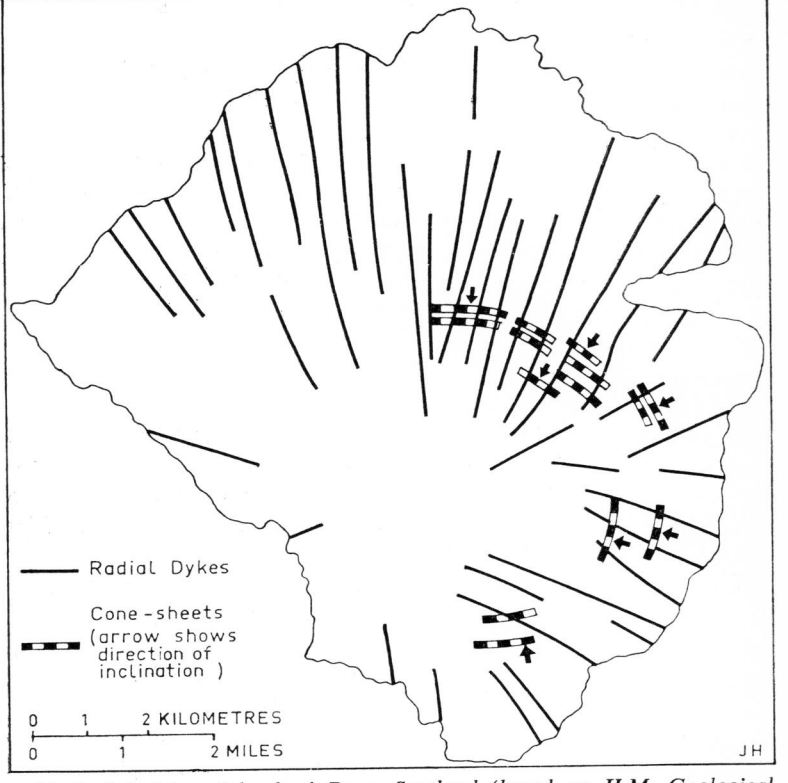

26 *Radial dykes, Island of Rum, Scotland (based on H.M. Geological Survey maps)*

even harder state when double walls are produced. Dykes usually fill gaps in the crust caused by tension, and the aggregate thickness of dyke swarms indicates the total extension of the crust. The Mull (Scotland) swarm has a total thickness of over 1000 m and indicates a stretching of the crust in the affected region of 3·8 per cent; the Arran swarm shows an extension of 7 per cent.

Although most dykes are intruded into bedrock, some actually penetrate into the volcanic pile above, and may even reach the surface exposed in a crater wall like that of Red Crater, Tongariro, New Zealand (Pl. 32). This dyke reveals a most interesting history: evidently the lava rose in the dyke, the edges were chilled and solidified, and then the lava drained away leaving the present hollow dyke.

SILLS

Intrusive rock may form nearly horizontal tabular bodies of rock called sills. These commonly follow the bedding of enclosing sedimentary rocks for considerable distances and are said to be concordant intrusions. Few remain concordant for their entire extent, however, and are locally transgressive where they cut across a bed and then spread along another bedding plane. Sills are particularly abundant in basins of thick, unfolded sediments such as those of South Africa, Tasmania, Antarctica, and Brazil, where conditions are ideal for widespread lateral intrusion.

Plateau basalt fields are built largely of innumerable lava flows, but also often contain thick sills of similar material intruded between previously erupted flows. Sills may be injected between earlier layers of a strato-volcano; one such sill exposed in the crater of La Soufrière, St Vincent, is said to be many tens of metres thick and to have columnar jointing.

Sills can be of very large dimensions, like the Jurassic sills of Tasmania which are up to 700 m thick. The sills in the Karroo of South Africa extend over an area of 500,000 km^2 and make up 15-25 per cent of the geological column in the area.

Because their heat alters the enclosing rock both above and below, whereas lava flows only bake underlying rocks, sills can be distinguished from thick lava flows. Sills also have chilled edges at both upper and lower surfaces while flows have distinct scoriaceous upper surfaces. When eroded, sills behave like any other body of hard rock in a sequence of layered rocks, and commonly give rise to a landscape of plateaux and cliffs. The very good jointing helps in maintaining steep, often vertical, escarpments.

In Tasmania the Jurassic dolerite mostly appears as a single body made up of interconnected sheets which resists erosion and tends to dominate the landscape; dolerite caps most of the highest mountains and underlies the great Central Plateau. In some parts of South Africa great mesas of intrusive dolerite are prominent in the scenery. The intrusion of these sills is thought to have occurred at the same time as the outpouring of the plateau basalts of which the Drakensberg is a remnant.

After prolonged erosion only small remnants of sills may remain. Browne (1933) described a number of sills from New South Wales, including Mt Dangar near Merriwa, Nullo Mountain in the Blue Mountains, Billyambija near Marulan, and Mt Bocobel in the

Cudgegong district, all of which have been very much reduced by erosion.

CONE SHEETS

These are curved concentric assemblages of dykes inclined inwards towards a common centre of eruption. They are inverted cones, becoming successively flatter away from the centre (Fig. 23), and the outermost cones also flatten towards the surface like an inverted trumpet. Presumably cones of country rock are displaced to allow the intrusion of the cone sheets. Individual cone sheets may be about 10 m thick.

Hotz (1952) and Walker (1958) have shown that the cone sheets of the Palisades (U.S.A.) and the Karroo (South Africa) have an inward dip of about 20° and an average diameter of 8-16 km, so if conical their apices would be at depths of about 3·5 km. The use of the term 'cone sheet' has been extended to much larger and more irregular intrusions, including some of the Jurassic dolerites of Tasmania. Carey (1958a) has suggested that when the dolerite magma was intruded it surged through the basement in a number of channels. On reaching the base of the horizontal Permian and Triassic sediments, the magma spread out laterally as a transgressive sheet, lifting and floating its roof of sediments. The dolerite in doing so formed a number of very large and shallow cone sheets, each cradling a central raft of sediments. Such a structure could be regarded as a lopolith.

RING DYKES

These structures are circular in plan and dip vertically or outwards at high angles. They appear to be filling a cylindrical fissure around a subsided mass. The material inside is generally (but not always) of volcanic origin and has inward dips, possibly due to drag caused by its downward movement. Subsidence of this kind is called cauldron subsidence, and is often associated with caldera collapse. A present-day example of the surface expression of a ring dyke is provided by the island of Niuafo'ou near Tonga. This is a basalt dome with a caldera surrounded by a complex of fissures 5 km across which has erupted lavas during the present century (Cotton, 1944).

Most ring dykes are revealed by considerable erosion, and stand as arcuate ridges above the surrounding country. These are now known from many parts of the world, and often have diameters up to 25 km. Branch (1966) has described many ring dykes from north Queensland. Stevens (1958) has described examples of both a simple ring dyke and a ring dyke complex from southwest of Brisbane.

LACCOLITHS

A body of intrusive rock that has a flat base but pushes overlying strata into a dome is called a laccolith. Many bodies originally thought to be laccoliths have since been shown to be other kinds of intrusions. The type area for them is the Henry Mountains of Utah, but these have since been shown to be fed laterally from a central stock, not from below. Edwards (1941) described two laccoliths from Stanley and Wynyard in northern Tasmania, but later workers interpret them as steep-sided bodies intruding horizontal Tertiary lavas and pyroclastics (Spry and Banks, 1962, p. 272).

However, there appear to be plenty of true laccoliths, and many have been described in New South Wales. Carne (1903) described a series of twelve laccoliths from the Barigan district in that state. The largest has a basal area of 5 km² and is at least 300 m thick. All have arched the overlying strata. From the Bald Mountain area, N.S.W., Carne (1908) described three laccoliths—Bald Mountain, The Pinnacle, and one unnamed, each of which intrudes the Coal Measures and wholly or partially uplifts the Triassic series, revetments of which are still to be seen on the shoulders of some. Jensen (1909) has described laccoliths of alkaline dolerite in the Nandewar Mountains, N.S.W.

LOPOLITHS

Enormous saucer-shaped intrusions are called lopoliths. Like laccoliths, they are becoming less common with further work, and the best known examples are proving to be structures of different form. The Sudbury Complex in Ontario is now thought to be a ring complex and the Bushveld Complex of South Africa is now thought to be a number of separate bodies, with thick dyke-like feeders. The Tasmanian dolerite sills, however, are locally transgressive and on the broad scale form a body that might well be regarded as a lopolith. Carey (1958) showed that regionally the bodies have the form of large cone sheets, but of course the scale is much larger than usual for such features.

PHACOLITHS

A phacolith is a concordant igneous intrusion in the crest of an anticline or the trough of a syncline. Phacolithic intrusions have been described from the Muswellbrook-Singleton area by Raggatt (1929).

BATHOLITHS AND STOCKS

These large bodies of igneous rock are formed deep in the earth's crust; they are plutonic rather than volcanic, so will not be discussed further in this book.

IX

HYDROLOGY AND DRAINAGE
OF VOLCANIC AREAS

GROUNDWATER

The water-holding spaces in a rock, such as joints, cracks, and the interstices between rock fragments, will generally form an interconnecting mesh of channels through which water can move. The percentage of total space in a rock is a measure of its porosity. The rate at which water can move through a rock is its permeability.

Some water is held by molecular attraction on to surfaces of rock fragments, and such water cannot flow freely. If the rock porosity is made up of many very small pores, as in fine ash, most of the water is held in this way and permeability will be very low. If the pores are large, as in blocky lava, the greater part of the water will be unaffected by molecular attraction and can flow freely.

A laboratory specimen of fresh dense basalt or rhyolite may show virtually no porosity, and the only water it could retain would be that wetting the surface of the block. Small specimens of such rock therefore indicate no water-holding capacity at all. In the field, however, such rocks may hold water in joints, cooling fractures, rubbly layers or other features, and they often contain a lot of water. The hydrological properties of a rock therefore depend on structure and field relationships as well as petrological type, though some generalisations can be made.

A rock with spaces that hold water is called an aquifer; an impermeable rock that may hold up or dam back water is called an aquiclude. The surface of the groundwater in an aquifer is known as the water table. Where the water table intersects the groundsurface, groundwater will emerge at a spring.

Water-bearing properties of igneous rocks

All except the most massive basalt flows are permeable, and the most significant hydrological feature of basalt is its great permeability. Cavities that hold water in basalt include interstitial spaces in clinker or flow breccia, cavities between flows, joints, gas vesicles, lava tubes, and vegetation-mould holes. Pillow lava is usually very permeable except where the interstices have been filled by secondary minerals, and most of the great springs in the Snake River Canyon near Twin Falls, Idaho, issue from pillow lava. Acid lava flows generally have low permeability because they are massive, though if they have a deep blocky layer on the surface this will be very permeable.

Pyroclastic fall deposits are very permeable, except for the finest ash. The permeability of the younger volcanoes of Hawaii is so great that no runoff occurs, and no well-defined stream channels exist even where the rainfall exceeds 5000 mm (Stearns, 1966).

The coarsest scoria is found close to vents and is of course extremely permeable, though the porosity may be reduced by lack of sorting of the deposit and the presence of fine material in the interstices. Some distance from the vent moderately coarse, well sorted lapilli and scoria are found, producing an excellent water-holding rock. Further still from the vent the ash is well sorted and fine. Pore spaces are small, so water is held by molecular attraction, and though porosity may be high, permeability is low. Fine ash is prone to fairly rapid weathering, alteration, and compaction, which tend to reduce permeability further.

Thus on a pyroclastic cone the upper and middle slopes tend to be very porous and good water holders, but the lower slopes tend to be more impermeable, so springs arise on the lower slopes at the top of the impermeable deposit.

Downstream of springs there is simple stream erosion, and basal sapping by the spring causes steepening of the headwall and gully retreat.

Pyroclastic flow deposits vary greatly in permeability. Unconsolidated pumice is extremely permeable. Welded zones of ignimbrites may also be sufficiently cracked to yield water freely, but may also be so massive as to be aquicludes considered safe even for dam foundations.

The water table

The water table is at its simplest on wide lava plains, where it is generally very flat with gradients of less than 1:1000. Because basalt is so permeable the level of the water table is rapidly adjusted to the level of the lowest outlet, and so if the lava is thick there may be a considerable depth to the water table. In the Snake River lava plain the depth to the water table is generally over 150 m. Because of the flatness of the water table, a few wells usually provide enough information to predict water levels over a considerable area, though complications can occur. Some complications are caused by perched water tables, the water being held up by sheets of impervious alluvium on top of the lava plain or interbedded with lava flows. Another complication occurs when the lava plain is divided into compartments by ridges of bedrock or by impermeable dykes. Such divisions may be quite invisible at the surface, for a lava plain may have a very smooth top but a quite irregular base.

Many rivers flowing from impermeable rocks will sink under-ground as soon as they reach a porous lava plain. If the river is carrying considerable sediment this will be deposited on the lava, and will slowly fill up the crevices and reduce the porosity of its bed. By continually silting its channel a river may extend across a

27 *Water table map, Mud Lake, Idaho. The lake is perched on clay beds on flat land, and the main water table is below with a groundwater cascade (after Stearns, 1942).*

permeable lava plain and deposit a veneer of sediment that can hold up surface water, which is said to be perched. A very good example of this is Mud Lake, Idaho (Fig. 27). On the north side of the lake there is only one water table, but on the south side there is a perched water table over the main water table, which here shows an exceptionally steep gradient.

In a simple volcanic island of perfect permeability the water table would rise slowly from sea level at the coast to a point beneath the wettest part of the island. Volcanic cones on land have a more irregular base, but in principle the situation is the same. The water table rises slowly from the level of springs around the base. The springs may be controlled by the contact with impermeable bedrock, by impermeable ash, or by other volcanic features such as dykes or impermeable flows.

Returning to the situation in volcanic islands, these hold a lens of fresh water within the rock, virtually floating on salt water. Like an iceberg, the floating water has a much greater part below

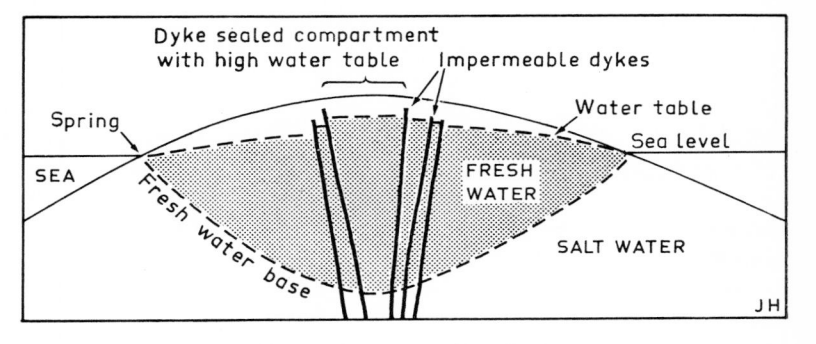

28 Fresh water distribution in a volcanic island

sea level than projecting above. Water leaks out at springs about sea level (Fig. 28), though more complicated situations are common where impervious sediments accumulate around the shore, as in Hawaii (Fig. 29). Springs may be due merely to variations in topography, as in ignimbrite regions, but they are found more commonly where an impermeable bed crops out at the surface. Lava flows, welded ignimbrite zones, or dense, impermeable pyroclastics are the commonest aquicludes. Composite cones, with their many alternations of porous and impermeable layers, lead to the common

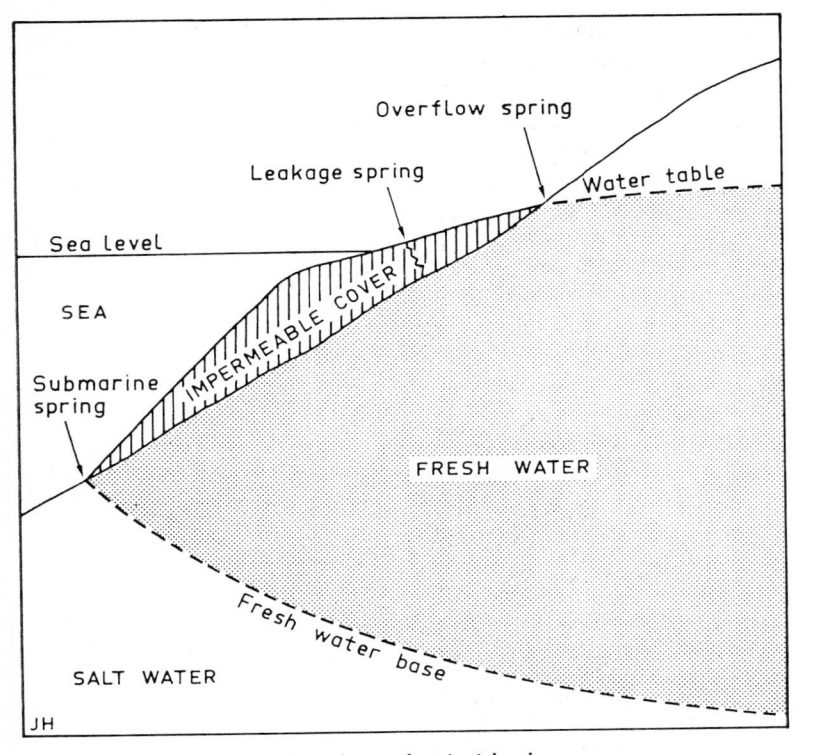

29 Discharge at the edge of a volcanic island

occurrence of springs, as for instance on the flanks of Tongariro and Ruapehu in New Zealand.

Some of the springs arising in volcanic country are extremely large, and according to Meinzer (1949) thirty-eight of the sixty-five first magnitude springs (100 cubic feet per second or more) are in volcanic rocks or associated gravel. These include Sheep Bridge Spring, Oregon, with a discharge of 791 m³ a day; Malade Springs, Idaho, discharging 2,761,000 m³ a day; and Thousand Springs, Idaho, discharging 2,112,000 m³ a day.

DRAINAGE OF VOLCANIC AREAS

Drainage patterns

Volcanoes have some very characteristic drainage patterns of which the most obvious is the radial drainage pattern on volcanic

cones. The streams originate some distance below the rim and run
with little sinuosity down the flanks (Pl. 34).

Even actively growing volcanoes of fine scoria and lapilli are
commonly dissected by numerous ravines, e.g. Ngauruhoe, New
Zealand, and Matupi, New Guinea.

When volcanic eruption is intermittent ravines may be cut
while the volcano is dormant; these are filled with tongues of lava
when activity is renewed. The tongues, which are usually convex

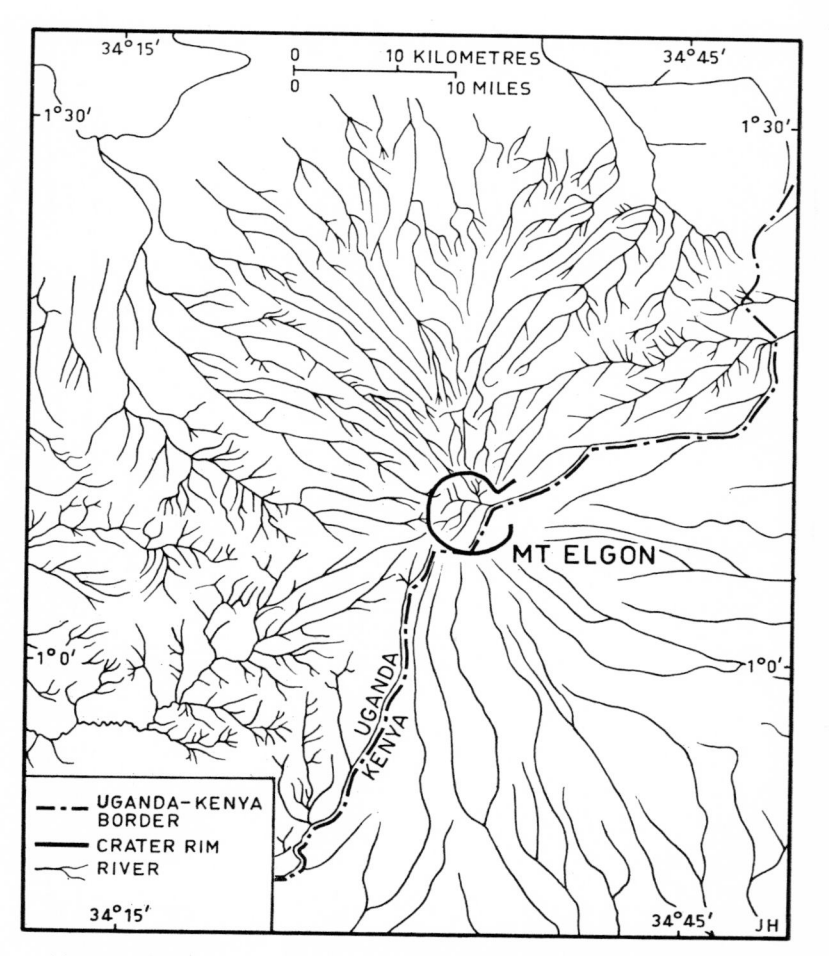

30 *Mt Elgon, East Africa. Radial drainage pattern and breached
crater.*

in section, then become divided and new valleys are excavated between them on the sites of the earlier ridges. This is simply an example of inversion of relief on the flanks of an active cone.

Inside craters and calderas the streams run from some distance below the rim towards the centre in a centripetal pattern. If a former crater lake overflows, the originally centripetal drainage becomes a

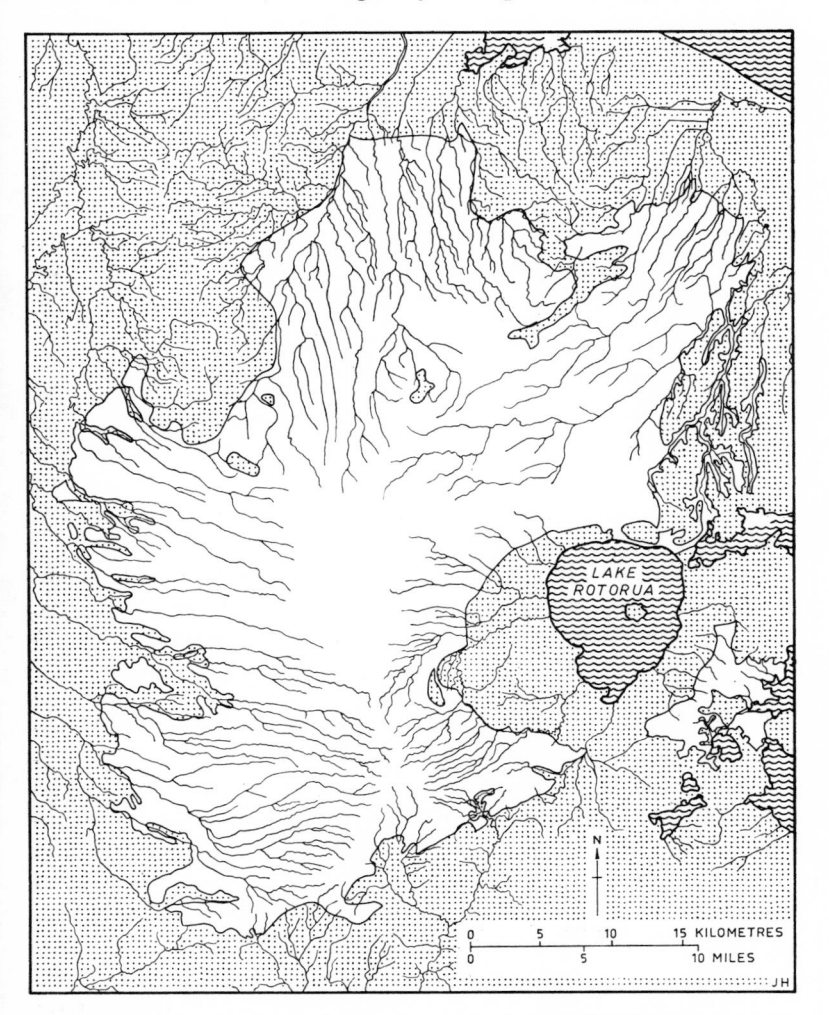

31 Mamaku ignimbrite plateau, New Zealand. The drainage pattern is radial overall, made up of a number of sectors with parallel drainage.

mere appendage at the head of a main stream that drains the crater through a breach (Fig. 30).

The crater rim may also be breached by headward erosion of one of the radial streams, which again leads to drainage of the crater and any lake it may have contained.

Volcanic plains of large size will develop an insequent drainage on their surface that follows irregularities of the type described in Chapter V. However, most of the drainage on lava plains is due to drainage displacement, as will be described in the next section.

On ignimbrite plateaux the upper zone of unwelded pumice is very porous, but water flows over the welded zone if one is present. This also tends to be flat (like the surface of the ignimbrite deposit) and a more or less insequent pattern may be expected. However, many ignimbrite areas have a markedly parallel drainage pattern (Fig. 31). This is presumably due to long and uniform slopes on uniform material.

Drainage density

Lava plains are often highly porous, especially at the base of flows, and layers of alluvium between flows may also provide aquifers. For this reason surface drainage is usually scarce on lava plains, and drainage density is low. For 320 km along the northern edge of the Snake River Plain, Idaho, all the rivers descending from the mountains sink into the porous lava, and at the end of the plain great springs discharge groundwater from the old lava-filled canyons. Only two rivers cross the Western District volcanic plains of Victoria from north to south.

One might expect that ignimbrite plains, having high porosity, should have a low drainage density, but this does not seem to be the case. To some extent this is because the welded zone of ignimbrites is relatively impermeable and holds up groundwater, and to some extent due to the mechanism of valley formation on ignimbrite plains. Many of the valleys are dry for long periods, and occasional floods, accompanied by much tunnelling and mass movement as well as normal erosion, may be largely responsible for the relatively high density of valleys.

Further generalisations about drainage density are hardly warranted, since it depends on so many factors, including amount and distribution of rainfall, permeability of rock, erodibility of rock, and topographic situations.

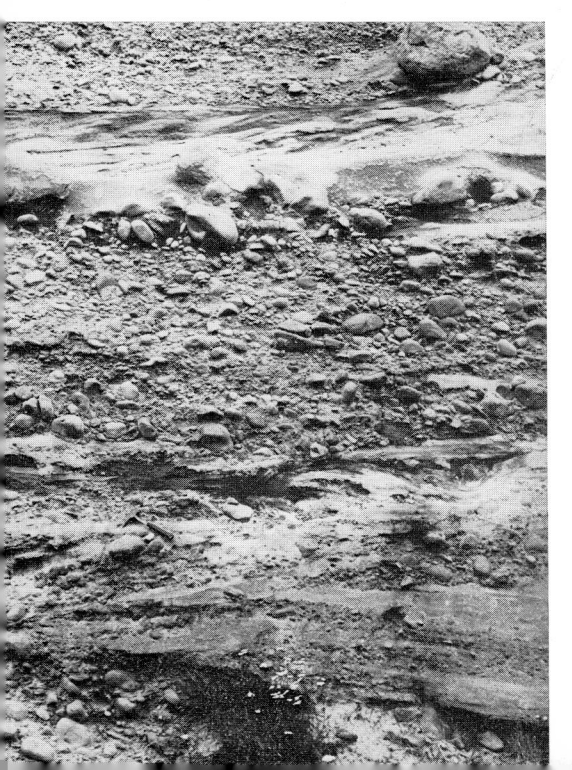

27 (Top) *Base of ignimbrite at Matahina dam, New Zealand. Strongly welded zone over less welded zone.*

28 (Left) *Typical lahar deposit, Waiouru, New Zealand*

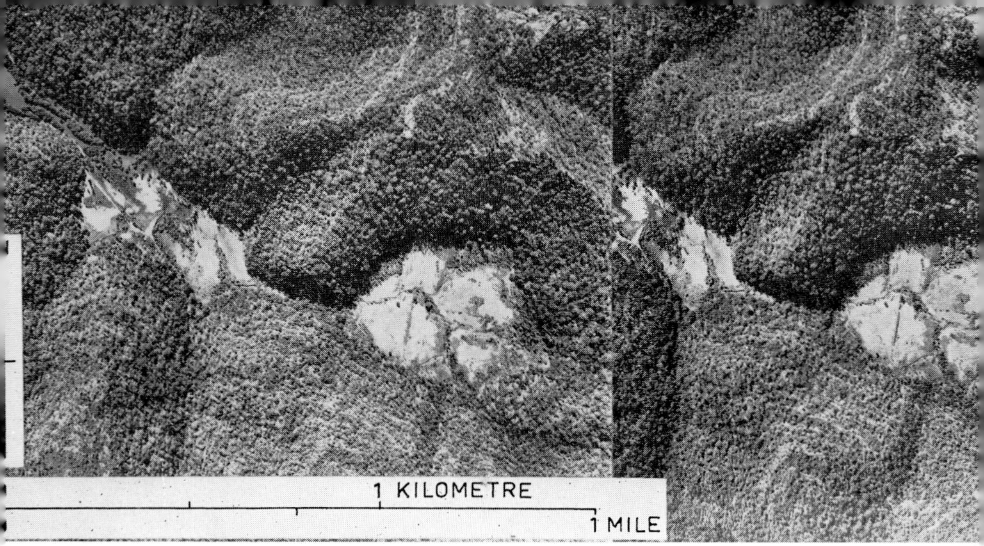

1 KILOMETRE

1 MILE

29 (Bottom) Volcanic necks: Crater Bluff (foreground) and Mt
Tonduron (background), Warrumbungles, N.S.W. (N.S.W. Government Tourist Bureau)

30 (Top) Eroded volcanic necks making basins below the general
level of the surrounding sandstone country, Hawkesbury River,
N.S.W. (Reproduction by courtesy of the Department of Lands,
New South Wales, Australia)

31 (Top) Dyke: the Breadknife, Warrumbungles, N.S.W. (N.S.W. Government Tourist Bureau)

32 (Bottom) Dyke exposed inside crater and partially drained, Red Crater, Tongariro, New Zealand

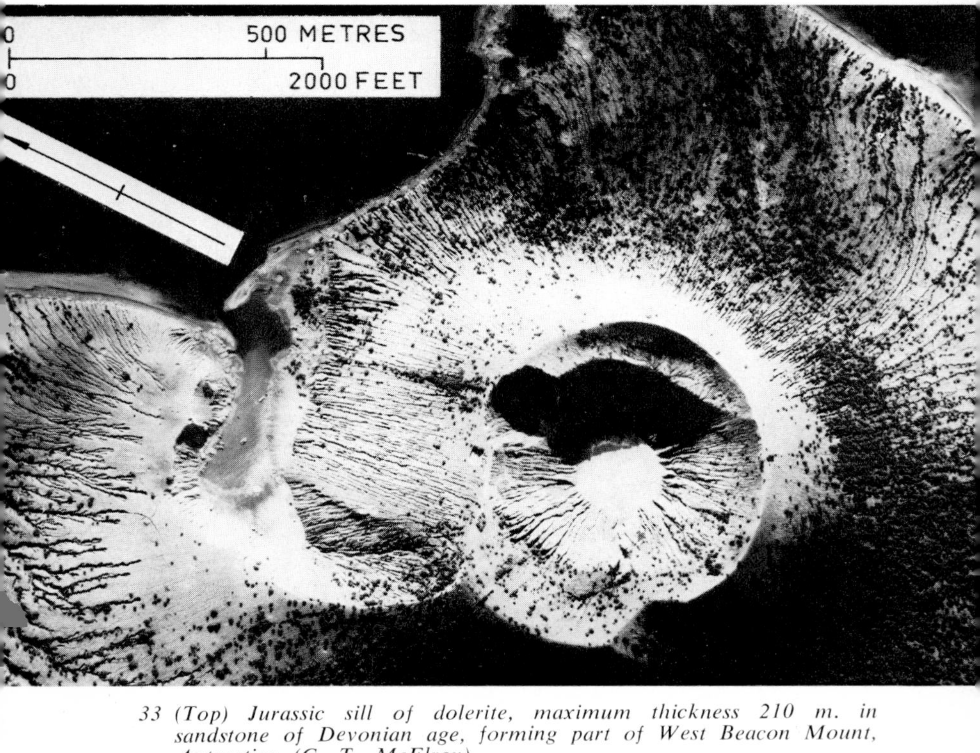

33 (Top) *Jurassic sill of dolerite, maximum thickness 210 m. in sandstone of Devonian age, forming part of West Beacon Mount, Antarctica (C. T. McElroy)*

34 (Bottom) *Radial drainage on Vulcan, Rabaul, New Guinea (Illinois Committee on Aerial Photography)*

Drainage diversion

Volcanic activity has a marked effect, sometimes utterly catas-trophic, on pre-existing drainage. If only small cones and flows are produced, streams may flow around them with but little shift from their old courses, but if enough lava is produced all pre-existing topography may be obliterated and a completely new drainage pattern initiated on the volcanic cones and lava plains.

A fairly simple example of drainage diversion is provided by the Warrumbungles, N.S.W., a mass of volcanics which erupted

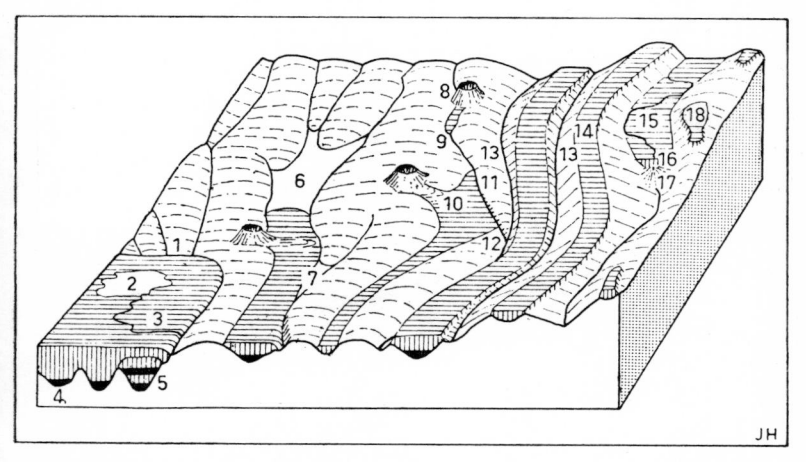

32 *Drainage and landforms associated with lava flows: (1) River diverted by lava plain. (2) Insequent lake on lava surface. (3) In-sequent stream in lava surface. (4) Deep lead. (5) Multiple lava flows and deep leads. (6) Lava dammed lake (main valley). (7) Lava dammed lake (tributary). (8) Stream flowing beneath cone and flow. (9) Spring. (10) Flow diverting river into next valley. (11) Lava diverted stream. (12) Probable site of gorge. (13) Twin lateral streams. (14) Inversion of relief. (15) Insequent stream on valley flow. (16) Waterfall. (17) Alluvial fan. (18) Residuals of older lava flow.*

on the course of the Castlereagh River. The waters had to find their way round the great effusive pile, and the new drainage—the Namoi and Macquarie rivers—flows in the same general direction as the original.

Lava flows displace rivers from their beds, and the water they carried must be accounted for in some other way. The various kinds of drainage diversion that can be caused by lava are shown diagrammatically in Fig. 32.

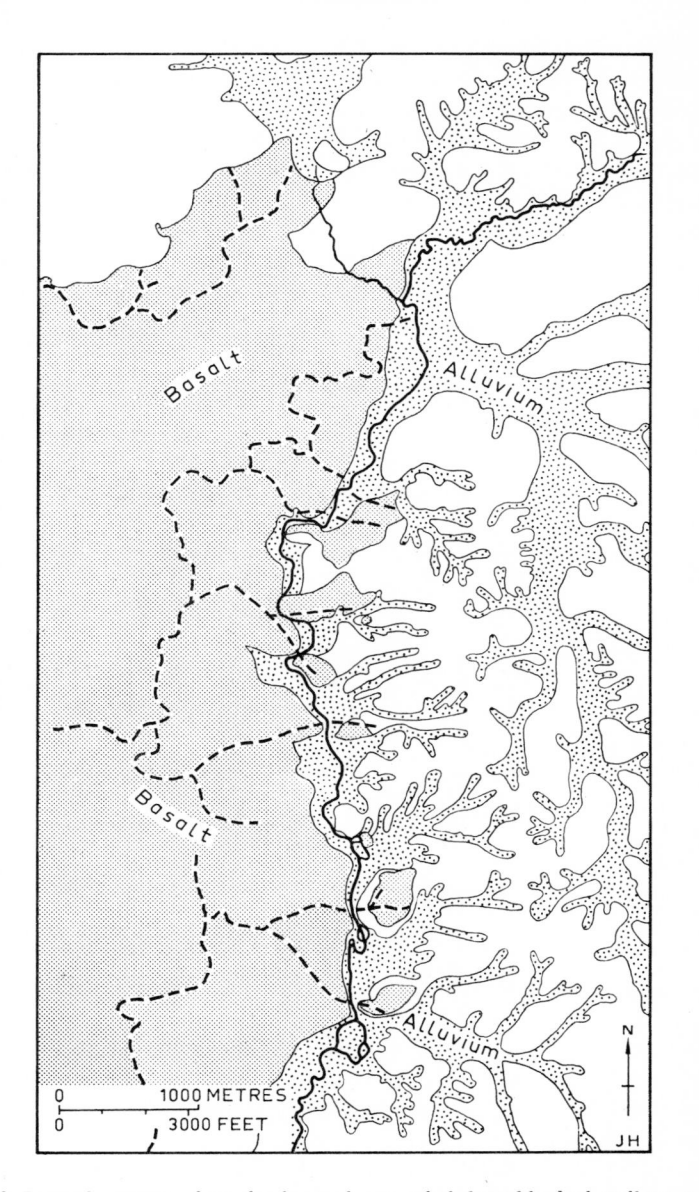

33 *Lateral stream, deep leads, and aggraded lava-blocked valleys near Ballarat, Victoria*

For a while the river may flow over the lava in an ill-defined course depending on minor irregularities in the lava surface. At this stage a thin layer of alluvium may be deposited haphazardly on the basalt, and this may account for the plentiful quartz and other unlikely minerals found in some 'basalt' soils. Eventually, however, the river will incise a well-defined valley either across the lava or around it.

Many lava flows are slightly convex so there is a shallow trench where the lava meets the old valley wall. This is commonly the place where diverted water flows in what is called a lateral stream (Fig. 33).

A simple example of drainage diversion is shown in Fig. 34. The ancestral Mt Emu Creek, Victoria, flowed southwards, with a

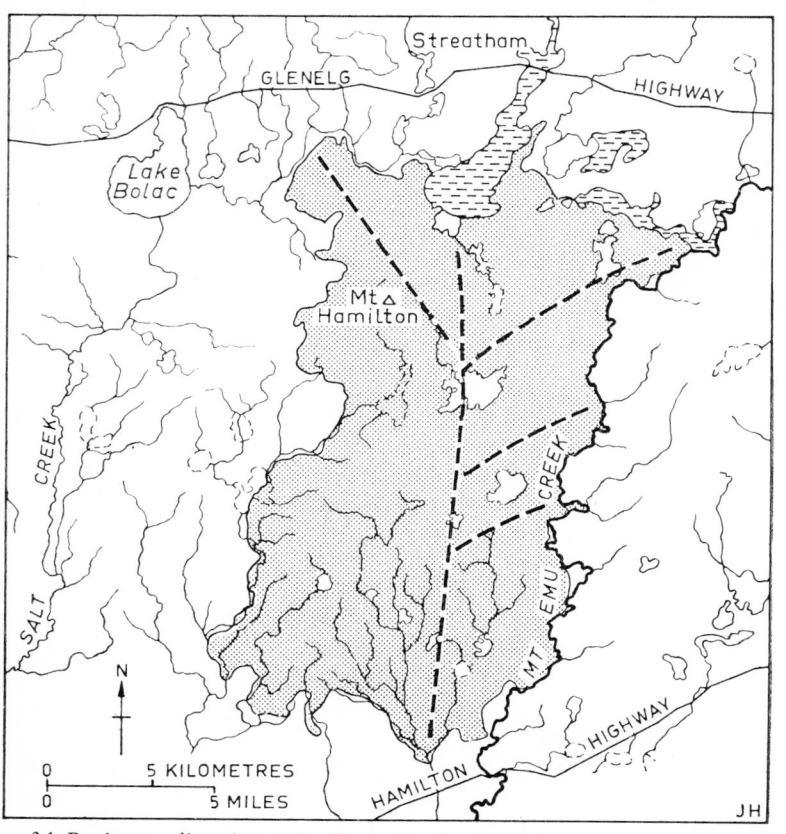

34 Drainage diversion, Mt Emu Creek, Victoria

number of tributaries from the east, one from the north, and one from the northwest. The course of this river was then blocked by extensive flows from Mt Hamilton and The Peak. Mt Emu Creek then flowed along the eastern edge of the flow, following the edge very faithfully, even where lobes from the lava flow extend up tributary valleys. The stream from the north now disappears in a series of swamps, some of which may overflow occasionally into some of the insequent lakes on the surface of the lava flow. The tributary from the northwest has been diverted to Lake Bolac, and then to Salt Creek, which is itself a lateral stream bounding an earlier flow. When a lava flow occupies a broad valley with tributaries on each side, lateral streams may develop on both sides of the flow as twin lateral streams.

Thick flows of lava may reach or overtop the old interfluve ridges, and streams may then be displaced entirely from their old valleys. Thus the Plenty River near Melbourne flows for some distance as a lateral stream on the east side of a lava flow, but eventually it is diverted into a neighbouring valley, from which point it flows in a gorge it has excavated in Silurian bedrock.

Very large sheet flows of basalt may divert rivers completely from their course so that they flow for many miles around the lava edge. The River Wannon in Victoria provides an example. Similarly the stream that used to flow down the Harman valley at Byaduk, Victoria, has been completely blocked by the lavas of Mt Napier. The flow that occupies the Harman valley therefore has no lateral streams.

Alluvial deposits in valley bottoms that are buried beneath lava flows are known as deep leads. Some contain economic placer deposits, such as tin at Herberton in Queensland, and gold in many places in Australia and California. Deep lead mining has provided a lot of information about pre-basaltic drainage patterns, even when lava plain formation has completely obliterated pre-existing topography.

The drainage pattern of deep leads may contain stream channels of several different ages, possibly reflecting lava diversion at several times, but nevertheless the drainage pattern revealed by deep lead maps is a useful tool for working out details of geomorphic histories. It may be compared with maps of modern drainage to see what changes have taken place since lava modified the drainage pattern. West of Ballarat, for instance, it can be seen that the position of the main divide has moved as much as 20 km to the north (Fig. 35).

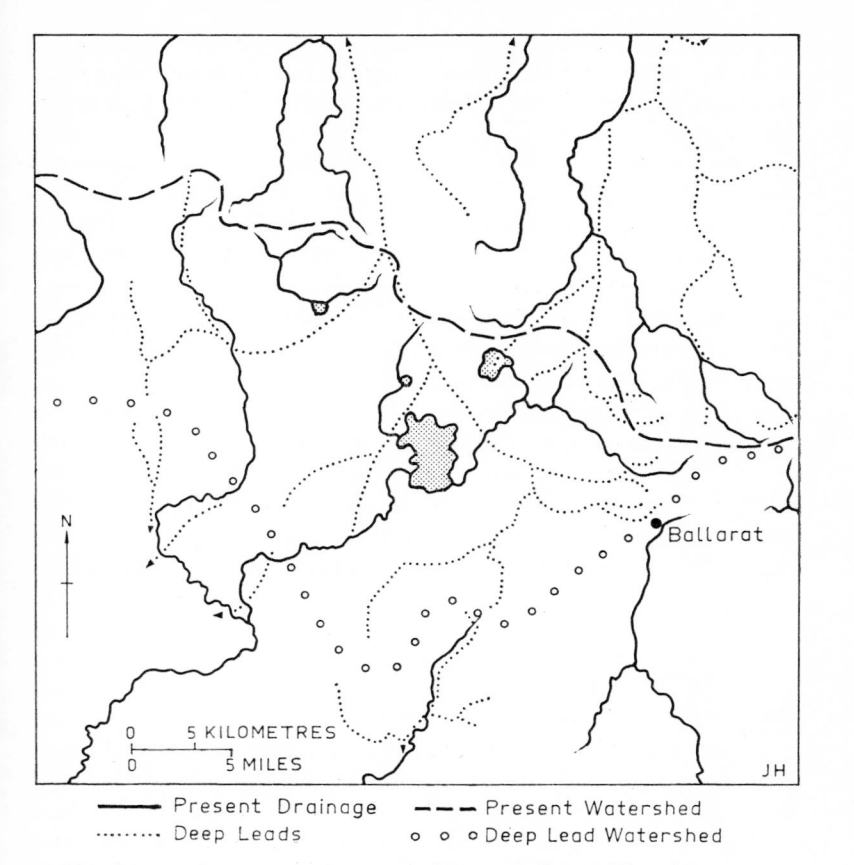

35 Change of position of watershed near Ballarat, Victoria

In some circumstances the direction of drainage may be completely reversed, usually in association with lake formation. In
New Zealand the upper Waitangi valley has been dammed by lava
to form Lake Omapere, which has a westward overflow now,
although the original Waitangi drainage was to the east. The
drainage of Lake Kivu described later in this chapter provides
another example. In Nicaragua volcanoes have ponded and reversed
drainage so that water now flows eastward across a former continental divide.

Drainage can be disrupted catastrophically during actual
eruptions. A lake that occupied the crater of La Soufrière, St
Vincent, was thrown out of the crater during the first phase of the

eruption of 1902, producing extensive hot mudflows that rushed down the mountain into the sea. The crater lake in Kelut, Indonesia, used to be similarly displaced during eruptions producing dangerous lahars.

Some of the ice-caps (jokulls) of Iceland are large, covering hundreds of square kilometres, and they may be partly melted from beneath by volcanic action to produce vast quantities of water in the so-called jokulhlaup (glacier burst) which devastates the country and leaves the landscape unrecognisable.

Estimates of the discharge rates of water in a jokulhlaup are almost incredible. The Grimsvotn jokulhlaup of 1934 discharged at an average rate of 100,000 m³ per second for two days, and the jokulhlaup of Katla in 1918 discharged at the rate of 400,000 m³ per second, also for a 2-day period. This is more than ten times the discharge rate of the Mississippi River and four times that of the Amazon. Katla produces the most dangerous and unpredictable hlaups because it has a greater gradient than others. The hlaups carry huge boulders; one of 400 m³ was carried 14 km by the hlaup of 1918.

LAKES

Crater lakes, caldera lakes, and maars

Closed depressions on impermeable rock may hold lakes. These of course are specially prominent in craters and calderas (Pl. 35). The craters of scoria cones may prove too permeable to hold water, as is the case with the many scoria cones of western Victoria, but some scoria cones hold lakes. Muhavura in Uganda is a symmetrical scoria volcano rising about 3000 m above the local bedrock, with a tiny but perfect crater lake at the top only about 10 m across. Most crater lakes are considerably larger than this, though their importance in the overall hydrology of volcanic areas is still slight. Caldera lakes, such as Crater Lake, Oregon, and Taal in the Philippines, are substantial bodies of water and important in regional hydrology.

Maars typically hold water and usually give rise to strikingly circular lakes such as Pulvermaar (Pl. 12, Fig. 11, p. 38). Where the maars are formed through irregular topography they may have more irregular outlines, like the Rubirizi volcanic lakes of Uganda. Others may be irregular due to the close eruption of several maars, as is the case at Bullenmerri and Mt Gambier. Some maars are almost perfect funnels, with only a small, flat base, like Pulvermaar, but many may have broad, very flat bottoms. The flat floor is probably made of pyroclastics that fell back into the crater, modified to some extent by alluvial fill.

Few crater lakes, caldera lakes, or maars have active overflow channels, for if overflow persisted for very long it would soon cut a channel that could drain the lake. A few have small overflow channels that are only used on rare occasions of high water. There is, for example, an overflow channel between the volcanic lakes Bullenmerri and Gnotuk in Victoria which is now about 22 m above the water surface of Bullenmerri and 65 m above Gnotuk, and which last overflowed in 1899.

Some maars may reflect the local groundwater level, but others are obviously isolated water bodies, and it is possible for two lakes only a few hundred metres apart to have completely different levels and different salinities, showing that the water bodies are not connected.

Crater lakes, perched high above the general ground surface, are clearly independent water bodies.

Lakes formed by volcanic damming

When volcanic products pile up in a valley they create a dam that holds back drainage and produces a lake.

On the largest scale a drainage system may be blocked by a whole volcanic field to form a huge lake like Lake Kivu which occupies a high valley that originally drained to the north, and so to the Nile. The eruption of the Birunga volcanic field, still active in parts, created a vast barrier to northern drainage, dammed back the water to form Lake Kivu, and now the drainage flows to the south through an older and lower volcanic barrier and eventually to Lake Tanganyika.

On a much smaller scale a single small volcanic cone may block a valley, as Le Tartaret in the Auvergne blocked the River Couze to form the Lac de Chambon, only 5·8 m deep.

More lakes are dammed back by lava flows than by cones. A main valley may be blocked by lava flows along its course forming a lake on the upstream side like Lake Bunyoni, Uganda, or lava may flow down a main valley and create many lakes where it blocks tributary valleys. The lakes accumulate silt which remains as alluvial flats when the lakes are drained, as they inevitably are, by cutting down of the overflow channel.

Lakes are normally drained by overflow as described above, but if evaporation removes most of the water a salt lake will be formed such as Lake Baringo in the Kenya Rift on the site of the much larger, lava-dammed, Pleistocene Lake Kamasai.

On complex initial topography more elaborate lakes may be formed, an example of which is Lake Lanao on Mindanao in the Philippines. Here the initial topography was an upland plateau cut by a deep ravine. A lava dam caused water to fill the ravine and spread out on to the plateau, so the lake now has a large expanse of water 4 to 10 m deep with a trough about 300 m deep on the site of the old ravine.

Lakes may form in valleys blocked by volcanic mudflows, as at Bandaisan, Japan. Ponding may also be due to river aggradation of volcanic fragments as in the Waikato valley, New Zealand. Great eruptions of pumice fragments added easily transportable material to the River Waikato, which rapidly aggraded its bed along a 130 km stretch. Tributary valleys, not supplied with sufficient volcanic fragments, were unable to build up their beds to the same level, and so formed shallow lakes (McCraw, 1967).

Volcanic activity is frequently accompanied by earth movements, and lakes may be caused by a combination of both effects; they are known as volcano-tectonic lakes. In New Zealand there is a large complex of volcano-tectonic depressions in the North Island, containing Lakes Rotorua and Taupo. Lake Toba in Sumatra, Indonesia, is of similar origin, and the many lakes of the Valley of Mexico are possibly volcano-tectonic too (but see p. 49).

The surfaces of lava flows may have many minor features and irregularities, described in Chapter V, and the drainage on some flows is insequent or almost random, with many small and shallow pools in irregularities of the surface. The volcanic plains of western Victoria contain many such lakes. Occasionally large but shallow lakes are maintained on the surface of volcanic flows, like Yellowstone Lake in Yellowstone Park, and Myvatn in Iceland which has an area of 27 km² and a maximum depth of only 2·3 m.

GEOTHERMAL ENERGY

In several of the world's volcanic areas there are resources of hot groundwater that can be used for the production of energy, known as geothermal energy.

Minor use has been made of such heat for a long time for such purposes as cooking, laundering, and bathing. Nowadays shallow bores provide domestic hot water to many homes in Rotorua, and the hot water needs of Reykjavík's 80,000 population are practically all met by the municipal water works from geothermal heat.

For the modern production of commercial energy, however, high pressure steam is required, which is only produced under special circumstances. The conditions required for geothermal energy fields are an efficient caprock, to seal the steam in; an underlying permeable aquifer in which hot water and steam may be

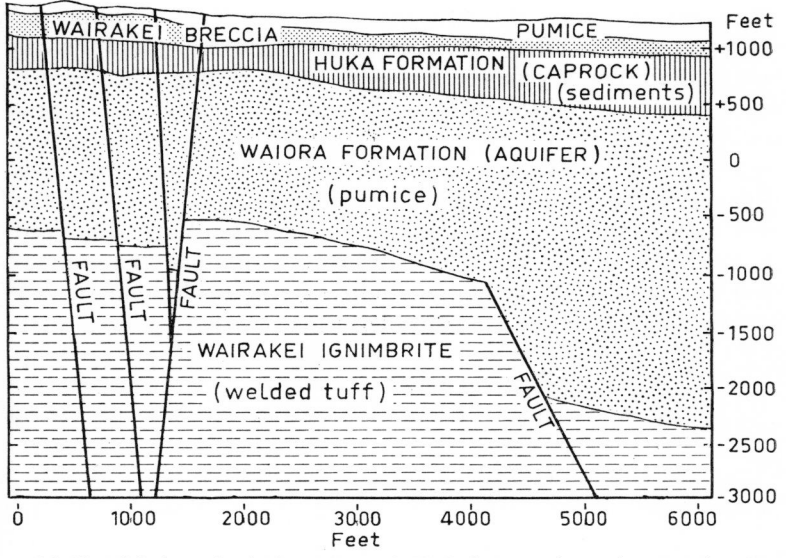

36 Simplified geological section of Wairakei geothermal area showing caprock, aquifer, and heat source

stored; a substantial thermal anomaly, to provide heat; and of course an adequate supply of water. This situation is illustrated at Wairakei, New Zealand (Fig. 36) where the caprock consists of the shales of the Huka Falls Formation and the aquifer is the Waiora pumice breccia. In practice although steam can be obtained almost anywhere from the breccia, power-producing hot water is obtained from deeper drills that tap fissures in the underlying ignimbrite. The water reaches the surface at a temperature of about 200°C where it is separated from steam (which is allowed to blow off), the superheated water is piped to the power station and there 'flashed' into steam which drives generators. Use of the water is complicated because of the corrosive chemicals dissolved in it.

The use of geothermal energy has increased very much in the last few decades: about a third of Italy's energy output is now geothermal, and about 11 per cent of New Zealand's energy requirements are met by geothermal sources (Pl. 36). At The Geysers in California, electrical energy is generated by geothermal heat at a cost 23 per cent cheaper than that from nearby conventional sources. Many other countries are now investigating the use of geothermal energy, including Japan, Chile, and Russia.

In New Zealand there are geothermal areas and geysers of great attraction to tourists. Tapping the steam reservoir for geothermal energy appears to affect the natural displays adversely and there is some danger that they may be destroyed. In any costing of geothermal energy the potential loss of tourism should be taken into account as well as the cost of the energy, though so far there appears to be little concern in New Zealand. Rotorua, for example, depends very much upon tourism, but there appears to be a *laissez-faire* attitude to tapping of steam for domestic use. With continued development it is possible that the town will eventually have abundant hot water in every house, at the expense of declining geyser activity and a declining tourist trade.

X

WEATHERING AND EROSION

The normal processes of weathering affect volcanic rocks much as any other, but basic rocks are more prone to chemical alteration than most. Both ferromagnesian minerals and feldspars are easily altered to clay minerals and iron oxides, with bases released in solution, and the ultimate weathering product is often a brown, base-rich, heavy soil. The high proportion of clay produced can impede further drainage, possibly causing reducing conditions to set in and so complicate the course of weathering. Weathering is therefore very dependent on drainage, which in turn is affected by topographic site and climate.

In tropical climate and in very leached sites, kaolin is the common end-product, accompanied by iron oxides. Laterite may be produced. In Australia many laterites appear to have been formed in the past on basalt, where the climate is no longer of the kind that would produce laterite. Around Toowoomba, Queensland, there are lateritised basalts with weathering profiles up to 30 m deep, and ferruginous zones up to 10 m thick. Side by side with these are basalts with relatively shallow black earths and brown lithosols. Two ages of basalt extrusion are thus indicated.

In extreme cases weathering goes beyond the laterite stage and produces bauxite on basalt. Raggatt *et al.* (1945) showed that the bauxite at Mirboo North, Victoria, could be derived from basalt by addition of water and removal of salts and silica in solution.

In temperate climates and in badly-drained sites montmorillonitic clays are often produced. In suitable environments carbonate may be precipitated at various parts of the weathering profile.

Basalt commonly gives rise to very productive soils of high fertility, though sometimes the physical properties of the soils are not good, especially on ill-drained lava plains. Basic pyroclastics can give rise to very fertile soils, as the distribution of cultivation around Tower Hill (Pl. 37) clearly shows. Of course pyroclastic deposits, with their high porosity, weather very much faster than solid rocks of the same composition. The composition of a rock plays a part in determining the fertility of the derived soil, however, and in general the more acid the rock the lower its subsequent fertility. Ignimbrite plains are not very fertile, being somewhat too freely drained and comparatively slow to weather, and possibly lacking in some plant nutrients.

Weathering profiles on old volcanic rocks can be very deep, frequently over 100 m, as on the agglomerates of the Sogeri Plateau, Papua. Weathering follows joints, and then attacks the individual joint blocks between. Successive layers of weathering are preserved as concentric shells around the central core of the joint block.

This feature is called spheroidal weathering, and it is very common in well-jointed basalts and dolerites (Pl. 38). Deep within weathering profiles the joint pattern of the rock is preserved in the weathered rock or saprolite. Occasional cores of joint blocks are preserved in unaltered rock, completely surrounded by totally altered rock. Such remnants are called corestones. Besides the well-rounded corestones, weathered basalt profiles occasionally contain irregular pieces of fresh basalt, sometimes known as floaters.

Weathering and erosion may combine to give peculiar landscapes under certain conditions. One such landscape is that developed on kaolinised pyroxene andesites of the Caliman Massif, Eastern Carpathians (Naum *et al.*, 1962). The landscape has many pseudo-karst features similar to those developed in areas of massive lime-stone, including lapies, alveoles, dolines, and even flowstone features developed from limonite. The name 'volcano-karst' was proposed for this kind of scenery. The 'stone forest' near Huaron, Peru, is a rugged topography of towers similar to some tropical karsts, but is produced by frost action on Tertiary ignimbrite (Tricart *et al.*, 1962).

Most of the normal coastal landforms can be produced on igneous rocks, and hard basalt commonly gives rise to well-developed cliffs and shore platforms. Basalt often shows many minor hollows suggestive of solution, and experimental evidence suggests that basalt is considerably more soluble in sea water than in fresh water.

Basalt can affect the weathering rate of adjacent rock—an example of 'incompatibility' of rocks. D. T. Currey (personal communication) found several examples at dam sites in Victoria. The situation is shown in Fig. 37, and two possibilities may be envisaged to account for the distribution of weathered rock beneath the basalt:

1. There has been an increase in the weathering of Ordovician rocks beneath the basalt.

2. The weathered material accumulated in low areas subsequently covered by basalt.

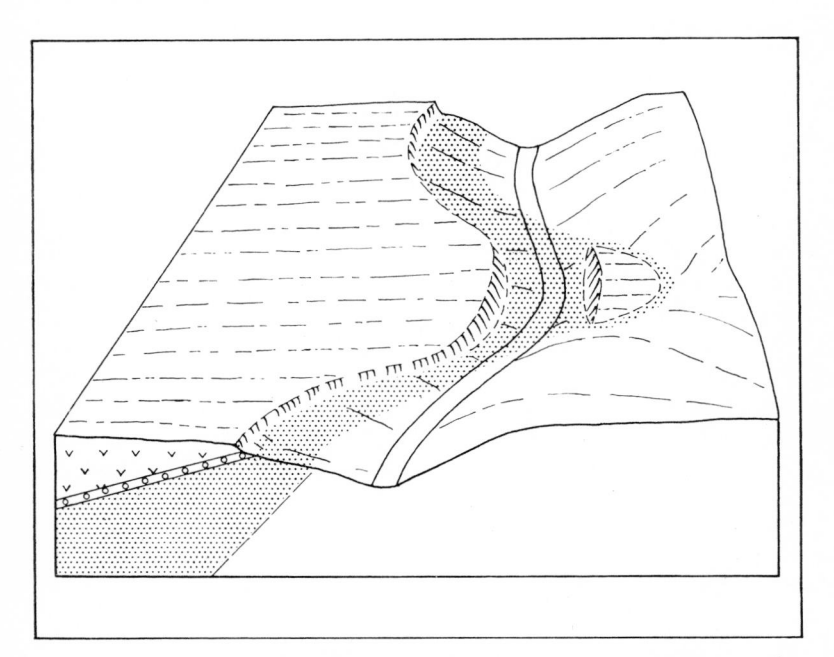

37 *Sub-basaltic weathering, Eppalock, Victoria. Weathered shale (stippled) extends to the original edge of the lava flow.*

Since the weathered rock is found under basalt both of the main flow and the outliers, and also on the eroded slopes between the main flow and the outliers, and yet is absent from all valley sides that never had a basalt cover, the first possibility seems the more probable. In excavations it was found that the base of the soft-weathered zone dipped steeply precisely at the presumed position of the basalt edge, at a gradient that could not have been parallel to an earlier valley side.

Silica dissolved out of weathering basalt may be re-precipitated in the underlying material as nodules or sheets of crypto-crystalline silica known in Australia as grey billy. This may be sufficiently massive to produce landforms of its own during later erosion, and grey billy may be used to deduce the former presence of a lava cover, even when no trace of igneous rock remains. Unfortunately grey billy is also produced by weathering mechanisms totally unconnected with vulcanicity, which can cause confusion, but in the future it should be possible to develop diagnostic tests for sub-basaltic billy.

EROSION OF CONES

Many young scoria cones are so porous that they suffer virtually no erosion, and Stearns (1966) says that the younger scoria cones of Hawaii are not eroded even under a rainfall of 5000 mm annually. On older volcanoes the weathering of ash and the formation of soil increases the clay content, lowers permeability, and thus leads eventually to erosion. On some volcanoes, however, erosion apparently sets in despite the porosity of the material: the small cone of Vulcan, New Guinea, for instance, is only thirty years old and made entirely of very porous pumice and ash, yet is already well gullied (Pl. 34). In complete contrast there are many scoria cones in Victoria of considerable age—perhaps half a million years or more old—that have not been gullied and undergo only slow rounding and reduction by weathering, mass movement, and sheet wash.

Lava cones, though not necessarily very permeable (see Chapter IX), will generally be more susceptible to erosion than scoria cones, and impermeable layers in the strato-volcanoes will tend to make them somewhat prone to erosion also.

Larger volcanoes will be more liable to erosion than small volcanoes made of the same material, for they have a larger catchment area and so water can more often accumulate to the stage of runoff, whereas small volcanoes may remain entirely within the hydrological limits of 'no erosion'.

Theoretically, when drainage is first initiated on a cone, there will be little erosion near the crater rim because there is no catchment for water collection, and also because the rim is often extremely porous. Somewhere on the mid-slopes of the cone erosion will be at a maximum, and will fall off towards the lower slopes because of declining gradient and deposition of material around the base of the volcano. Gullies will therefore be deepest on the mid-slopes, and when these coalesce to form valleys they will produce a concave long profile.

Larger valleys on volcanoes of fairly uniform rock will tend to be typically V-shaped in cross-section. On some volcanoes such valleys run almost from top to bottom of the slopes, with the valley sides intersecting in sharp-edged ridges. The radial pattern of uniform sized valleys, with regularly spaced ribs between them, gives rise to what has been called 'parasol ribbing'.

There appear to be two erosional mechanisms that can cause parasol ribbing. According to Cotton (1944) it is caused not by

38 Parasol ribbing, Mt Batok (2420 m), Java

normal erosion but by an avalanching process associated with hot ash. The grooves formed by avalanching are entirely due to gravity and not to any explosive propulsion, although avalanching takes place while the ash is still hot. Each groove can carry many slides and the ash comes to rest in fans or irregular heaps around the base of the cone.

But some examples of parasol ribbing appear to be definitely due to fluvial erosion by radial ravines, including those on Batok (Fig. 38) and Bromo in Indonesia.

Perhaps the two types of parasol ribbing may be distinguished by the valley pattern. From the pictures of the avalanche-formed grooves on Vesuvius figured by Cotton (1944, p. 238) it seems thât all grooves originate at the crater rim. Photographs of Batok show shorter valleys on the lower slopes that appear as if inserted between the longer valleys, and originating on the middle and lower slopes.

In lava cones and strato-volcanoes structural control by hard lava beds will commonly lead to steep-sided, gorge-like valleys.

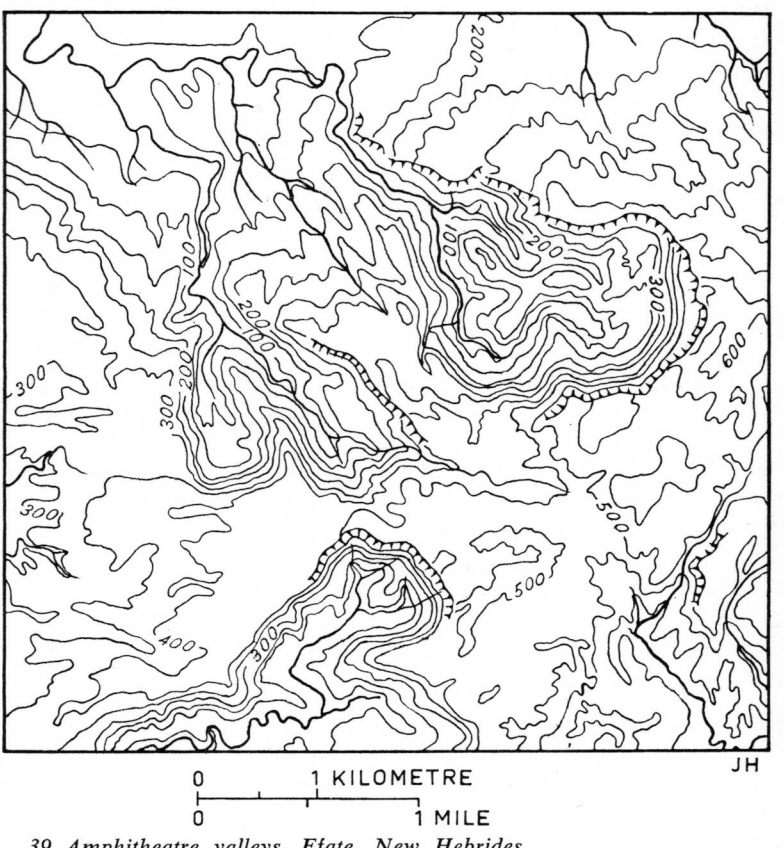

39 Amphitheatre valleys, Efate, New Hebrides

One distinctive variety of valley of this kind is known as an amphi-theatre-headed valley (Stearns, 1966) and is found on most of the larger islands of Hawaii and on many other volcanoes, including those of the New Hebrides (Fig. 39).

Alternate resistant and nonresistant beds, usually dipping downstream, are especially favourable for the development of these

35 *Crater Lake, Mt Ruapehu, New Zealand (foreground) and Lake Taupo (occupying a collapse depression) in the background (New Zealand Geological Survey)*

36 *Wairakei Geothermal Power Station, New Zealand. The clouds of waste steam mark bores. Superheated water is passed along the pipes to the power station at the top of the picture, conveniently situated next to a river for cooling and waste discharge. The U-bends in the pipes are to allow for expansion.*

valleys. The nonresistant beds are undercut and give rise to waterfalls. As such falls erode headwards they tend to coalesce into one big fall. Eventually the streams reach the stage where they have a 'fall point', above which the stream continues to cut down, and below which lateral erosion is dominant. Haiku Stream, Oahu, has a gradient of 2° below the fall point and a gradient of 41° above. River capture on upper slopes of a volcano, where the streams are converging upwards, helps the valley to enlarge into an amphitheatre near its source. Captured tributaries form coalescing plunge pools, with narrow ridges in between which are easily undercut.

According to Stearns (1966) such amphitheatre valleys do not develop where the original slope of the groundsurface was 3° or less. The steep headwall and sides of the amphitheatre valleys are dissected into many spurs by close-set ravines, chutes, or 'flutes' so precipitous that they are sometimes called 'vertical valleys'. At a later stage of denudation, the side and head walls of the valleys retreat, and the lower gentler slopes come to occupy a larger part of the landscape. The steeper upper slopes are still dissected by many steep gullies, but at this stage they will no longer be eroded by plunge pools and collapse. However, according to Wentworth (1943), they will be eroded by a process of shallow landsliding which periodically, during very heavy rains, cleans out each gully as a 'soil avalanche'. When the steep edges of neighbouring valleys retreat far enough they will intersect to form steep ridges, which will eventually be consumed. On the northeastern, most rapidly eroded side of Oahu, former ridges have apparently been reduced in this way. The ridges between the lower valleys have been destroyed, but the valley heads, which are still very steep, coalesce to make a continuous cliff. This cliff, or 'pali' as it is called, is still retreating and consuming what is left of the earlier dome.

Occasionally one amphitheatre valley may grow to enormous size, far outstripping its neighbours. This is especially probable if it breaches a crater and thus extends its catchment. Such enormous valleys are then bordering on the scale of so-called 'erosion calderas'. The Caldera of La Palma (Canary Islands), which supplied the general term for great depressions, appears to be of this kind. A number of amphitheatre valleys are combining to erode an interior lowland in Réunion. The so-called 'crater' or 'caldera' of Haleakala on the island of Maui (Hawaiian Islands) is formed basically by the meeting of two amphitheatre valleys, Kaupo valley and Keanae valley, working backwards from opposite sides of the island.

It is of great significance that the drainage pattern on cones is
radial, and the valley heads converge towards the top of the cone
(Fig. 40). As they erode headwards they come closer together, and
eventually stream abstraction and river capture are inevitable.
This process is particularly effective on those cones of sufficient
size to induce orographic rainfall, for the upper slopes will of course

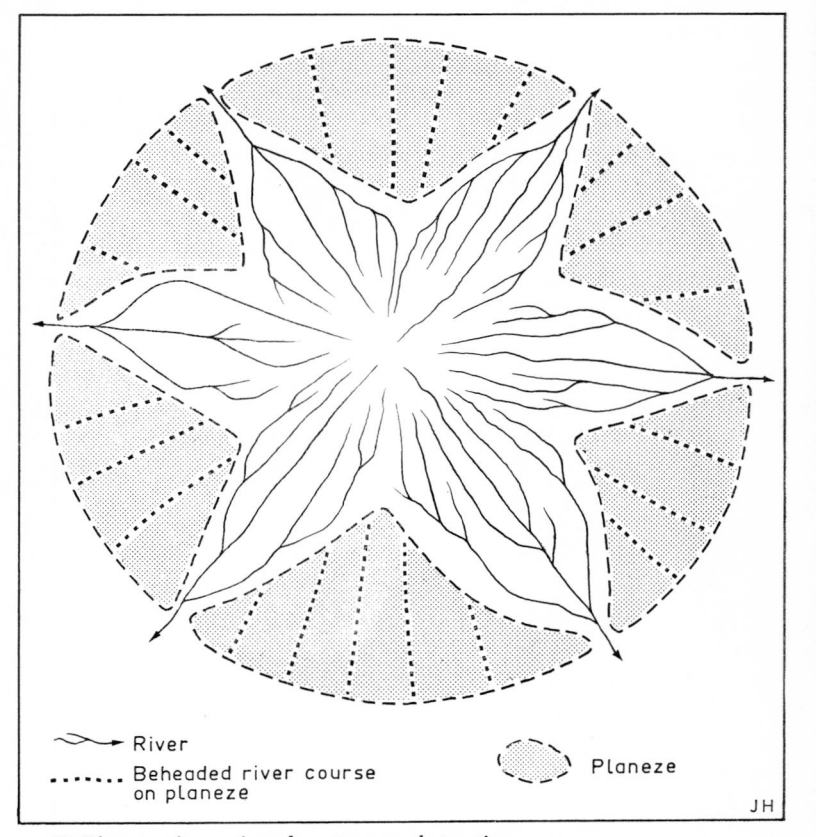

River

...... Beheaded river course
on planeze

Planeze

JH

40 Planeze formation by stream abstraction

get more water, increasing the drainage density and thus the inci-
dence of abstraction and river capture. Since this process is most
effective on the upper slopes it is there that the original surface
of the volcano is first removed. On lower slopes the valley sides
have not met, and large triangular facets of the original volcano
surface are preserved, often for considerable periods of time.

These triangular facets of original volcano surface are called planezes. Of course the surface of a planeze will seldom be completely uneroded, but such gullies as dissect it are very much smaller than the large valleys between planezes. Some of them may be small channels which flowed before stream abstraction and capture; others are small channels which developed later to carry runoff from the planeze surface itself.

A secondary cone on the slopes of a large volcanic dome deflects drainage to form two main channels, one on each side. These concentrate the drainage and give rise to valleys larger than unconcentrated radial valleys. After considerable erosion a wedge-shaped remnant of the secondary cone remains, and even if it should be entirely eroded the drainage pattern will continue to indicate its former presence. A lava fill in the crater of a scoria cone can affect the course of subsequent erosion. The 'Mount Holden' type of volcano in Victoria refers to a group of such volcanoes, which have a flat top and one flank of lava, the rest of the volcano being of scoria. It is thought that these volcanoes were scoria cones with breached craters from which a lava flow issued, and then by a kind of inversion of relief caused by sheet erosion of the scoria the lava became a caprock.

In those volcanoes with closed craters, erosion will eventually lead to breaching of the crater. This erosion may be brought about by overflow from a crater lake, or by headward erosion of a radial valley. The first radial valley to notch the crater thereby increases its catchment considerably, which consequently increases its erosion rate. This valley therefore becomes much larger than the other valleys on the cone, and the eroded volcano thus becomes typically horseshoe shaped.

Centripetal drainage of the crater also erodes, and makes the crater even larger. In the course of time a large erosional basin takes the place of the crater, surrounded by remnants of the old volcano flanks. These basins, which may be several kilometres in diameter, were once known as erosional calderas, a term not now in favour as the term caldera has come to have the more specific usage as described in Chapter IV.

The Banks Peninsula, New Zealand, provides an excellent example. It is made up of two shield volcanoes, Lyttelton which was active between 10 and 12 million years ago, and Akaroa which was active between 7·5 and 9·5 million years ago (Stipp and McDougall, 1969). The central regions of both volcanoes have been very deeply eroded and subsequently drowned to form the harbours of Lyttelton and Akaroa.

A volcano may go through a number of stages during the course of erosion (Fig. 41). Starting from a complete volcano, the next stage would be a gullied volcano, followed by a volcano dissected by large valleys with planezes around the edge. Eventually all the

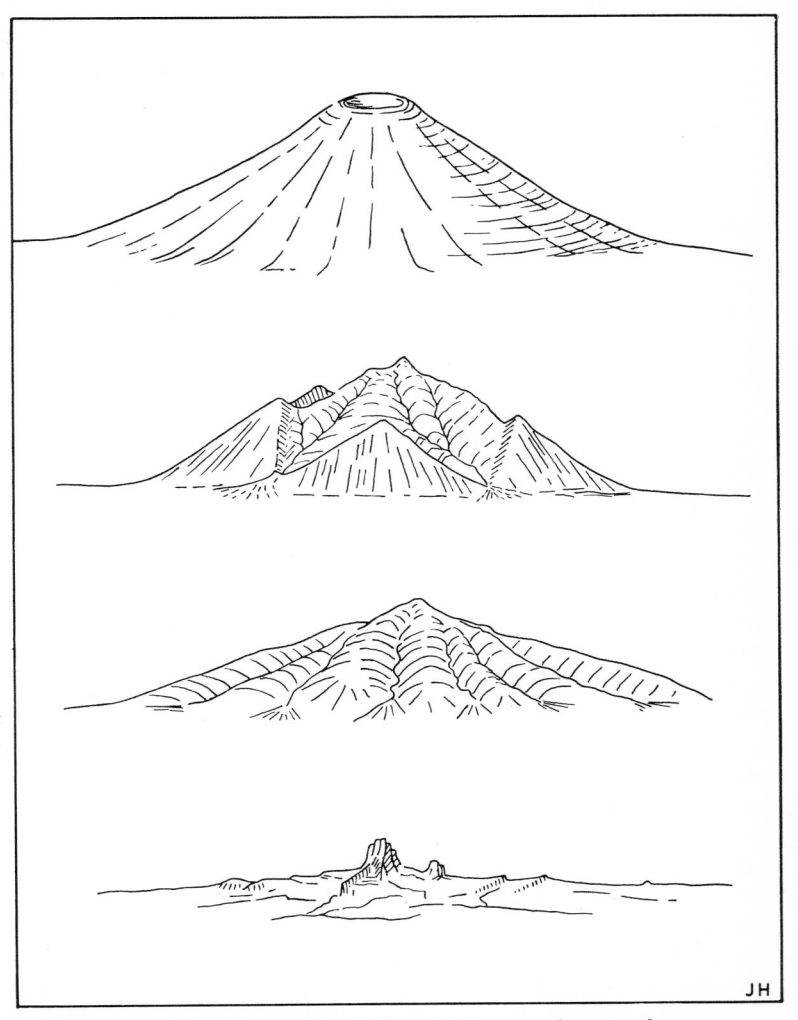

41 *Stages in erosion of a volcano: intact volcano, planeze stage, residual volcano, volcanic skeleton*

planezes would be eroded away, leaving an irregular hilly mass that may be termed a residual volcano, and after further erosion only a few necks, dykes, and sills would rise much above the general level of erosion. This may be called the skeleton stage.

In New Zealand Kear (1957) believed that the different stages of dissection could be related to the length of time since the volcano erupted, and the different stages indicated the following ages:

> Volcano—Holocene
>
> Planeze—Middle Pleistocene to Holocene
>
> Residual—Plio-Pleistocene
>
> Skeleton—Upper Miocene

It must be realised that this idealised sequence of erosional forms does not hold in all, or even in most cases. The course of erosion depends on many factors including the size and structure of the volcano, climate, vegetation, and setting. The style of erosion varies from place to place, for reasons we do not always fully understand.

In some volcanoes a small number of main valleys are responsible for most of the erosion, and such circumstances lead to the preservation of planezes. On the other hand it is possible for many valleys to be eroded simultaneously, producing the parasol-ribbing effect when a planeze stage would be virtually non-existent. In some volcanoes practically all the volcanic edifice is removed before the intrusive necks and dykes are exposed, in others they may be exposed by erosion of the heart of the volcano while extensive planeze remnants are preserved.

It is thus possible for different parts of a large volcanic mass to be at different stages of erosion—some parts may be completely removed exposing underlying bedrock, elsewhere intrusive rocks may be exposed, while in some places considerable remnants of the volcano may be preserved.

The Nandewar Mountains near Narrabri, New South Wales, are a dome-shaped mass reaching about 1500 m at the highest point, Mt Kaputar. Erosion has cut right through the volcanic pile and carved valleys up to 600 m deep in the underlying basement, which consists of sandstone injected by numerous sills of trachyte and dolerite. Many of the valleys are gorges with steep or even vertical sides. A similar story is found in the Warrumbungles, N.S.W., but there the exposure of more necks, cumulo-domes, and dykes has produced even more spectacular scenery, and yet some planezes remain.

The large Tertiary Napak volcano of Uganda still has planeze-like remnants (Fig. 42) even though it is estimated that no less than 97 per cent of the original volcano has been removed by erosion, together with a large quantity of bedrock (King, 1949).

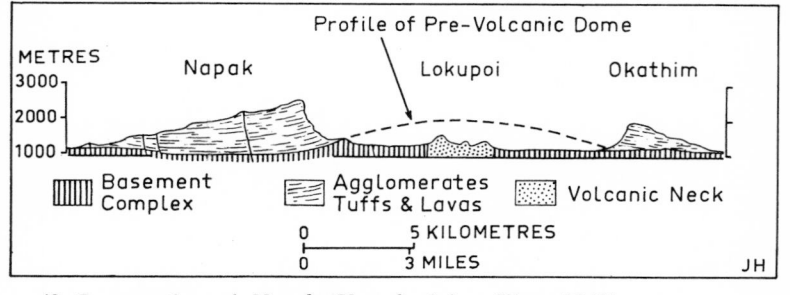

42 *Cross-section of Napak, Uganda (after King, 1949)*

Erosion of geologically much older volcanic complexes can produce topography similar in a general way to that of a younger complex. In the Mullaley area of New South Wales, for instance, Dulhunty (1967) has described a Mesozoic volcanic complex where streams have excavated valleys exposing up to 300 m of lava flows,

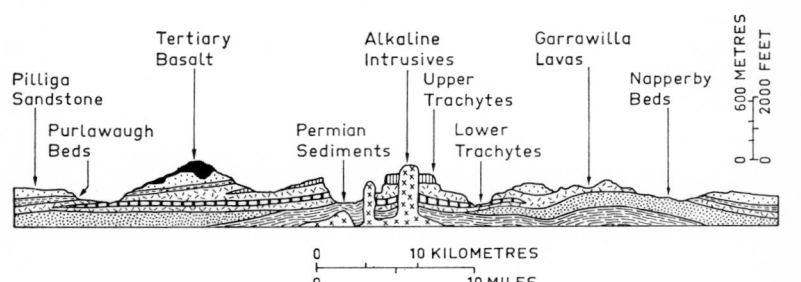

43 *Generalised geological section in the Mullaley area, N.S.W. (after Dulhunty, 1967)*

and eroded plugs now stand up to 450 m above the valley floors. Despite the age of these volcanics, erosion has reached the underlying sediments in only a few places within the volcanic area (Fig. 43).

The course of erosion becomes especially complicated when the volcano continues to be active during erosion, or resumes activity after a period of erosion, which can of course happen many times.

A sequence of erosion and later eruption appears to be typical of some of the volcanic masses of New South Wales. At Canobolas, for instance, there is an approximately level plateau of Silurian and Devonian rocks about 1000 m high on which stands a pile of Tertiary 'earlier lavas' and tuffs rising to a height of about 500 m above the plateau (Old Man Canobolas). The 'earlier lavas' are not found below the plateau level at 1000 m. A later period of erosion reduced the volcanic pile and cut valleys into the plateau. 'Later basalts' then flowed down these valleys at altitudes below 1000 m, sometimes filling them completely and overflowing on to the tableland and lapping around the old volcano.

Aspect is very important in controlling the degree of erosion of slopes. The northeastern slopes of the larger Hawaiian islands may be incised by deep canyons because of the high rainfall, whereas leeward slopes remain relatively undissected, provided they have both been eroded for the same length of time. However, on the Waianae Range, Oahu, the leeward slope is older and hence much more eroded than the windward side. The rate of erosion on a volcano may be reduced by the growth of another volcano to the windward, as happened when the Koolau dome cut off the trade winds from the Waianae dome.

Large volcanoes have significant climatic changes at different altitudes and on different aspects, which affect the type and degree or erosion. On El Misti, Peru, for example, a composite cone of lava and ash, there are larger and more persistent snowfields on the western side, and consequently a much more advanced state of erosion (Bullard, 1962b).

Kilimanjaro, Tanzania, shows a whole range of glacial erosion forms, including cirques, U-shaped valleys, pavements, striations, roches moutonnées, lateral moraines, kettle holes, and crag-and-tail (Downie, 1964). Six episodes of glaciation are recognised, of which the last two are post-Pleistocene.

A glacier that taps the crater of a large volcano, as does the Weyprecht Glacier on the Beerenberg, Jan Mayen, obtains a big advantage over other glaciers because of its increased area for névé accumulation. The Weyprecht valley is much deeper than that of other glaciers on the mountain as a result.

The planezes that extend up to about 3000 m on glaciated Mt Rainier, U.S.A., are known as 'wedges'. On higher slopes, between 3000 and 4000 m, the wedges are replaced by long walls of rock arranged radially from the summit known as 'cleavers', for they

split the descending ice into lobes (Fig. 44). The cleavers appear
to be remnants of the original volcano surface, for although their
walls can be over 300 m high, their upper surfaces are uneroded
dip slopes (Coombs, 1936).

There may be interaction of vulcanicity and glaciation as
described from the Santiago Basin of Chile by Tricart (1965).
Glaciers were already in decay at the end of the Wurm glaciation,

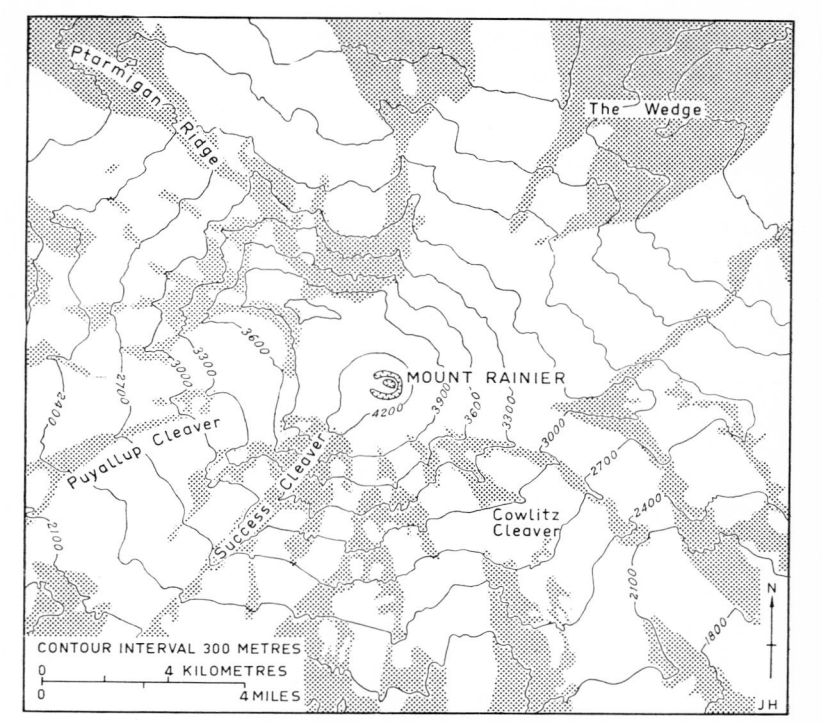

*44 Mt Rainier, Washington, U.S.A., showing radial ridges and cleavers
of rock (stippled) separated by glaciers*

but ash eruptions catastrophically increased the rate of deglaciation,
and a very large area is covered by ashes that were transported
by the water so produced.

Periglacial action, with frost and solifluction causing screes
and blockfields, can occur on volcanics in suitable locations, as
for instance in the Ardèche, France (Bozon, 1963).

Occasionally a number of different modes of erosion combine
to dissect a volcano and provide a measure of the effectiveness of

different agents under the prevailing conditions. An example is provided by Ross volcano in the Auckland Islands, about 400 km south of the South Island of New Zealand. Ross volcano was originally dissected by a typical radial series of valleys. Most of these were later glaciated, and some were beheaded by marine erosion which produced precipitous cliffs up to 500 m high on the west coast. Some of the ridges were reduced to saddles by the erosion of tributaries. In unglaciated areas the interfluves are strongly dissected, but where interfluves were covered by snow they have been protected and remain as gentle-sloping undissected ridges between glaciated troughs (Wright, 1967).

The Piton des Neiges forms the northwest part of the island of Réunion, and overall is a shield 50 km across at sea level. The amount of erosion varies enormously from place to place on this volcano, and while many young flows and pyroclastics are preserved on its flank, elsewhere there are deep gorges with amphitheatre-shaped heads exposing sections of the lava succession up to 2500 m high. On this volcano there is considerable erosion even of the summit, and it is probable that a summit cone rose 300 m higher than the present summit at the time when activity ceased (Upton and Wadsworth, 1966).

Many strato-volcanoes have a very long active life, and their story is usually one of gullying, then filling the gully with a flow, and later formation of new gullies, the sequence being repeated many times and varied periodically by occasional pyroclastic deposits or parasitic cone formation. In this sort of volcano a sort of steady state is achieved; so long as the volcano remains active no major change of form will be produced by erosion.

EROSION OF LAVA FLOWS AND LAVA PLAINS

The streams that drain lava plains, whether insequent, lateral, or complex types, will erode their valleys and modify the landscape. In many instances the basalt is harder than the surrounding bedrock, so the latter is eroded fastest. The amount of incision of lateral streams will depend on the size of the catchment, amount of runoff, hardness of rock, age and other factors. When there is sufficient available relief, lateral streams may incise valleys hundreds of metres deep. This process can eventually lead to 'inversion of relief' whereby the lava flow which originally occupied a valley bottom comes to

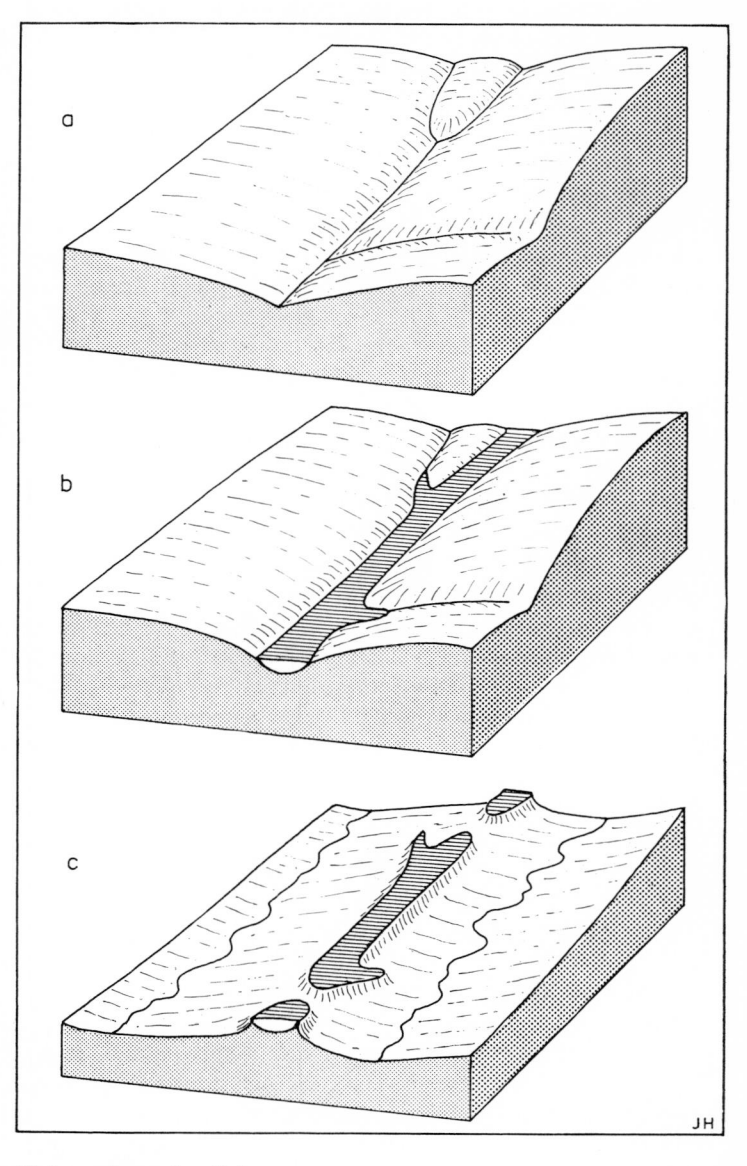

a

b

c

JH

45 Inversion of relief

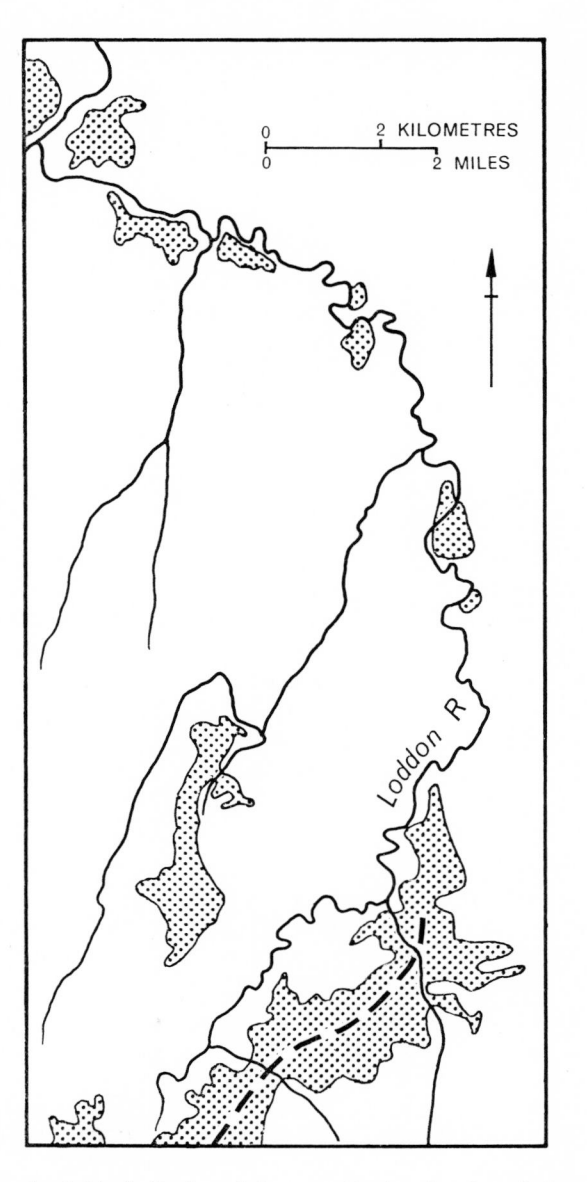

46 Deep lead (dash line) and lava residuals, showing drainage modifications on the Loddon River, Victoria

mark a ridge top (Fig. 45). Eventually a string of basalt-capped hills may be all that remains to indicate the early drainage system.

An excellent example is shown in Pl. 39. El Capitan is a hill 50 km northeast of Cobar, N.S.W., capped by fine-grained basalt. The shape of the hill in plan clearly indicates the remains of a main valley with a tributary, and indeed river deposits have been found below the basalt. The lava is probably of Tertiary age, and the surrounding plain is eroded across Silurian sedimentary rocks.

By using such hills, and also deep lead information, early drainage can often be worked out, and the course of erosion determined in some detail. Thus Fig. 46 shows part of the course of the Loddon River and its associated outcrops of basalt. Near the headwaters in the south the old valley is still filled with basalt, and the deep lead has been mapped, predictably, along the centre of the flow. The present river is here a lateral stream, with tributaries flowing over the basalt. Further downstream to the north the river originally meandered over the lava surface, but it has now cut down to a level below the deep lead, leaving remnants of lava as flat-topped hills in meander cores.

The area shown in Fig. 47 was originally drained by the Campaspe, which took most drainage, and by the small Coliban River in the north. The old courses can be traced from the deep leads. After the valleys were filled with lava, no tributaries from the west seemed able to cross the basalt to join the Campaspe; they were diverted north as a lateral stream, and eventually joined the Coliban which became much larger and cut deeply through its lava. The Campaspe, deprived of its tributaries, failed to cut down very much and still flows over the basalt in most of its upper reaches, occasionally crossing on to bedrock.

Lava diversion and stream incision may be repeated many times in areas of continuing volcanic activity, as exemplified by the Snake River in southern Idaho. The Snake River first cut a canyon at least 30 m deep. Then came the Malad basalt, entirely filling the canyon for at least 16 km of its length and displacing the river southwestwards. The river then cut a canyon about 70 m deep, which was interrupted by the outpouring of the Thousand Springs basalt and further displacement to the southwest. The next canyon was eroded to a depth of over 170 m and then blocked by three further flows. The river flowed around the southwest of the latest barrier, and tumbled back into its old course at Thousand Springs.

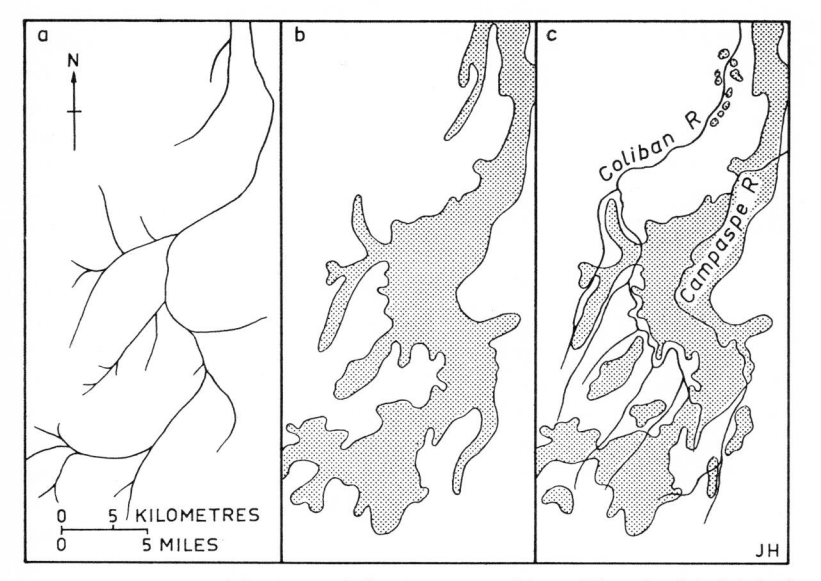

47 Drainage modifications of the Campaspe River, Victoria: (a) Original drainage as indicated by deep leads. (b) Maximum extent of lava. (c) Present-day drainage.

The many changes in drainage that accompany volcanic action and the repeated damming and downcutting of rivers lead to the formation of many alluvial and lacustrine terraces. When a diverted stream falls back into its old channel the sudden decrease in gradient causes deposition of an alluvial fan, which is itself destroyed as the river continues its vertical erosion.

Basalt often gives rise to very steep, frequently vertical slopes, because it is hard rock and commonly has vertical joints. Where a stream leaves a basalt flow or sheet there is often a waterfall (Pl. 40). The edges of lava plateaux frequently stand out as vertical escarpments, especially where the underlying material is softer sedimentary rock. Vertical jointing in other igneous rocks—agglomerate, dolerite, and the welded zone of ignimbrites for instance—can give rise to similar escarpments.

Basalt sheets are often superimposed one upon another, with zones of weathering, alluvial deposition, or pyroclastic deposits in between. In this case the interbedded soft material is a line of weakness attacked by erosion, spring sapping, and undercutting. The landscape comes to look like a series of giant steps, each flow producing a steep escarpment and a flat top. Step topography is known as *treppen* in German, from which comes the word 'trap', once used to mean basalt, as in the Deccan Traps. Many eroded lava plains or flows often retain a flat top making typical mesas and buttes capped with basalt.

The many joints in basalt render it permeable and springs emerge at the base where it overlies impermeable bedrock. These springs erode headwards, and in the Snake River region give rise to typical 'alcoves', vertical-sided, round-ended side valleys, at the head of which issues a large spring (Fig. 48). Similar sapping occurs round many lava sheets in other parts of the world, but is seldom so spectacular.

Valleys in lava plains are commonly modified by landslides. In Iceland, where landslides (mainly slumps and rock slides) are particularly common, they attain dimensions up to 2 km broad, and most of them appear to be about 9000 years old. In most valleys there is some initial dip on the layers of plateau basalt exposed on valley walls, and landslides are confined to the side of the valley where the layers dip towards the valley. The slides have typical cirque-like scars, and moraine-like debris heaps up to 70 m thick. It seems that initial valleys were cut by water erosion, and then glacial erosion oversteepened the valley sides. When the ice melted the unstable valley sides collapsed, possibly triggered by earth movements of post-glacial isostatic uplift. Landslides and avalanches are found in Hawaii, but are not as common as might perhaps be expected from the steep slopes. The relative stability is largely due to the low angles of dip of the beds and the scarcity of slippery ash beds and clays between lava beds.

The McPherson Range in the south of Queensland consists largely of flat-topped spurs radiating to the north and separated by valleys which in some places are gorges some hundreds of metres deep. A feature of the physiography is the presence along the sides of these valleys of enormous old landslides now established by vegetation. Irregular terraces, more or less flat topped, have thus been formed at various levels (Stephenson, Stevens, and Tweedale, 1960).

The Tamar River, Tasmania, is an example of a river that closely follows its pre-basaltic course, and is superimposed on the basalt filling its old channel. As a result the base of the basalt slopes downward towards the river on both sides of the valley.

Columns tend to be normal to the base, and so are slightly overhanging; downward slope of sheet jointing parallel to the base

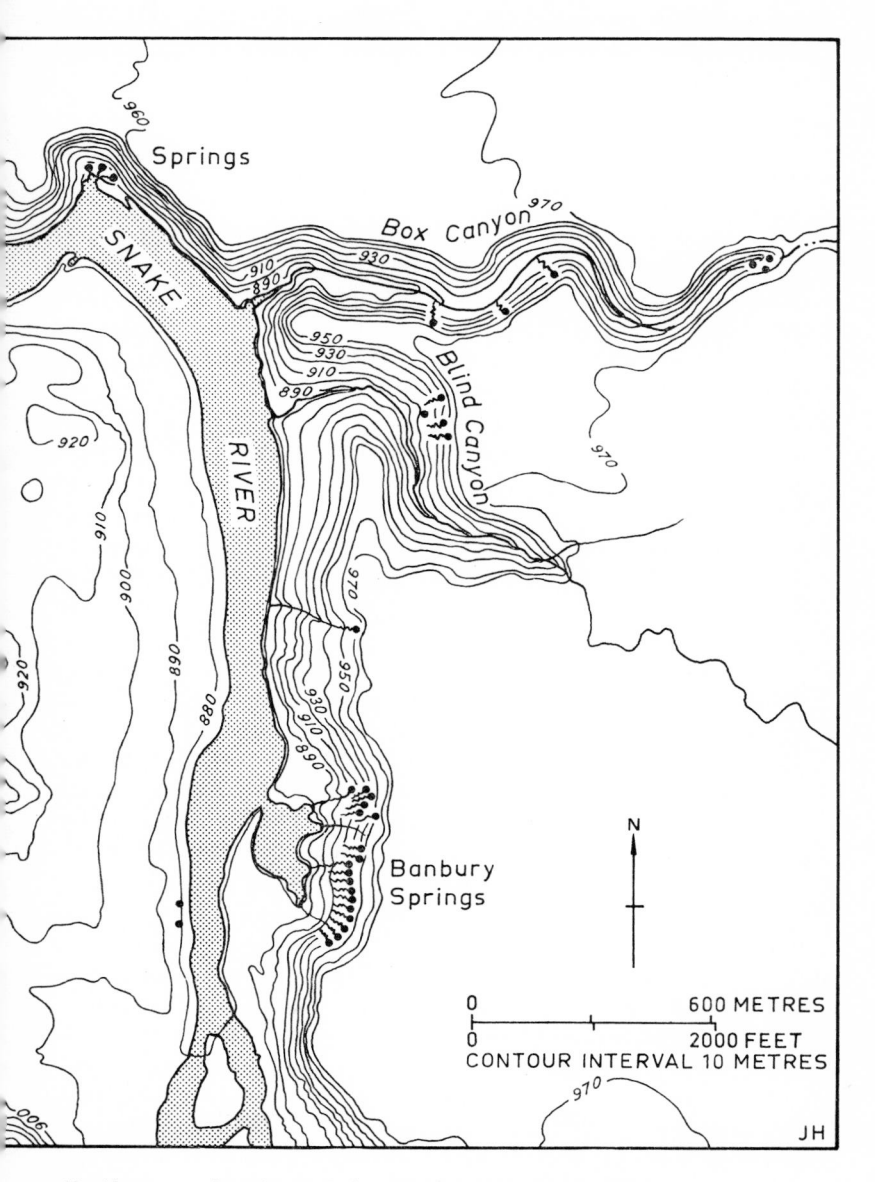

48 *Alcoves and springs of the Snake River, Idaho, U.S.A.*

also helps to provide conditions extremely favourable for sliding. Failure takes place both by backward rotational sliding and by forward toppling, and valley sides have widespread mantles of basalt float (Sutherland, 1966).

EROSION OF PYROCLASTIC DEPOSITS

There is very marked differential erosion between the welded and non-welded parts of a pyroclastic flow. The welded zone is generally resistant to erosion and stands out as a prominent landscape feature, and the vertical jointing assists the general resistance to erosion in forming vertical cliffs. These may be undermined by the washing out of material from the underlying, unwelded zone.

The unwelded parts of flows may weather to produce silicic solutions that can be reprecipitated at the ground surface causing case hardening; in other words a crust forms at the ground surface that is harder than the rock behind. In some areas, such as the Bandelier area of New Mexico, this gives rise to a 'Swiss cheese' effect, when the skin is broken at weak spots and the softer material behind removed to form cavities up to cave size, possibly assisted by wind erosion.

A feature described from the New Mexico flows is the formation of tent hills, conical hills resembling wigwams. These are closely packed, and are in fact the interfluves between closely spaced gullies. Blocks in the ash may act as caprocks, and give rise to earth pillars, steep-sided columns of soft ash protected from erosion by a large rock on top. Well-known examples include The Pinnacles in Crater Lake National Park, U.S.A., and the fields of huge earth pillars in Cappadocia in Turkey, famous for the villages, monasteries, and churches carved in them.

In New Zealand thick pumice deposits produce a distinctive kind of scenery with well-rounded hills as seen in Pl. 41. When a welded zone is exposed, however, it gives rise to vertical cliffs of bare rock often following joint patterns. These are often found on mid-slopes, but in many places the upper pumice has been completely removed so that the welded ignimbrite makes a caprock. Here it gives rise to plateaux, mesas, and buttes very similar to those produced by basalt. However, these buttes seem to be able to withstand reduction to a very small size without collapse and produce the ignimbrite tors, typical of parts of the North Island. A typical tor is shown in Pl. 42. It can be seen that no fallen columns of welded ignimbrite accumulate around the base of the tors; some are buried

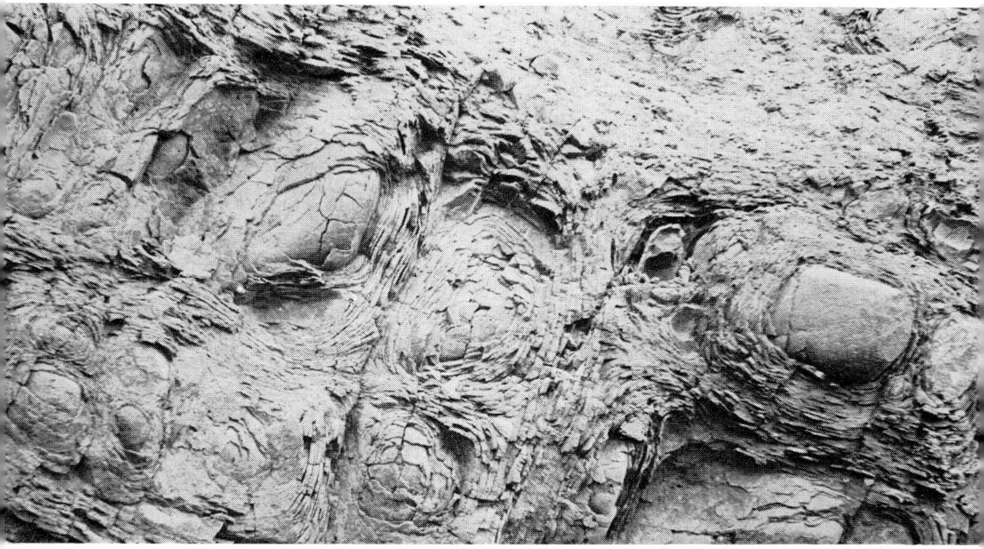

37 (Top) Tower Hill, Victoria. Vertical photograph showing the
asymmetrical distribution of ash reflected in the intensity of cultivation. (Crown copyright. Courtesy of the Director of National
Mapping, Department of National Development, Canberra.)

38 (Bottom) Spheroidal weathering in basalt, Bacchus Marsh, Victoria
(A. A. Baker)

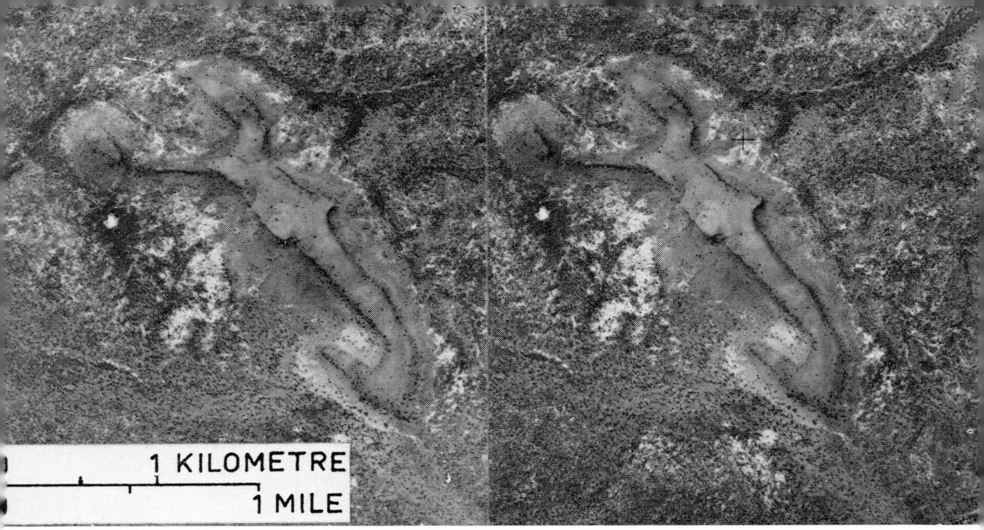

39 (Top) Inversion of relief. Stereo-pair showing the basalt-capped El
Capitan, near Cobar, N.S.W., which originally was a valley flow.
(Crown copyright. Courtesy of the Director of National Mapping,
Department of National Mapping, Canberra.)

40 (Bottom) Waterfall at the edge of a basalt flow, Campaspe River,
Victoria

by later ash falls but they presumably weather away much faster once they have fallen. Some tor topography may result from original variability in the welded zone, which can change rapidly over short distance and is therefore susceptible to differential erosion.

In hard welded ignimbrites the valleys are steep-sided, and if narrow may be gorge-like. Where welding is not so intense resistant slopes may have angles of about 30-35° and have a thin soil cover. These slopes often have ribs of more resistant rock that look like dykes, but are usually the hardened rock formed along a cooling joint.

In the conversion of land into pasture in the pumice lands of the central North Island the yellow-brown pumice soils lose their structure, become less able to retain moisture, runoff increases and erosion is accelerated forming spectacular gullies up to 25 m deep and 150 m long (Selby, 1966).

Gullies cut in the pumice are characterised by vertical headcuts and sidewalls. They are commonly discontinuous in their early stages, each short length of gully having a very low fan at its downstream end. With time such gullies coalesce to form continuous gullies (Blong, 1966).

RATES OF WEATHERING AND EROSION

Volcanoes provide some very good opportunities for quantitative studies on rates of weathering and erosion.

Some rates can be determined by direct observation of processes on recently produced deposits. Others can be determined from a study of historically active volcanoes for which the date of eruption is known. For yet others it may be possible to determine the age of volcanic deposits by other means. The age may be determined stratigraphically, from the age of fossils found included in the volcanics or in deposits definitely associated with the volcanics.

For deposits up to about 45,000 years old it is often possible to use carbon dating. It is not uncommon to find charcoal beneath volcanic deposits, charred by the volcanic heat, and this carbon can provide a date for the volcanic event itself. Vegetation carbonised by the most recent lava flow from Puy de la Vache, Auvergne, France, gave a date of 7650 ± 350 years. The eruption that produced the caldera of Crater Lake, Arizona, took place about 6600 years ago. Pyroclastics of Mt Gambier, South Australia, overlie carbon that gave a date of 1410 ± 90 (Blackburn, 1966).

For older volcanoes the potassium/argon method may be used, and this method can be applied to whole rock samples. Potassium/ argon dating can be applied to very old rocks and can be used on rocks as young as perhaps 100,000 years. Some approximate ages of Australian volcanics obtained include Mt Warning, 22 million years; Glasshouse Mountains, 25 million years; Warrumbungles, 14 million years; lava at Panmure, near Mt Warrnambool, Victoria, 0·58 million years (McDougall, 1969).

Weathering rates

In St Vincent, West Indies, it was found that a fertile soil had formed within twenty years of eruption on andesitic ash, and some plants can grow almost as soon as ash is cold.

The rate of weathering of andesitic ash was studied in detail in St Vincent by Hay (1960), who found that a 4000-year-old ash had weathered to form a clayey soil 2 m thick. The soil formed at a rate of 0·45 to 0·6 m in 1000 years. Glass decomposed at a rate of 15 $g/cm^2/1000$ yrs.

Ruxton (1968) worked on the weathering rates of some ash layers in Papua that could be carbon dated. The ash layers are nearly all derived by ash fall from Mt Lamington, 20-28 km to the north-west, at a fairly uniform accumulation rate between 12 and 19 cm/ 1000 yrs over the last 90,000 years. By analysis and calculation of the loss of mobile elements, principally silica, it was shown that the weathering rate decreased exponentially and the average rate of weathering is halved about every 5000 years. The rate of clay formation, up to 14 $g/cm^2/1000$ yrs, is similar to that calculated by Hay from St Vincent.

On a longer time scale Ruxton (1968) determined rates of weathering of rocks of The Hydrographers strato-volcano, Papua, potassium/argon dated at 650,000 years. The weathering profiles on sites with little or no erosion have an upper zone of 1·5-7·5 m of silty clay over a lower zone of 15-30 m of clayey silt with rock structure preserved. The average loss of silica per unit area is 4-6 $g/cm^2/1000$ yrs, which compares with 3·8 $g/cm^2/1000$ yrs in Oahu, Hawaii, and 4 $g/cm^2/1000$ yrs in St Vincent (Ruxton, 1968).

Erosion rates

The rate of erosion immediately after an eruption can be found by direct observation. There do not appear to be any quantitative results available from such observations, but qualitative observations give some idea of the obviously rapid erosion rates in the early stages of dissection of newly deposited volcanic material. As an example, the erosion of deposits laid down by Barcena, Mexico, has been reported by Richards (1965). The eruption of Barcena started on 1 August 1952, and covered Isla San Benedicto with tephra. Until mid-September wind erosion was dominant, but then the first rain came, which formed a crust when it dried out. The ash mantled pre-existing valleys, and later erosion caused gullies to appear, the formation of which can be dated:

12 September 1952: there was no evidence of drainage on the island.

20 September 1952: a number of gullies were present, with irregular courses, and dry waterfalls up to 10 m high.

May 1955: the gullies were now well established, with fairly smooth long profiles, and few waterfalls remained.

The rim of the crater also showed rates of erosion. It was at first a sharp, knife-like rim, and could only be traversed by straddling it up to December 1952, but by March 1953 it was well rounded. Tholoids appeared in the crater in November and December 1952, creating a V-sectioned fosse between the tholoid and the crater wall. By 1954 this had been filled in by erosion of the crater wall.

To get quantitative erosion rates one needs to know the original form of a landsurface, the present form, and the time that has elapsed between the two surfaces. Volcanoes have particularly simple original forms in many instances, and so provide an excellent starting point for such calculations.

A simple example is provided by the scoria cone Vulcan near Rabaul, New Guinea (Ollier and Brown, in press). It is known that the volcano was originally smooth, and indeed much of the original surface is preserved. The cross-sectional area of all the gullies in a section is calculated, and if this is averaged out along the total length of the section, an average amount of surface lowering is obtained. In this instance the average amount of surface lowering was as much as 101 cm. The volcano erupted in 1937, and the survey was carried out in 1967, so this amount of lowering took thirty years. Erosion rates are conventionally expressed in centimetres per thousand years, and the maximum rate for Vulcan works out at over 30m/1000 yrs. This is a fantastically high rate of erosion, and suggests that at the start of erosion the rate is very high, and falls off later on, as at Barcena.

A similar technique using a longer time scale has been used by Ruxton and McDougall (1967) to measure the rate of erosion of The Hydrographers, an andesitic strato-volcano in northeast Papua. This volcano is in a late planeze stage of dissection, and the original surface can be reconstructed for the eastern flanks by drawing generalised contours. The amount of ground lowering of concentric sectors was measured as the difference between the present cross-sectional areas of the sectors and the original cross-section. The volcano was dated by the potassium/argon method, and assuming an age of 650,000 (the youngest date obtained) for the beginning of dissection, denudation rates range from 8 cm/1000 yrs at a relief of 60 m to 75 cm/1000 yrs at a relief of 760 m. There is a linear correlation between the rate of denudation and the relief, the average maximum slope angle, and the average slope length. The range of variation is generally similar to that found on other rocks in similar climatic environments.

Rates of marine erosion can be measured on volcanic rocks, and provide interesting information on erosion rates on newly formed land masses, uncomplicated by previous geomorphic history. The eruption of Barcena, Mexico, extended the shoreline 275 m seaward between 1 and 11 August 1952 (Richards, 1965). Erosion then set in, and was at a rate of 90 cm/day between 11 August and 15 November. From then until 10 December the rate averaged 170 cm/day. In February 1953 a lava flow put an end to this rapid erosion, and provided a new datum for measuring erosion rates. Erosion of the flow between 16 April and 20 May was 21-46 cm/day, but by September the rate had dropped to 12 cm/day.

The speed with which erosion can reduce a volcano to a flat-topped shoal like a guyot has been demonstrated by many 'hide and seek' volcanoes. Grahams Island, which appeared between Sicily and Africa in 1831, was reduced very rapidly. Bogoslov in the Behring Sea has a long history of dome building and erosion. Falcon Island, Tonga, has a remarkable history of eruption and erosion, which may be summarised as follows:

1867   A new shoal reported.
1877   Smoke seen to rise.
1885   An island appeared, and reached a height of 80 m.
1895   The island was reduced to 8 m.
1898   Once more a shoal.
1913   The shoal had disappeared.
1927   Renewed eruption, and a cone 100 m high built.

Volcanic activity may be sometimes useful in measuring erosion rates of neighbouring rocks. In the Massif Central, France, for instance, vulcanicity in Villafranchian times partially buried pre-existing topography and provided a datum to measure subsequent erosion. Slopes on crystalline rocks have retreated only a few metres, whereas calcareous marls are much dissected and have been lowered by about 100 m (Bout, Derruau, and Fel, 1960).

Another way to determine rates of erosion is to determine the rates of infilling of a sedimentary basin. If the catchment has remained the same, then changes in rates of sedimentation would correspond roughly to changes in rate of erosion. Pullar (1967) has used layers of volcanic ash and buried soils to date rates of infilling of the Gisborne Plains, New Zealand. As there are five different marker beds he was able to work out accumulation for five different periods, going back to 1400 B.C. as follows:

Stage	Marker bed	Infilling rate (million m³/year)
1932-1950	Matawhero soils	1·14
1820-1932	Matawhero friable soils	0·13
1650-1820	Waihirere soils	0·17
130-1650	Taupo Pumice	0·11
1400 B.C.-A.D. 130	Waimihia Lapilli	0·21

The rate of present sedimentation is 5 to 10 times that of previous stages and is attributed to accelerated erosion following large-scale deforestation at the time of European settlement. Sedimentation during stage 1650-1820 is attributed to catastrophic storm damage about 1650, and that during stage 1400 B.C.-A.D. 130 is attributed to tectonics shortly before the Taupo Pumice eruptions.

XI

PATTERNS OF VOLCANIC DISTRIBUTION

When the distribution of volcanoes is examined, either in detail or on the world scale, several significant patterns are revealed. Some of these show local structural controls of various kinds, and the world patterns are significant in considerations of morphotectonics and earth evolution at the largest scale.

LINEAMENTS

A lineament is a significant line in the earth's surface which may be expressed topographically, by river pattern, or in the present case by a line of volcanoes. Aligned volcanoes immediately suggest fissures through which lava has emerged. In some instances there is observational proof that this is the case. Many fissure eruptions have been witnessed in Iceland, and in Hawaii numerous eruptions have started as a 'curtain of fire' fissure eruption, up to 22 km long, but usually within a day this has become sealed except for a few points of eruption. Of course these remaining points are on a line.

Lava shields are typically built from fissures, which are concentrated in narrow zones called rift zones. Most Hawaiian islands have two or three rift zones, from 100 m to 3 km wide. Rift zones are marked at the surface by lines of cinder cones, pit craters, lava cones, and open fissures. Working back from volcanic patterns to determine the underlying fracture patterns is not always so easy, especially where there are many closely spaced volcanoes and a number of different lineaments can be inferred. Figure 49a shows a number of volcanoes in central Victoria, and in experiments Ollier and Joyce (1964) found little agreement between the interpretations of different people. However, once the lineaments are drawn in as by Coulson (1953) the map Fig. 49b looks quite convincing.

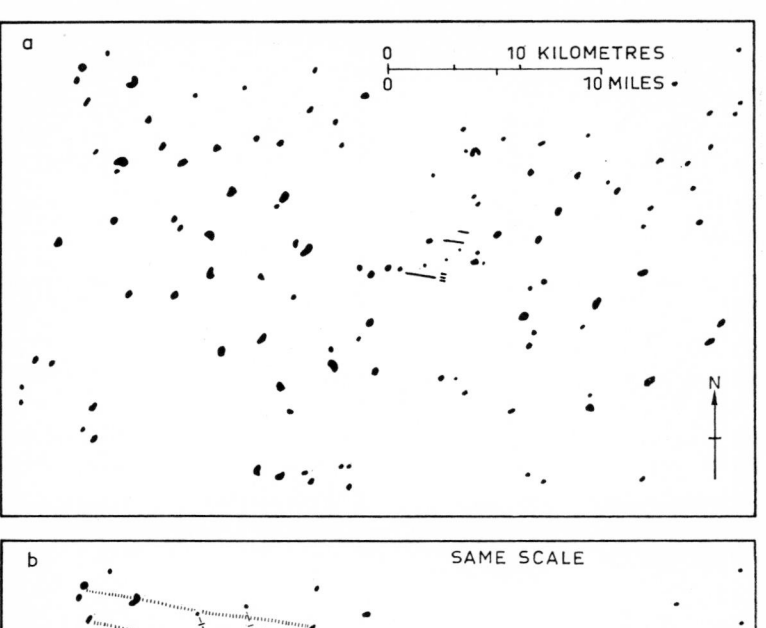

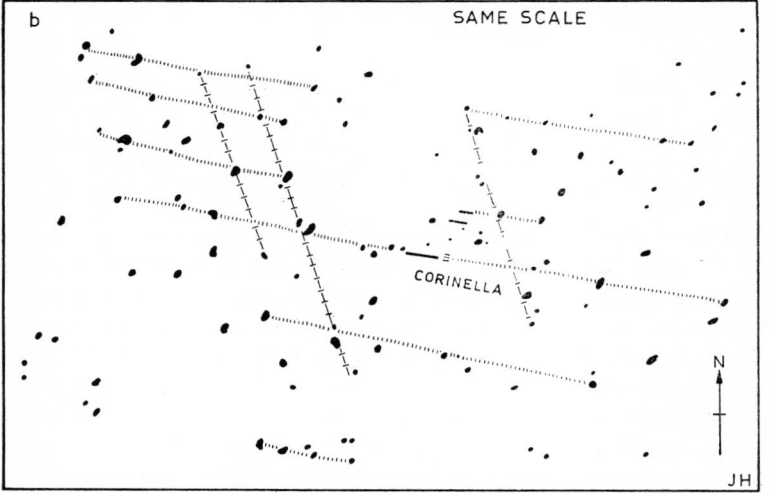

49 (a) Volcanoes of central Victoria; (b) lineaments of central Victoria (after Coulson, 1953)

Such interpretations are always open to question, and it is a matter of judgment how far they should be pursued.

An interesting pattern was presented by Shand (1938) for the Galapagos Islands (Fig. 50). The intersecting lineaments, possibly fissures, divide the crust of the earth into blocks. Shand reasons

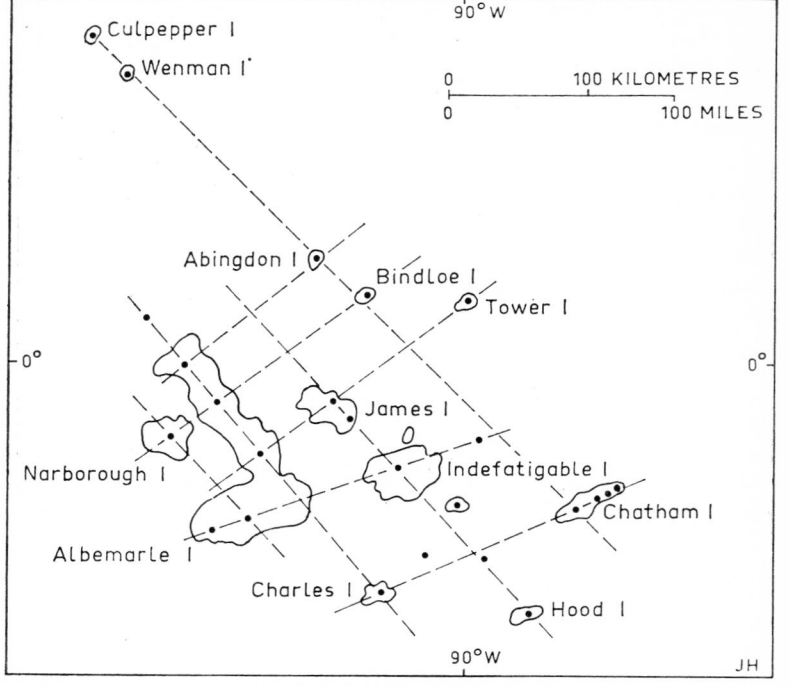

50 *Spacing of volcanoes in the Galapagos Islands*

that these blocks have a distinctive size depending on the thickness of the crust. Just as in breaking a slab of chocolate or toffee there is a smallest size that can be broken, approximately equal to the thickness of the slab, so one might conclude that the distance across the Galapagos blocks is approximately the same as the thickness of the earth's crust.

Volcanoes of Mexico fall on to two lineaments. One is east-west, possibly an extension of the Clarion Fracture Zone, a zone of transverse faulting that can be traced for 3000 km into the Pacific. Popocatepetl, Colima, and Barcena (born 1952) are on this line. The second lineament is NNW to SSE, parallel to the structural trend of the Mexican plateau, and Jorullo and Parícutin are on this line.

The Azores show three structural trends: a dominant east-west trend along one of the transverse zones; a pattern of concentric faults; and a pattern of radial faults. Minor eruption centres often occur at the intersection of concentric and radial faults.

Fault lines would seem to be likely lineaments for volcanoes to follow, and there is frequently a close association of vulcanicity and faulting. Volcanoes often fall not right on the fault line, but a little to one side on either the upthrown or downthrown block. Along the fault bounding the Western Rift Valley in Uganda, for example, there are volcanoes both in the graben and on the upthrown block, but not actually on the line of the fault. The Brisbane Ranges monocline in Victoria has volcanoes on both sides but not on the line. Possibly the fault line is a zone of local shearing and compression, while on each side is a zone of slight tension. The Western Volcanic District of Victoria considered as a whole exhibits a similar

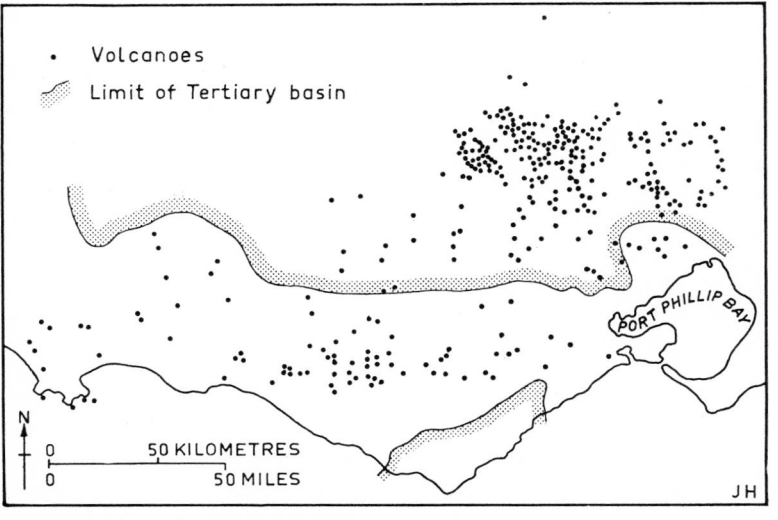

51 Map of volcanoes of western Victoria

pattern. Figure 51 shows that the Western Plains are a relatively downwarped area, a syncline of Tertiary sediments. To the north of the syncline on the upthrown block there are many volcanoes, there are few volcanoes around the edge of the syncline, and there is another maximum along the deepest part of the syncline. No explanation has so far been offered for the occurrence of many volcanoes along the line of the syncline.

When the type of volcano is taken into consideration, further patterns become evident. The maars of the Western Plains are concentrated along the synclinal axis, and they also seem to be arranged along short north-south lineaments (Fig. 52).

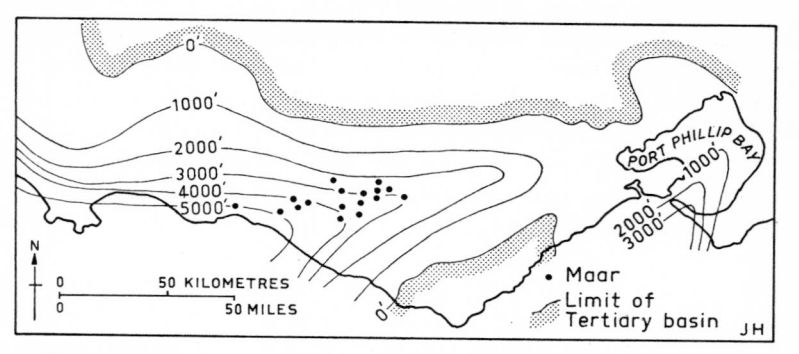

52 *Concentration of maars along the synclinal axis of Tertiary sediments, western Victoria*

Distribution patterns may be accompanied by petrological and structural contrasts among volcanoes within quite small areas. In Guatemala, for instance, there is a line of large, composite, andesite cones in the west, parallel to the coast, but in the east most volcanoes are smaller, basaltic, and more scattered than those to the west (Williams and McBirney, 1964).

In New South Wales and Queensland an interesting relationship between volcanic distribution and the axis of uplift was pointed out by Jensen (1909). The Tertiary volcanics generally lie immediately east or west of the line of most uplift and not on it. Jensen provides the following examples:

1. The Fassifern trachytes lie immediately to the east of the Darling Downs uplift.

2. The Glasshouse Mountains lie east of the Woodford uplifted peneplain.

3. The Yandina trachytes lie east of the Blackall Range and Cooran uplift, and west and south of the Woondum horst.

4. The Nandewars lie west of the New England uplift.

5. The Clarence trachytes lie east of the New England uplift.

6. The Warrumbungles are some distance west of the New England uplift.

7. The Gib and the Canobolas lie west of the Blue Mountains uplift.

Kear (1964) has proposed that there are at least three kinds of alignments:

a. Volcanic vent alignments. These are thought to be tensional features usually parallel to the principal horizontal stress direction.

b. Volcanic centre alignments. These are probably related to underlying pre-existing faults that became fissures during eruption.

c. Regional volcanic alignments. These probably indicate the location of the major fractures that acted as conduits from depth to minor fault systems nearer the surface.

WORLD PATTERNS

The active volcanoes of the world are shown in the frontispiece but in order to understand their distribution it is necessary to consider other major features of the earth's crust.

The most obvious single feature is the division of the earth's surface into land and sea, continents and oceans. This is no mere accidental distribution, with water filling chance depressions on an otherwise continuous earth crust, but reflects a fundamental division between continents and oceans.

Geological and geophysical studies have combined to give the modern picture of the earth's crust, in which the continents, predominantly granitic in composition, float like rafts on a layer of basalt which forms the surface of the crust beneath the oceans. The granitic continents, consisting largely of silica and alumina, are said to form the *sial* layer; the basalt layer, rich in silica and magnesia, may be called the *sima* layer. Figure 53 illustrates the concept of sial and sima, and Fig. 54 shows approximate dimensions of the layers. Note that the thickness of solid crust, that is to the Mohorovičić discontinuity (the Moho), is very small under the ocean, and that the basalt layer is thicker under the continents. We might therefore expect a notable difference between continental vulcanicity and oceanic vulcanicity, a difference which is indeed well marked.

Pure oceanic volcanoes are almost entirely basaltic, being derived directly from the sima basalt. Continental volcanoes may be of all kinds: basaltic if deep-seated basalt manages to reach the surface without contamination, or various kinds of intermediate or acid rocks if either basalt is contaminated by admixture with continental rocks, or if a magma is produced by actual melting of continental rocks.

There are marked differences between the Atlantic and Pacific oceans. Structures such as the grain of mountain ranges run roughly

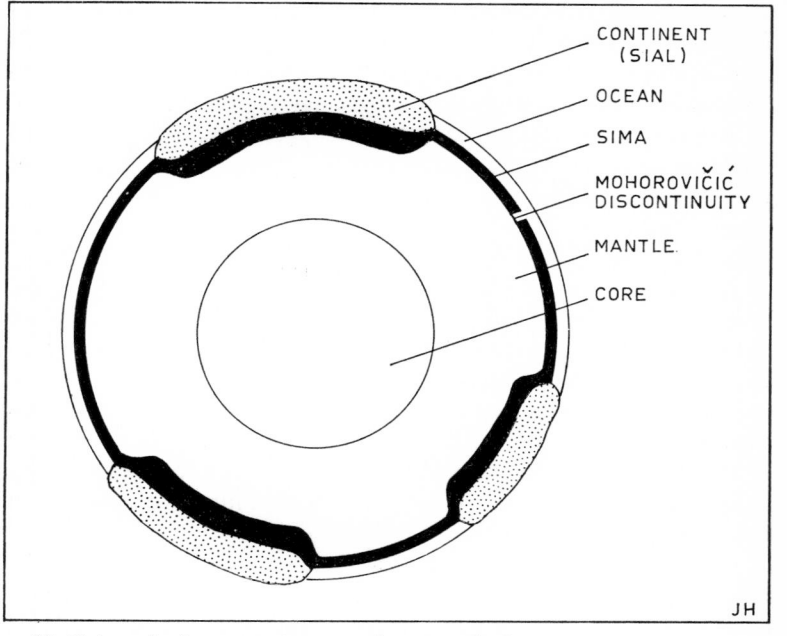

53 *Sial and sima, continent and ocean basin*

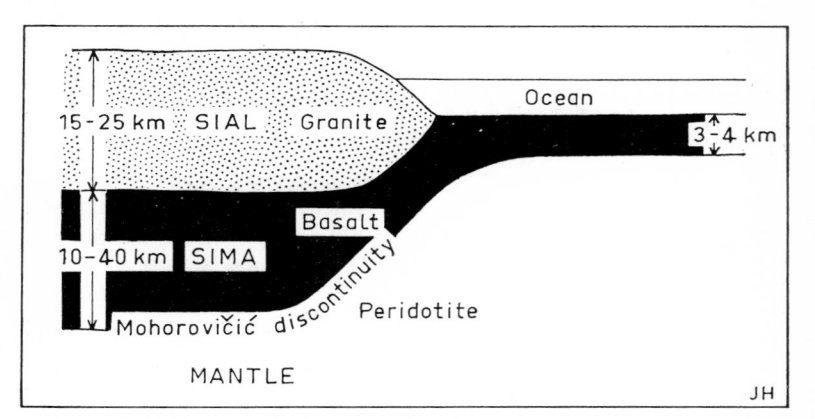

54   *Thicknesses of layers of the earth's crust*

parallel to the coast around the Pacific, but on land masses bordering
the Atlantic the mountain grain and other structures normally abut
at a considerable angle to the coastline. Volcanoes in the Atlantic
are confined to the middle of the ocean, but the Pacific is ringed by

volcanoes as well as having numerous volcanic chains in mid-ocean. Of the approximately 450 volcanoes that have been active in historical times about 350 are in the Pacific hemisphere, and of about 2500 recorded eruptions over 2000 took place in the Pacific.

Around the Pacific it is possible to draw a line—the so-called Andesite Line—that separates the central area of basaltic volcanoes from the surrounding area characterised by highly explosive andesitic volcanoes (although other kinds of volcanoes are found within the andesitic area). The Andesite Line is shown in Fig. 55.

Off the east coast of the Asian mainland there are many islands arranged in festoons, convex to the east. These are the so-called island arcs (Fig. 56) which run from the Aleutians, through Kamchatka, the Kuriles, Japan, etc. to New Guinea. In the Aleutians the simplest kind of arc is found. In Indonesia there are complicated double arcs.

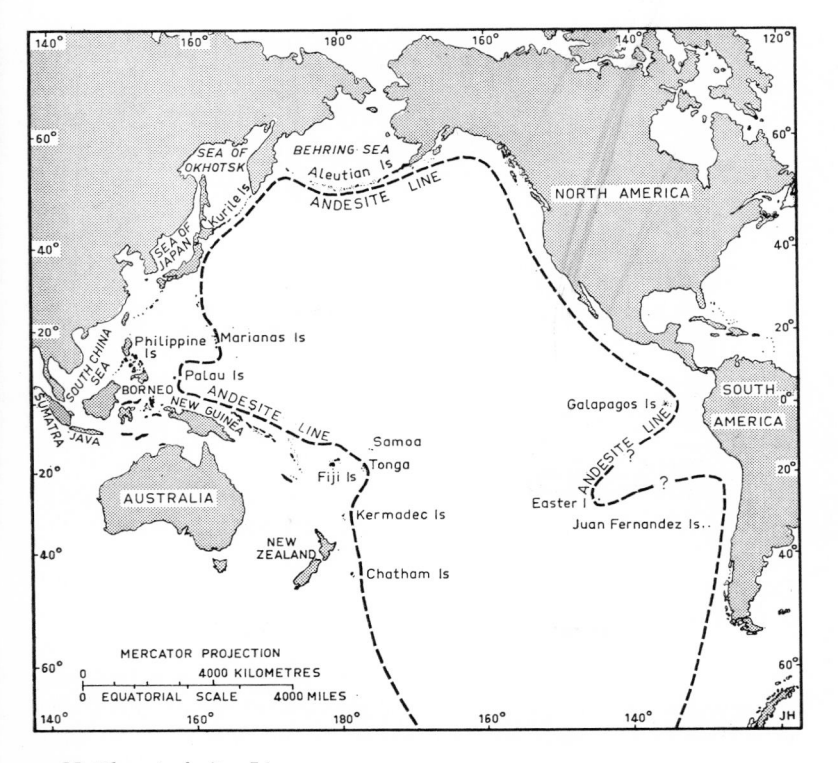

55 *The Andesite Line*

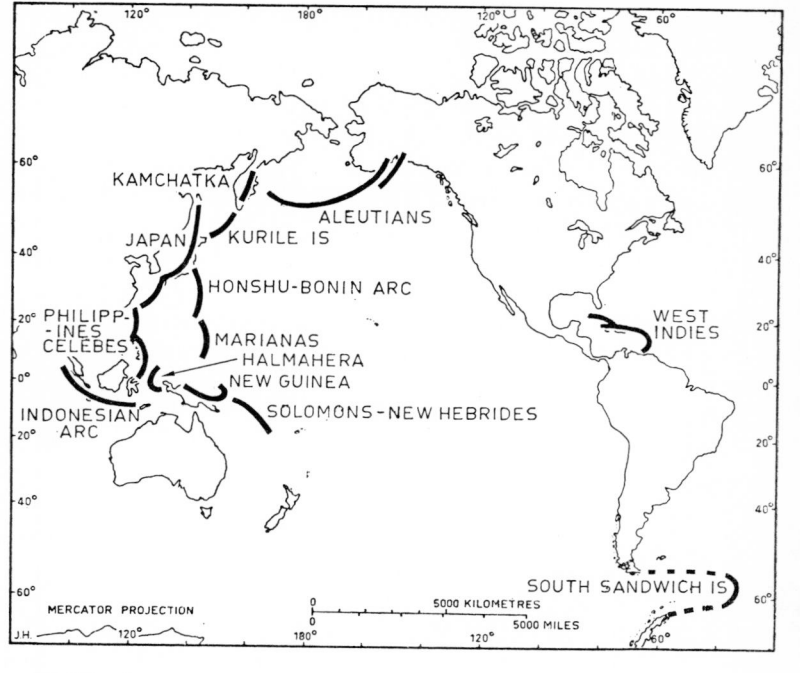

56 Island arcs

The American coast of the Pacific does not have island arcs, but two notable arcs appear to have been pushed from the Pacific beyond the American continents. These are the Caribbean arcs and the South Sandwich Island arc.

Island arcs are the site of many large deep-seated earthquakes, and when the epicentres of these are plotted they are found to fall on a surface sloping down towards the continent at 30-35°, to depths of 700 km, that is one-tenth of the earth's radius. The most plausible explanation for this is that these planes are major fault planes, and movement along them causes earthquakes, pushes the continent towards the ocean (or the ocean under the continent) and topographically gives rise to the arc (Fig. 57).

Geometrical considerations show that a plane surface at the angle of dip determined from earthquake plots would intersect the earth's curved surface in a much broader arc than the island arcs actually have. To account for the curvature of the arcs one must presume that the fault planes are actually parts of conic surfaces.

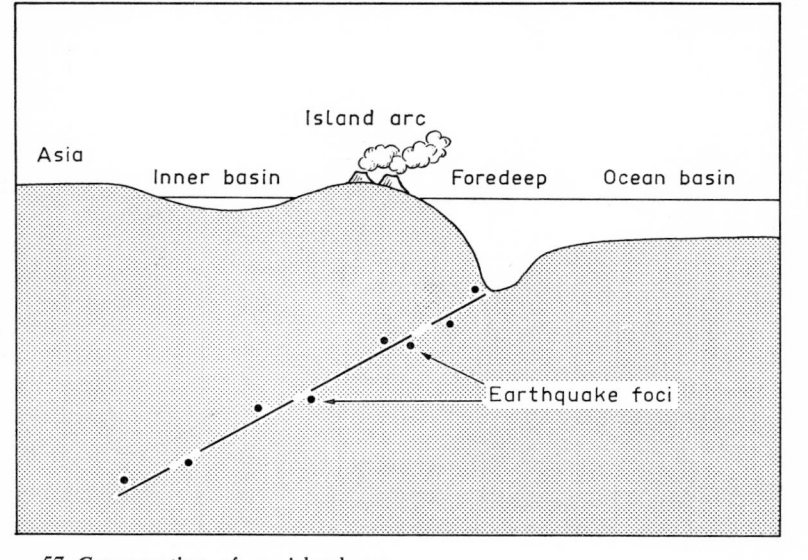

57 Cross-section of an island arc

La Soufrière and Mont Pelée are almost 250 km apart on the same island arc, and it was probably movement along the associated fracture that caused them to erupt within one day of each other in 1902.

On the outside of island arcs the greatest ocean depths are found, rather suggesting that the ocean is being dragged or pushed down.

Running down the centre of both the north and south Atlantic Ocean is a ridge, submarine for most of its length. Iceland may be considered as an emergent portion of the ridge and so offers clues as to its nature. The island is traversed by a rift zone of neovolcanics which runs between areas of Tertiary plateau basalt. However, the neovolcanic zone is quite wide and sinuous, and eruptions take place over a wider area than the active part of the ridge. Furthermore, well defined magnetic anomalies of the ridge to the south are not present in Iceland (Björnsson, 1967). The Atlantic ridge is remarkably situated half-way between opposing land masses, and so is sometimes known as a mid-ocean ridge. The ridge is, however, only part of a world-wide system of ocean ridges, and although many appear to be equidistant from pairs of landmasses the system breaks down in the Pacific, so the term mid-ocean ridge is not always appropriate (Fig. 58).

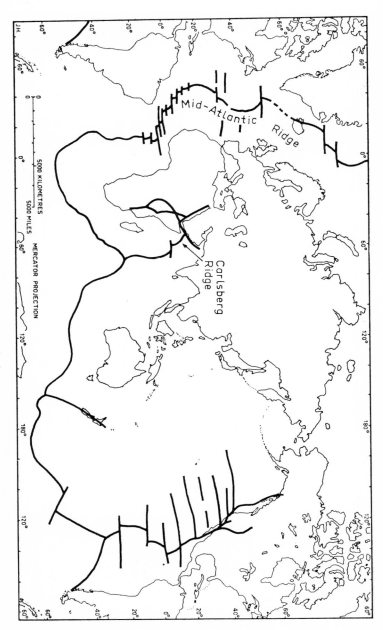

58 Sub-oceanic ridges and shear zones

41 (Top) *Rounded hills on eroded pumice deposits, near Lake Rotoiti, New Zealand*

42 (Bottom) *Ignimbrite tor. A small remnant of welded zone over rounded lower slopes on unwelded Mamaku ignimbrite, 25 km northwest of Rotorua, New Zealand.*

43 (Top) *Cast of victim of eruption of Vesuvius, A.D. 79, at Pompeii. The attitude of many victims, with hands close to mouth, indicates death by suffocation (Ente Provinciale per il Turismo, Naples).*

44 (Bottom) *Destruction caused by the eruption of Mt Arenal, Costa Rica, 1968. Note the defoliation of trees and the thin cover of ash. (Courtesy of U.S. Department of the Interior, Geological Survey, and the Smithsonian Institution Center for Short-Lived Phenomena.)*

In the Atlantic, it is found that not only does the ocean ridge remain remarkably equidistant from the continents, but that the opposing continental outlines have remarkably similar shape. Carey (1958c) has shown that if the edges of the continental jigsaw pieces are taken to be the middle of the continental slope, rather than the accidental sea level shapes, then the 'fit' between South America and Africa is within $\frac{1}{2}°$ over 45° of arc. This must be more than coincidence. Bullard, Everett, and Smith (1965) have shown an

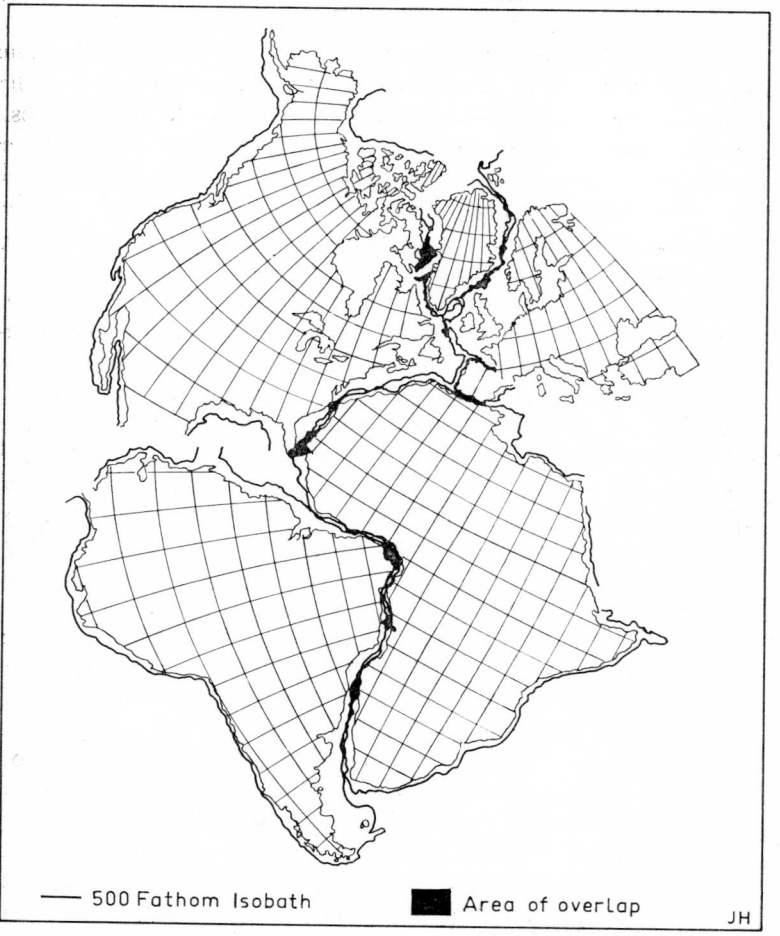

—— 500 Fathom Isobath   ■■ Area of overlap

JH

59 The 'fit' of the continents around the Atlantic (Bullard, Everett, and Smith, 1965)

equally good fit for all the land masses bordering the Atlantic (Fig. 59).

These relationships are part of the evidence for the theory of continental drift, which supposes that the continents were once united and have since drifted apart. This theory and the many different lines of evidence that support it are described in an excellent summary by Holmes (1965). So far as the Atlantic is concerned, one can postulate that the Americas have drifted west from the ocean ridge and Eurafrica has drifted east, the ocean ridge marking the original line of junction.

Wilson (1963) has drawn attention to the fact that the numerous volcanoes of the Atlantic appear to be youngest on the ocean ridge and get progressively older towards the continents. This suggests that the Atlantic has progressively opened up, forming new volcanoes on the ridge periodically, and these volcanoes have then drifted away from the ridge with the continents, to be replaced by younger volcanoes on the ridge. The ocean floor appears to be spreading from the ridge to the continents.

Supporting evidence for the spreading of ocean floors comes from modern studies of palaeomagnetism. It has been shown that there have been several reversals of the earth's polarity in the past few million years as shown in Fig. 60. Work on ocean ridges has revealed that this same pattern is found symmetrically on each side of the ridge (Fig. 61), suggesting that new basalt has been injected at the centre, taking on the polarity prevailing at the time, and then drifted away to be replaced by a new line of injected basalt. By dating the rocks (by the potassium/argon method) and measuring the distance apart of corresponding bands of sea floor, it is even possible to work out the rate of ocean floor spreading.

Magnetic patterns over the Pacific ridge suggest that the Pacific expanded at 4·5 cm/yr for ten million years, making a total of 45 km of movement. This may be compared with 1-2 cm/yr for the North Atlantic and 2-3 cm/yr for the South Atlantic and the Indian Ocean.

In the Pacific there is another pattern of volcanic distribution, first discovered by Chubb (1957), which may have some bearing on ideas of sea floor spreading. Many Pacific volcanoes have a linear arrangement and there is a progressive change in age along the line. Thus in the Hawaiian Islands the most active vulcanicity is to the east on the island of Hawaii itself. The centre of activity appears to be still moving and there are active submarine volcanoes further east. To the west of Hawaii are older islands which are extinct

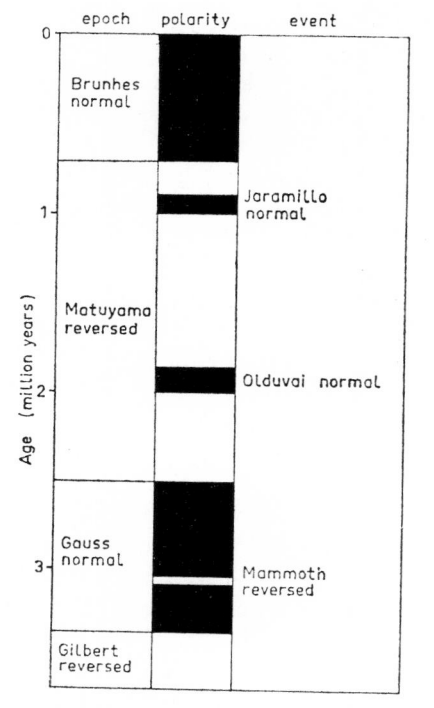

60 *Palaeomagnetic reversals of the earth's field
in the last 4 million years*

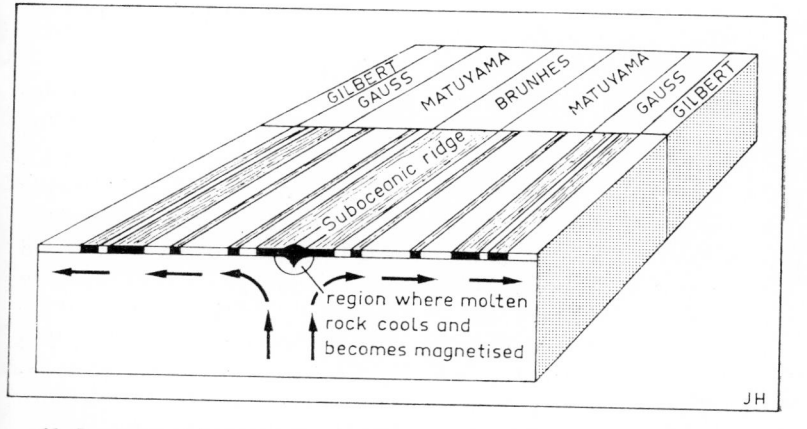

61 *Symmetry of magnetic reversals across a sub-oceanic ridge*

volcanoes. These show progressively more erosion and subsidence, with drowned valley coasts. Fringing coral reefs come in next and beyond the chain of volcanic islands there are coral atolls further to the west.

These observations fully support Darwin's theory of atoll formation by simultaneous coral growth and subsidence. Each volcano in turn appears to go through a sequence of eruption, erosion, coral growth, and subsidence.

As we have seen, several ocean ridges tend to be equidistant between land masses, but on Fig. 58 it can be seen that the Carlsbad ridge in the Indian Ocean heads right into land on the Red Sea. Geophysical work has shown that the Red Sea has a high positive gravity anomaly, and is most probably floored by sima. The Red Sea therefore may represent a very early stage of ocean spreading when sima has reached the surface, but the land masses have only just started to drift apart. The continuation of the same line into the ocean marks the line from which India and the Horn of Africa have drifted. The Red Sea rift is accompanied by vulcanicity in neighbouring land areas.

Another branch of the system can be traced through Abyssinia into the rift valley system of Africa. The rift valleys are long fault troughs (grabens) with fault movement of several thousand metres. The fault troughs are filled with great thicknesses of sediment so they have a negative gravity anomaly (unlike the Red Sea), and the rift valleys may mark an even earlier stage in the dismemberment of continents. They are accompanied by vulcanicity, of basic type but different from oceanic basalt in being of alkaline rather than of calc-alkaline suites.

Carey (1958c) has reported that although individual continental assemblages often show a remarkably good fit, he was unable ever to assemble *all* the continents into one large land mass on the globe. However, on a globe of smaller size he obtained an excellent fit. This leads to a theory of an expanding earth which supposes that the earth once had a continuous sial cover, but by expansion of the earth this has been fragmented, and the oceans have grown, and are growing, in between. With a simple drift idea, it is hard to see how the Atlantic could expand without at the same time causing other oceans to shrink, and yet all oceans seem to be expanding. The expanding earth hypothesis would remove this problem. The expansion of the earth could be caused by phase changes giving rise to minerals of lower density; the ultimate cause might be a decline

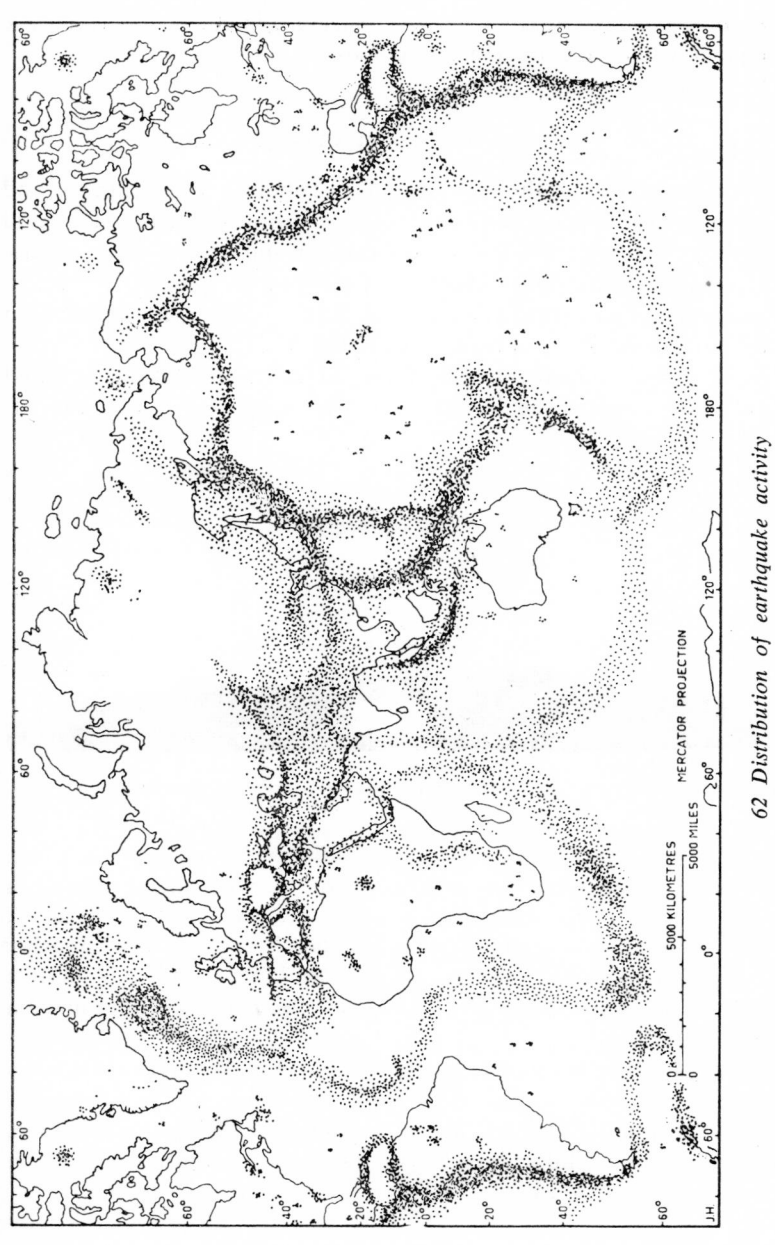

62 Distribution of earthquake activity

in the force of gravity, as Dirac has proposed. These ideas are further elaborated by Holmes (1965).

VOLCANOES AND EARTHQUAKES

To a large extent the patterns of distribution of volcanoes and earthquakes coincide, and indeed observation of earthquakes and tremors is one of the main tools the vulcanologist uses to predict eruptions. There are, however, some notable exceptions where vulcanicity and earthquakes do not occur together, as can be seen by comparing the frontispiece with Fig. 62.

The circum-Pacific belt is followed by both earthquakes and volcanoes, as are the island arcs. The ocean ridges and the rift

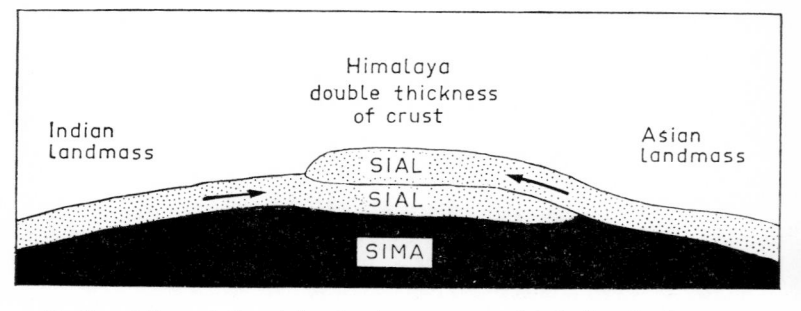

63 Overriding of the Asian landmass on to the Indian landmass

valleys are also lines of volcanic eruption and earthquake activity. Another notable earthquake zone is the Mediterranean-Himalaya belt, but this is only volcanic at the Mediterranean end. The Himalaya appears to be an area where one crustal block has overridden another —the Asian block overlies the Indian block—and this double thickness of crust is too great for penetration by ascending magma (Fig. 63).

Antarctica is remarkably devoid of earthquakes, yet does have a small amount of vulcanicity, notably the active Mt Erebus. Some major eruptions, such as that of Coseguina in Nicaragua in 1835, appear to have taken place with little or no forewarning from earthquake activity.

XII

ASPECTS OF VULCANOLOGY

Active volcanoes are dangerous, sometimes spectacularly destructive (Pl. 43). Whole towns may be destroyed, probably the best known example being Pompeii, obliterated by the eruption of Vesuvius in A.D. 79.

Pompeii, 8 km from the eruption centre, was completely buried under the fallout of ash over a period of two days, and completely forgotten until rediscovered in 1595. The eruption seems to have been quiet enough at the start for many people to leave, but those who stayed too long, perhaps to save their possessions, had great trouble because of the darkness and increasing violence of the eruptions. About 16,000 people perished, and many of the bodies later excavated were clutching bags of coins or jewels. Hundreds of casts have been made from the moulds left by bodies.

The 1783 eruption of Skaptar Jokull was a national disaster for Iceland and a fifth of its inhabitants (10,000) died from its effects. Half the cattle, three-quarters of the horses, and four-fifths of the sheep population also perished, and dust even destroyed crops in Scotland, 1000 km away.

The 1815 eruption of Tamboro, Indonesia, killed 12,000 people by direct effects and up to 70,000 died from famine following the spoliation of land and crops. The 1902 eruption of Mont Pelée killed 30,000 people in a minute and left only two survivors in the town of St Pierre. In the same year the eruption of La Soufrière (St Vincent) took 2000 lives and caused the extinction of the Caribs, the original inhabitants of the island when Columbus discovered it. In 1909 Kelut (Indonesia) killed 5500 people.

Volcanoes continue to be a menace up to the present time. The eruption of Mt Lamington, Papua, in 1951 killed 6000 people; Mt Agung, in Bali, Indonesia, killed 1500 people in 1963; Villarica, Chile, caused 30,000 people to evacuate their homes in 1963 and 1964; Taal, Philippines, took another 500 lives in 1965.

The menace of volcanoes is greater than would be supposed from the disasters that have happened so far. In Chapter VII we saw that some ignimbrite deposits are on a tremendous scale. Most of these are prehistoric, and by good fortune most of the large historical eruptions—such as the 1912 eruption of the Valley of Ten Thousand Smokes and the 1956 eruption of Bezymianny, Kamchatka—have taken place in uninhabited areas. If such an eruption should occur—as it has before—in Japan, New Zealand, California, or some other densely populated area there would be a catastrophe of unheard-of proportions.

For this reason the main bread-and-butter work of vulcanologists is to predict eruptions, and all the ancillary research is justified if it helps towards this aim.

PREDICTION OF ERUPTIONS

Observations of many volcanoes have led to the discovery of various phenomena that may be taken as warning signs of impending eruption. These are seldom certain, and frequently there is very little time between warning and eruption—the 1872 eruption of Vesuvius gave no warning up to the previous night, even to trained observers—but at least people may be given such warning as is possible.

Warning signs include the melting of snow caps, the disappearance of crater lakes, the drying up of wells and springs, death of surrounding vegetation, and movement of animals and birds. It seems that many animals left Mont Pelée before its eruption in 1902. The sort of observation described above depends on special circumstances, and for most volcano prediction more routine methods must be used, as will be described below.

Seismic methods

The measurement of earth tremors is now the commonest method of eruption prediction. The ascent of magma causes tremors, and before an eruption there is usually a marked increase in the number and violence of local tremors with a focus at shallow depth. A number of synchronised seismographs can give an accurate location of the eruption point, and seismic shocks may give several days' warning. The method cannot be certain, however. Some eruptions, such as that of Coseguina (1815), apparently take place without preliminary tremors. On the other hand Vesuvius has given strong warning tremors on several occasions in the past few years without producing an eruption.

When an elaborate seismic net is utilised, quite remarkable feats of forecasting can be achieved. In the eruption of Kilauea in December 1959 seismographs provided six months' notice of eruption by recording tremors from the remarkable depth of 50 km. As time went by the focal depth of tremors became less and less, and by measuring the speed of the rise the date of eruption could be forecast. Extra field seismographs were used to locate the epicentres accurately, and the exact point of eruption (Kilauea Iki) and time of eruption were predicted with unprecedented accuracy. Furthermore, when the eruption stopped the time and place of a recurrence were forecast, and the village of Kapoho, 15 km from Kilauea Iki, was evacuated with sufficient warning to allow removal of portable belongings before the area was buried by lava.

The possibility of using long-range forecasting of volcanic activity (several months, to possibly several years) was presented by Blot (1964) and is based on the apparent relationship between some deep (550-650 km) and intermediate (150-250 km) seismic effects and certain eruptions in the New Hebrides group. In the first three years of observations since publishing the hypothesis the volcanoes Gaua, Ambrym, and Lopevi have erupted on dates forecast months in advance. The relationship between volcanic eruption and deep effects cannot be direct since magma does not originate at these great depths, but some sort of activity is traced in depth and direction, and appears to take 12 ± 2 months to travel from 650 to 200 km depth, and 6 ± 2 between 200 km and eruption at the surface.

Tilt measurements

Before an eruption a volcano is liable to swell because of lava pushing up inside it. This swelling or tumescence can be measured by tiltmeters. After eruption the volcano sinks back, often below its original position. Changes observed in Hawaii amount to -2 ft (0.6 m) and $-3\frac{1}{2}$ ft (1 m). Such changes could be determined by occasional surveys, but a quicker method is needed for volcanic prediction, preferably a single measurement. Tiltmeters measure very accurately the tilt of the ground and any change in tilt may be regarded as a warning. By careful placement of tiltmeters some information may be gained about the possible location of an eruption. On Hawaii they are placed so that tumescence of Kilauea gives a northward tilt, while swelling of Mauna Loa gives an eastward tilt. Tiltmeter readings on Manam Island volcano, New Guinea, showed a slow rise of 30 seconds during the five months preceding the climactic explosions of 1958. A rise of 8 seconds preceded the eruption of March 1960, and then during the initial lava outpourings there was a fall of 11 seconds.

Uplift and outward tilting of caldera edges prior to eruption causes horizontal expansion, which can be measured by tellurometers. Distance measurements across Kilauea caldera, Hawaii, showed a line of 3098 m lengthened by 12 m prior to eruption and then rapidly shortened by 28 cm during and after eruption. The method is said to be accurate to four parts per million (Decker, Hill, and Wright, 1966).

Swelling and sinking of the land is most easily observed at the coast, for a change in relative sea level has very marked effects. The sea is said to have retreated some distance the day before the eruption of Monte Nuovo near Naples in 1538; in all probability it was the land swelling. The Temple of Serapis at Naples records many changes of sea level by the level at which marine borers have lived on its pillars during their numerous submergences. Much of the movement in this area is probably related to volcanic activity.

Temperature measurement

The temperature of crater lakes, hot springs, and fumaroles often shows a sharp increase before eruption. By constant or regular readings it may be possible to give some warning.

However, in both Indonesia and in New Guinea it has been found that there is no good correlation of temperature increase (measured in summit craters) and eruption, so the general reliability of the method is in considerable doubt (Neumann van Padang, 1963).

Gas composition

The composition of gases erupted from craters or fumaroles may vary before eruption. There is likely to be an increase in the amount of HCl. The composition of gases emitted from volcanoes depends on the temperature. Iwasaki, Ozawa, and Yoshida (1966) say that high temperature emanations include H_2O, HCl, HF, SO_2, CO_2, H_2, H_2S, N_2 and others, but low temperature emissions have only CO_2 and H_2S as main components.

A great deal of water is produced by volcanoes, though it is not easy to determine whether this is original water or if some has been recycled from sedimentary rocks. In the eruption of

Bezymianny, Kamchatka, 1956, for instance, it was estimated that 2·5 per cent by weight of the eruption products consisted of water, and that 2·7 per cent of the original magma was water (Markhinin, 1962).

A very good correlation between composition and amounts of gas, and eruptive activity and the composition and amounts of gas, was demonstrated at Mt Mihara, Japan, by Noguchi and Kamiya (1963). From April to early July 1957, amounts of F, Cl, and S were low. They increased markedly from 17 to 30 July, and eruption took place on 5 and 6 August. The increase in the amounts of these gases was repeated in early October, and eruption occurred on 13 October.

Tazieff and Tonani (1963) used rapid methods of gas analysis and could trace changes in content of H_2O and CO_2 over a three-hour period inside the crater of Stromboli. The range and rapidity of changes were amazing: CO_2 went from 0 to 25 per cent in less than 3 minutes, H_2O from 0 to 45 per cent in a similar period. This appears to diminish the value of the almost isolated analyses obtained previously by conventional methods.

Gravity and magnetism

Movements of lava at depth cause slight changes in local gravity and magnetic fields, and so measurements of these effects may give some way of predicting possible eruption. At present such measurements are not very much used, perhaps because they are not sufficiently sensitive indicators. The potential value of magnetometric work is discussed by Bernstein (1960).

Regular behaviour of volcanoes

If some pattern could be found in the times of eruption of a volcano, if some rhythm or cyclical behaviour could be demonstrated, then prediction would be very much easier. There have been many attempts at finding periodicity, varying from wild numerology to serious scientific attempts, and also efforts to link volcanic activity with other events such as sunspots or phases of the moon.

Jaggar (1931) believed that Hawaiian eruptions exhibited 11- and 132-year cycles, corresponding with sunspot cycles. However, Stearns and Macdonald (1946) found no support for this claim, and maintain that 150 years of observations are not enough for such speculation.

Mt Etna has a fairly regular pattern within individual eruptions. Each starts with a fracture on the flank. Lava flows out at the bottom and a scoria cone is built up at the top. Succeeding eruptions occur at higher and higher spots along the rift until the fracture is sealed. Imbo (1928) has suggested that the periodicity involves cycles with eruptions at fairly regular intervals:

> 1755-1809 a 54-year cycle with 9-year intervals
> 1809-1865 a 56-year cycle with 6-year intervals
> 1865-1908 a 43-year cycle with 7-year intervals

We are now supposed to be in a cycle with 7-year intervals. Each new cycle starts on a new fissure.

Vesuvius has the best long-term records of any volcano. Even from early days the dates of eruption are known because of the strange fact that the relics of St Januarius were paraded at eruption time to quell the activity. No kind of mathematical periodicity fits all the events, but a rough general sequence of events can be made out as follows:

Period of repose	average 7 years
Explosions build cinder cones on the crater floor	average 30 years
Crater fills with lava and may overflow	
Earthquakes, explosions, cone splits and great floods of lava erupt	average a few weeks
Gas 'blow off'—a continuous emission of high pressure gas	average a few hours

The last great eruption of Vesuvius was in 1944 when the towns of Massa and San Sebastian were destroyed. Since then the volcano has been quiet, and eruption appears long overdue. Whatever one may think of the scientific value or otherwise of the search for periodicity it is hard not to be somewhat alarmed, and fear that the next eruption will be particularly violent.

WHAT TO DO WHEN A VOLCANO ERUPTS

Vulcanologists spend a lot of time trying to predict eruptions. When an eruption seems imminent evacuation will usually be advised. Little can be done to save property, but many lives may be saved. Thus in the 1914 eruption of Sakurajima, Japan, seven out of eighteen villages were destroyed on the island, property damage was estimated at $19,000,000 and nearly 25 km² were covered by new lava, but no lives were lost and an estimated 15,000 people were evacuated from within the death radius of the volcano (Wilcoxson, 1967). When eruption actually occurs instrumental observations become secondary to direct observations, and the vulcanologists' work changes from prediction to actively warning people of possible dangers from flow, explosions, and ashfall (taking into account the effect of wind), and drainage diversion and flooding. Let us consider these aspects a little further.

Flows

Flows usually move sufficiently slowly for people to get out of their way. It may be possible to move to higher ground, making sure not to be surrounded by lava and possibly engulfed. It is normally better to get right away. Although people generally escape from flows, their homes and farms cannot be moved and will generally be destroyed. However, if natural and political circumstances permit, it may be possible to prevent such destruction.

The 1669 flow of Mt Etna threatened the town of Catania. A man called Pappalardo, deservedly a hero of vulcanology, took fifty men to divert the flow. Covered with wet skins to protect them from the heat and armed with iron bars they breached the skin and diverted part of the lava at least, so that the main flow slowed down. Unfortunately the diverted lava headed for the town of Paterno, and five hundred Paterno citizens drove off the Catanians. The flow then destroyed a large part of Catania.

In Hawaii Jaggar organised the bombing of flows during eruptions in 1935 and 1942. By making extra breaches the lava spread out laterally and eventually stopped. In this sort of experiment it can always be argued that the flow would have stopped anyway, but at least the bombing may have helped. In 1955 Macdonald had low walls built that proved sufficient to divert flows, and thus saved large areas of plantations. Bombing and diversion are only useful if there is sufficient waste land to receive the lava. If a flow is advancing across valuable land this policy is no use, and then dams may be built to prevent its spread, as reported by Macdonald (1962) from Hawaii. In January 1960 eruption in the eastern rift zone, 40 km east of Kilauea caldera, produced 113 m³ of lava covering 5-6 km². A number of walls were built, several hundred metres long, 5 m high and 20 m wide. These were not diversions but simply dams impounding the lava. In fact lava overflowed the dams, but it is thought that it was sufficiently slowed down to justify the dam construction. It was found that such walls need to be heavy and broad-based to withstand the thrust of lava flows, and that overflow causes erosion of the walls.

On strato-volcanoes, flows run down radial valleys, and may possibly be diverted into neighbouring valleys of less value. The 1929 Vesuvius flow could have been diverted into earlier lava fields where no harm would be done, but military authorities refused to allow it. Villages in the main Vallone Valley were therefore evacuated and were extensively damaged.

Explosions, pyroclastics, and gas

Pyroclastic eruptions are very hard to deal with, and early evacuation is the best policy, especially if there is any danger of pyroclastic flows. Once a nuée ardente erupts there is nothing, absolutely nothing, that can be done except to look for possible survivors around the edge of the flow.

In the town of St Pierre, prior to the eruption of Mont Pelée, many people were quite anxious to evacuate, for there were plenty of warning signs. Horses were dropping dead in the street, dead birds fell from the sky, a fine ash covered the city, there were muted sounds, the air was sulphurous, and an incandescent mass could be seen rising in the volcano. However, the Governor was anxious that people stay for the elections to be held on 10 May.

On 6 May troops were stationed to prevent people leaving town.

On 7 May Professor Landes of the Lycée opined in the local newspaper that 'The Montagne Pelée presents no more danger to the inhabitants of Saint-Pierre than does Vesuvius to those of Naples'.

On 8 May at 7.30 a.m. four great explosions came from Pelée, one of which shot laterally to St Pierre. The town clock stopped at 7.32, when the town's 30,000 people were killed.

In quiet ash falls evacuation is still the best policy. If this is impossible light protection should be sought—during the eruption of 4 April 1906 Neapolitans went about with umbrellas to keep off the rain of volcanic sand. It may even be possible to spend some time shovelling ash from the roofs of houses. It is probably not a good idea to go to church for shelter or prayer. During the 1906 eruption of Vesuvius villagers of San Giuseppe assembled in church for refuge, but the weight of ash on the roof caused the building to collapse, and 105 people were killed.

It must not be forgotten that even quiet eruptions can do a lot of damage. The volcano Irazu is only 30 km from San José, capital of Costa Rica, with a quarter of a million inhabitants. Eruptions of ash and gas between 1963 and 1965 were not fatal, but were nevertheless a great nuisance to everyday life and many crops and much good land were ruined. Losses were estimated at $150,000,000.

Santiago, Nicaragua, was a quiet volcano in the solfataric stage, but the fumes did a great deal of damage, estimated at $10,000,000 between 1946 and 1951. Many solutions were considered for stopping or ameliorating the nuisance, but in 1953 the emissions fortunately stopped of their own accord.

Pyroclastic eruption can produce total darkness, and artificial light is of little help. If people were aware of this possibility it might at least prevent some panic, which is an incidental danger in all eruptions. In the 1835 eruption of Coseguina, Nicaragua, the tremendous noise and ashfall was taken to indicate the coming of Judgement Day, and 'the terror of the inhabitants of Aloncho was so great, that three hundred of those who lived in a state of concubinage were married at once' (Galindo, 1835, quoted in Wilcoxson (1967), p. 320).

Floods and lahars

Drainage diversions can be a great danger. The commonest kind is the sudden displacement of a crater lake, producing a lahar, either hot or cold, which flows in very mobile fashion though carrying large boulders. Lahars are fairly common on strato-volcanoes. Attempts may be made to divert them by walls, but little success has been achieved by such structures. Furthermore, there is not sufficient warning for most lahars. A known lahar path ought not to be inhabited, though in many instances it is.

In Kelut, Indonesia, which has a long history of lahar eruptions, massive walls were built, 3 m high, but proved useless against lahars. Later the crater lake was drained by tunnels and the next eruption caused significantly less damage than usual. However, this eruption destroyed the tunnels. A new set of 'seepage pipes' was constructed which, while not actually reaching the crater, would drain it if the rock were permeable. However, Zen (1965) reported that the pipes had failed to drain the lake, so lahars are again a potential danger.

In Iceland the Jokulhlaup, produced when sub-ice volcanoes melt great quantities of water, causes total devastation, but fortunately of uninhabited areas.

Secondary effects of an eruption may present serious problems to inhabitants, and to some extent modify landforms. The increased runoff caused by the destruction of vegetation can cause flooding, rapid erosion, and silting up of stream beds.

G. A. M. Taylor has described how such flooding after the disastrous 1951 eruption of Mt Lamington, Papua, caused some loss of equipment and necessitated removal of one of the evacuation camps. Mudflows frequently descended the mountain as roaring torrents, disrupting communications, and at river crossings a permanent labour force was needed to remove the debris left by daily flash floods.

In case this parade of disasters should be too depressing, we might briefly try to see volcanic damage in perspective. In the past 500 years volcanoes have probably killed, directly or indirectly, over 200,000 people, of whom about half died in the eruptions of Tamboro, Krakatoa, and Mont Pelée. This toll is in fact very low when compared with those of earthquakes, floods, wars, or road accidents.

On the credit side volcanoes produce fertile land, energy and materials for industry, and a livelihood for many people in the tourist trade. Even when activity has long ceased, most volcanic regions retain a great natural beauty, and frequently display most spectacular scenery. Such areas are often tourist attractions, and a large number of National Parks are located on volcanic centres. On balance, volcanoes do more good than harm.

BIBLIOGRAPHY

The scientific literature on volcanoes is scattered in a wide range of journals and books. The main journal devoted to volcanic studies is the *Bulletin Volcanologique*, published in Italy. The *Catalogue of the Active Volcanoes of the World*, published by the International Association of Volcanology, consists of a number of volumes, each devoted to a particular area, in which brief accounts of all volcanoes regarded as active are catalogued and described. Other work is published in various journals of geology, geophysics, and geography. Most work on volcanoes appears to concern vulcanology and petrology, with smaller amounts on geophysics and geochemistry and very little on geomorphology. Such articles as are published on geomorphology may be traced through the relevant section of *Geographical Abstracts (A) Geomorphology*, published by K. M. Clayton (University of East Anglia, Norwich, England). The *Bibliography of (North American) Geology* and the *Bibliography and Index of Geology Exclusive of North America*, both published by the Geological Society of America, contain many abstracts of papers on volcanoes, and appear as annual volumes.

The only book mainly concerned with the geomorphology of volcanoes is that by Cotton (1944). Wilcoxson (1967) recounts many human interest stories of eruptions in a book which is at once popular and technically accurate. Rittmann's book (1962) is a standard reference on volcanoes, though less concerned with landforms than with fundamental mechanisms. Bullard (1962a) is especially concerned with a number of selected eruptions, but also presents a broad account of the subject. Of general geology books that deal with volcanoes that of Holmes (1965) is outstanding. Tazieff's book (1962) is perhaps the best of the highly illustrated artistic books on volcanoes.

Glossaries of Definitions and Geological Terms

American Geological Institute. 1957. *Glossary of Geology and Related Sciences*. NAS-NRC Pub. 501.

————— 1962. *Dictionary of Geological Terms*. Dolphin Books, New York. An abridged version of the above glossary.

Baulig, H. 1956. *Vocabulaire Franco-Anglo-Allemand de Géomorphologie*. Colin, Paris.

Challinor, J. 1962. *A Dictionary of Geology*. University of Wales, Cardiff.

Rice, C. M. 1941. *Dictionary of Geological Terms*. Edwards, Ann Arbor.

Schieferdecker, A. A. A. G. (ed.). 1959. *Geological Nomenclature*. Royal Geological and Mining Society of the Netherlands.

Stamp, L. D. (ed.). 1961. *A Glossary of Geographical Terms*. Longmans, London.

Stokes, W. L. and Varnes, D. J. 1955. Glossary of Selected Geologic Terms. *Colorado Scientific Society Proceedings*, Vol. 16. Denver.

164   *Bibliography*

The following books and papers are referred to in the text:

Adamson, C. L. 1969. Crushed stone and gravel resources of the Sydney region. *Rec. geol. Surv. N.S.W.* **11**. In press.

Aramaki, S. 1961. Classification of pyroclastic flows. *Int. Geol. Rev.* **3**, 518-24.

—— and Yamasaki, M. 1963. Pyroclastic flows in Japan. *Bull. volcan.* **26**, 89-99.

Baker, P. E. and Harris, P. G. 1963. Lava channels on Tristan da Cunha. *Geol. Mag.* **100**, 345-51.

Bemmelen, R. W. van. 1930. The volcano-tectonic origin of Lake Toba (North Sumatra). *Proc. Pacif. Sci. Congr.* **2**, 115-24.

Benson, W. N. and Turner, F. J. 1940. Mugearites in the Dunedin District. *Trans R. Soc. N.Z.* **70**, 188-99.

Bernstein, V. A. 1960. On magnetometric investigations in vicinity of volcanoes. *Bull. volcan.* **23**, 129-33.

Björnsson, S. (ed.). 1967. *Iceland and Mid-ocean Ridges.* Report of a symposium. Leiftur, Reykjavík.

Blackburn, G. 1966. Carbon date of Mt Gambier. *Radiocarbon* **8**, 61.

Blong, R. J. 1966. Discontinuous gullies on the volcanic plateau. *J. Hydrol. (N.Z.)* **5**, 87-99.

Blot, C. 1964. Origine profonde des séismes superficiels et des éruptions volcaniques. *Bur. Central seismol. Intern.* **A23**, 103-21.

Bordet, P. 1965. Nomenclature volcanologique. *Bull. volcan.* **28**, 151-7.

Bout, P., Derruau, M., and Fel, A. 1960. The use of volcanic cones and lava flows in the Massif Central to measure the recession of slopes in crystalline rocks. *Z. Geomorph.* **Supp. 1**, 140-55.

Boutakoff, N. 1963. The geology and geomorphology of the Portland area. *Mem. geol. Surv. Vict.* **22**.

Bozon, P. 1963. Contribution to the study of volcanic landforms in the Ardèche. *Revue Géog. alp.* **51**, 591-647.

Branch, C. D. 1963. The emplacement of acid magma in the epizone, and the relationship with ignimbrites, North Queensland, Australia. *Bull. volcan.* **25**, 47-60.

—— 1966. Volcanic cauldrons, ring complexes and associated granites in the Georgetown Inlier, Queensland. *Bull. Bur. Miner. Resour. Geol. Geophys. Aust.* **76**.

Breed, W. J. 1964. Morphology and lineation of cinder cones in the San Franciscan volcanic field. *Museum of Northern Arizona Bulletin* No. 40, 65-71.

Brown, M. C. 1962. Discussion—nuées ardentes and fluidization. *Am. J. Sci.* **260**, 467-70.

Browne, W. R. 1933. An account of post-Palaeozoic igneous activity in New South Wales. *J. Proc. R. Soc. N.S.W.* **67**, 9-95.

Bucher, W. M. 1933. Cryptovolcanic structures in the United States. *Proc. Int. geol. Congr.* 16. **2**, 1055-84.

Bullard, E., Everett, J. E., and Smith, A. G. 1965. The fit of the continents around the Atlantic. *Phil. Trans. R. Soc.* **1088**, 41-51.

Bullard, F. M. 1962a. *Volcanoes; in History, in Theory, in Eruption.* Nelson, Edinburgh.

—— 1962b. Volcanoes of Southern Peru. *Bull. volcan.* **24**, 443-53.

Carey, S. W. 1958a. Note on the columnar jointing in Tasmanian Dolerite. *Dolerite Symposium.* University of Tasmania, Hobart, 229-30.

—— 1958b. The isostrat, a new technique for the analysis of the structure of the Tasmanian dolerite. *Dolerite Symposium.* University of Tasmania, Hobart.

—— 1958c. The tectonic approach to continental drift. *Continental Drift: a symposium.* University of Tasmania, Hobart, 177-355.

Carne, J. E. 1903. The kerosene shale deposits. N.S.W. Geological Survey, *Mem. Geol. Surv.* No. 3, 236-40.

—— 1908. Geology and mineral resources of the Western Coalfield. N.S.W. Geological Survey, *Mem. Geol. Surv.* No. 6.

Chubb, L. J. 1957. The pattern of some Pacific Island chains. *Geol. Mag.* **94**, 221-8.

Colton, H. S. 1930. Lava squeeze-ups. *Volc. Lett. Hawaii Volc. Res. Ass.* **300**, 3.

Cook, E. F. 1966. Paleovolcanology. *Earth Sci. Rev.* **1**, 155-74.

Cook, P. J. 1968. The Gosses Bluff cryptoexplosion structure. *J. Geol.* **76**, 123-39.

Coombs, H. A. 1936. The geology of Mount Rainier National Park. *Univ. Washington Publ. Geol.* **3**, No. 2, 131-212.

Cotton, C. A. 1944. *Volcanoes as Landscape Forms.* Whitcombe and Tombs, Christchurch.

—— 1962. The volcano tectonic theory of block faulting no longer tenable. *N.Z. Sci. Rev.* **20**, 48-9.

Coulson, A. 1953. The volcanic rocks of the Daylesford district. *Proc. R. Soc. Vict.* **65**, 113-24.

Cucuzza-Silvestri, S. 1963. Proposal for a genetic classification of hyaloclastites. *Bull. volcan.* **25**, 315-21.

Davies, K. A. 1952. The building of Mount Elgon. *Mem. geol. Surv. Uganda* **7**.

Dawson, J. B. 1962. The geology of Oldoinyo Lengai. *Bull. volcan.* **24**, 349-87.

—— 1964. Carbonatitic volcanic ashes in Northern Tanganyika. *Bull. volcan.* **27**, 81-91.

Decker, R. W., Hill, D. P., and Wright, T. L. 1966. Deformation measurements on Kilauea volcano, Hawaii. *Bull. volcan.* **29**, 721-30.

Downie, C. 1964. Glaciations of Mount Kilimanjaro, northeast Tanganyika. *Bull. geol. Soc. Am.* **75**, 1-16.

—— and Wilkinson, P. 1962. The explosion craters of Basotu, Tanganyika Territory. *Bull. volcan.* **24**, 389-420.

Dulhunty, J. A. 1967. Mesozoic alkaline volcanism and Garrawilla lavas near Mullaley, New South Wales. *J. geol. Soc. Aust.* **14**, 133-8.

Edwards, A. B. 1941. The crinanite laccolith of Circular Head, Tasmania. *Proc. R. Soc. Vict.* **53**, 403-15.

Finch, R. H. 1933. Block lava. *J. Geol.* **41**, 769-70.

Fisher, R. V. 1966. Rocks composed of volcanic fragments and their classification. *Earth Sci. Rev.* **1**, 287-98.

Fitch, F. 1964. The development of the Beerenberg Volcano, Jan Mayen. *Proc. Geol. Ass.* **75**, 133-65.

Galloway, R. W. 1967. Pre-basalt, sub-basalt, and post-basalt surfaces of the Hunter Valley, New South Wales. Ch. 13 in *Landform Studies from Australia and New Guinea*, ed. J. N. Jennings and J. A. Mabbutt. Australian National University Press, Canberra.

Gèze, B. 1964. Sur la classification des dynamismes volcaniques. *Bull. volcan.* **27**, 237-57.

Gibbs, H. S. and Wells, N. 1966. Volcanic ash soils in New Zealand. *Bull. volcan.* **29**, 669-70.

Griggs, R. F. 1921. Our greatest national monument. *Natn. geogr. Mag.* **40**, 219-92.

Grindley, G. W. 1965. Wairakei geothermal field, Taupo. N.Z. Dept Sci. & Ind. Res. *Geol. Survey Bull.* **75**.

Hay, R. L. 1960. Rate of clay formation and mineral alteration in a 4000-year-old volcanic ash soil on St. Vincent, B.W.I. *Am. J. Sci.* **258**, 354-68.

Holmes, A. 1965. *Principles of Physical Geology.* Nelson, London.

Hotz, P. E. 1952. Form of diabase sheets in southeastern Pennsylvania. *Am. J. Sci.* **250**, 375-88.

Hunt, C. B. 1938. A suggested explanation for the curvature of columnar joints in volcanic necks. *Am. J. Sci.* **236**, 142-9.

Imbo, G. 1928. Variazioni cicliche nella successione dei periodi di riposo etnei. *Bull. volcan.* Nos. 15-18.

Iwasaki, I., Ozawa, T., and Yoshida, M. 1966. Differentiation of volcanic emanation around the boiling point of water in geothermal regions. *Bull. volcan.* **29**, 517-27.

Jaggar, T. A. 1931. Volcanic cycles and sunspots. *Volcano Letter*, No. 326.

Jensen, H. I. 1909. Notes on the geology of the Mt. Flinders and Fassifern districts, Queensland. *Proc. Linn. Soc. N.S.W.* **34**, 67-104.

Kaizuka, S. 1965. Some problems of tephrochronology in Japan. *VII Conf. int. Ass. Quatern. Res. Boulder Abstracts.*

Karapetian, K. I. 1964. Some regularities in areal volcanism. *Bull. volcan.* **27**, 381-3.

Kear, D. 1957. Erosional stages of volcanic cones as indicators of age. *N.Z. J. Sci. Technol.* **B.38**, 671-82.

—— 1964. Volcanic alignments north and west of New Zealand's central volcanic regions. *N.Z. Jl Geol. Geophys.* **7**, 24-44.

Kennedy, W. Q. and Richey, J. E. 1947. Catalogue of the active volcanoes of the world. *Bull. volcan. Supp.* Ser. II, **Tome VII.**

King, B. C. 1949. The Napak area of southern Karamoja, Uganda. *Mem. geol. Surv. Uganda* **5**.

Kjartansson, G. 1966. Sur la récession glaciaire et les types volcaniques dans la région du Kjölur sur le plateau centrale de l'Islande. *Revue Géomorph. dyn.* **16**, 23-39.

Kuno, H. *et al.* 1964. Sorting of pumice and lithic fragments as a key to eruptive and emplacement mechanism. *Jap. J. Geol. Geogr.* **35**, 223-38.

Lewis, J. F. 1968. Tauhara volcano, Taupo Zone. I Geology and Structure. *N.Z. Jl Geol. Geophys.* **11**, 212-24.

Lipman, P. W. 1967. Mineral and chemical variations within an ash-flow sheet from Aso Caldera, southwestern Japan. *Contr. Mineral Petrol.* **16**, 300-27.

McBirney, A. R. 1963. Factors governing the nature of submarine volcanism. *Bull. volcan.* **26**, 455-69.

—— and Williams, H. 1965. Volcanic history of Nicaragua. *Univ. Calif. Publs. geol. Sci.* **55**, 1-65.

McCall, G. J. H. 1963. Classification of calderas—Krakatoan and Glencoe types. *Nature, Lond.* **197**, 136-8.

—— and Bristow, C. M. 1965. An introductory account of Suswa Volcano, Kenya. *Bull. volcan.* **28**, 333-67.

McCraw, J. D. 1967. The surface features and soil pattern of the Hamilton Basin. *Earth Sci. J.* **1**, 59-74.

Macdonald, G. A. 1953. Pahoehoe, aa, and block lava. *Am. J. Sci.* **251**, 169-91.

—— 1962. The 1959 and 1960 eruptions of Kilauea volcano, Hawaii, and the construction of walls to restrict the spread of lava flows. *Bull. volcan.* **24**, 249-94.

—— 1967. Forms and structures of extrusive basaltic rocks. In *Basalts*, ed. H. H. Hess and A. Poldervaart. Wiley, New York, 1-61.

McDougall, I. 1969. Potassium argon dates from Victoria. In press.

——, Allsop, H. L., and Chamalaun, F. H. 1966. Isotopic dating of the Newer Volcanics of Victoria, Australia, and geomagnetic polarity epochs. *J. geophys. Res.* **71**, 6107-18.

McTaggart, K. C. 1962. Nuées ardentes and fluidization—a reply. *Am. J. Sci.* **260**, 470-6.

Markhinin, E. K. 1962. On the possibility of estimating the amount of juvenile water participating in volcanic explosions. *Bull. volcan.* **24**, 187-91.

Marshall, B. 1967. Kink bands and other syn-depositional structures in Recent tuffs at Tower Hill, Victoria. *ANZAAS 39th Congress*, Section C (abstract).

Mathews, W. H. 1947. 'Tuyas', flat-topped volcanoes in North British Columbia. *Am. J. Sci.* **245**, 560-70.

Meinzer, O. E. (ed.). 1949. *Hydrology.* Dover, New York.

Menard, H. W. 1964. *Marine Geology of the Pacific.* McGraw-Hill, New York.

Moore, J. G. 1967. Base surge in recent volcanic eruptions. *Bull. volcan.* **30**, 337-63.

———, Nakamura, K., and Alcarez, A. 1966. The 1965 eruption of Taal volcano. *Science, N.Y.* **151**, 955-60.

Morimoto, R. and Ossaka, J. 1964. Low temperature mud-explosion of Mt. Yaké. *Bull. volcan.* **27**, 49-50.

Murai, I. 1961. A study of the textural characteristics of pyroclastic flow deposits in Japan. *Bull. Earthq. Res. Inst. Tokyo Univ.* **39**, 133-254.

Murata, K. J., Dondol, C., and Saenz, R. 1966. The 1963-65 eruption of Irazú volcano, Costa Rica. *Bull. volcan.* **29**, 765-93.

Naum, T. R. *et al.* 1962. Volcanic karst in the Caliman Massif, Eastern Carpathians. *Anal. Univ. Bucuresti. Ser. Stiint. Nat. Geol. Geog.* **32**, 143-79.

Neumann van Padang, M. 1963. The temperatures in the crater region of some Indonesian volcanoes before the eruption. *Bull. volcan.* **26**, 319-36.

Nichols, R. L. 1936. Flow units in basalt. *J. Geol.* **44**, 617-30.

——— 1939. Squeeze-ups. *J. Geol.* **47**, 421-5.

Ninkovich, D., and Heezen, B. C. 1965. Santorini tephra. *Submarine Geology and Geophysics*, ed. W. F. Whittard and R. Bradshaw. Butterworths, London, pp. 413-52.

Noguchi, K., and Kamiya, H. 1963. Prediction of volcanic eruption by measuring the chemical composition and amounts of gas. *Bull. volcan.* **26**, 367-78.

Ōba, Y. 1966. Geology and petrology of Usu volcano, Hokkaido, Japan. *J. Fac. Sci. Hokkaido Univ.*, Ser. IV, **13**, 185-236.

Ollier, C. D. 1964a. Tumuli and lava blisters of Victoria, Australia. *Nature, Lond.* **202**, 1284-6.

——— 1964b. Caves and related features of Mount Eccles. *Victorian Nat.* **81**, 64-71.

——— 1967a. Landforms of the Newer Volcanic Province of Victoria. Ch. 14 in *Landform Studies from Australia and New Guinea*, ed. J. N. Jennings and J. A. Mabbutt. A.N.U. Press, Canberra.

——— 1967b. Maars. Their characteristics, varieties and definition. *Bull. volcan.* **31**, 45-73.

——— and Brown, M. C. 1965. Lava caves of Victoria. *Bull. volcan.* **28**, 215-30.

——— and Brown, M. J. F. Erosion of a young volcano in New Guinea. *Z. Geomorph.* In press.

——— and Joyce, E. B. 1964. Volcanic physiography of the western plains of Victoria. *Proc. R. Soc. Vict.* **77**, 357-76.

O'Shea, B. E. 1954. Ruapehu and the Tangiwai disaster. *N.Z. Jl Sci. Technol.* **B36**, 174-89.

Prider, R. T. 1960. The leucite lamproites of the Fitzroy Basin, Western Australia. *J. geol. Soc. Aust.* **6**, 71-118.

Pullar, W. A. 1967. Uses of volcanic ash beds in geomorphology. *Earth Sci. J.*
    1, 164-77.

Raggatt, H. G. 1929. Notes on the structural and tectonic geology of the Hunter
    Valley between Scone and Muswellbrook, with special reference to the
    age of the diastrophism. *Proc. Linn. Soc. N.S.W.* **54**, 273-82.

————, Owen, H. B., and Hills, E. S. 1945. The bauxite deposits of the Boolara-
    Mirboo North area, South Gippsland, Victoria. *Comm. Australia Dept.
    Supply Shipping Min. Res. Bull.* **14**.

Re, M. D. 1963. Hyaloclastites and pillow lavas of Acicastello (Mt. Etna).
    Bull. volcan. **25**, 281-4.

Reck, H. 1915. Physiographische Studie über vulkanische Bomben. *Z. vulk.*
    Ergänzungsband, 1914-1915, **1**, 124.

Richards, A. F. 1965. Geology of the Islas Revillagigedo, 3. Effects of Erosion
    on Isla San Benedicto 1952-61 following the birth of Volcan Barcena.
    Bull. volcan. **28**, 381-403.

Rittmann, A. 1962. *Volcanoes and their Activity*, tr. E. A. Vincent. Interscience,
    New York.

Ruxton, B. P. 1968. Rates of weathering of Quaternary volcanic ash in north-
    east Papua. *Int. Congr. Soil Sci., Trans. 9th*, Adelaide, **4**, 367-76.

———— and McDougall, I. 1967. Denudation rates in northeast Papua from
    potassium-argon dating of lavas. *Am. J. Sci.* **265**, 545-61.

Saggerson, E. P. 1963. Geology of the Simba-Kibwezi area. *Geol. Surv. Kenya.*
    Report No. 58.

Searle, E. J. 1964. *City of Volcanoes*. Paul, Auckland.

Selby, M. J. 1966. Soil erosion on the pumice lands of the central North Island.
    N.Z. Geogr. **22**, 194-6.

Shand, S. J. 1938. *Earth Lore*. Dutton, New York.

Skeats, E. W. and James, A. V. G. 1937. Basaltic barriers and other surface
    features of the Newer Basalts of Western Victoria. *Proc. R. Soc. Vict.* **49**,
    245-78.

Spry, A. 1962. The origin of columnar jointing, particularly in basalt flows.
    J. geol. Soc. Aust. **8**, 191-216.

———— and Banks, M. R. 1962. The geology of Tasmania. *J. geol. Soc. Aust.* **9**,
    107-362.

Standard, J. C. 1961. Submarine geology of the Tasman Sea. *Bull. geol. Soc.
    Am.* **72**, 1777-88.

Stearns, H. T. 1926. Volcanism in the Mud Lake area, Idaho. *Am. J. Sci.*
    211, 353-63.

———— 1935. Geology and ground-water resources of the island of Oahu,
    Hawaii. *Hawaii Div. Hydrog. Bull.* **1**, 479 pp.

———— 1949. Hydrology of volcanic terranes. Ch. 15 in *Hydrology*, ed. O.
    E. Meinzer. Dover, New York.

———— 1966. *Geology of the State of Hawaii*. Panin Books, Palo Alto,
    California.

———— and Macdonald, G. A. 1946. Geology and ground-water resources of
    the island of Hawaii. *Hawaii Div. Hydrog. Bull.* **9**.

Stephenson, P. J. *et al.* 1967. The Ambrym Island Research Project (New
    Hebrides). *ANZAAS 39th Congress*, Section C (abstract).

————, Stevens, N. C. and Tweedale, G. W. 1960. Geology of Queensland.
    Lower Cainozoic igneous rocks, ed. D. Hill and A. K. Denmead. *Geol.
    Soc. Aust. J.* **7**, 355-69.

Stevens, N. C. 1958. Ring-structures of the Mt. Alford district south-east Queensland. *Geol. Soc. Aust. J.* **6**, 37-49.

—— 1962. Upper Cainozoic volcanism near Gayndah, Queensland. *Proc. R. Soc. Qd* **62**, 75-82.

Stipp, J. J. and McDougall, I. 1969. Geochronology of the Banks Peninsula volcanoes, New Zealand. *N.Z. Jl Geol. Geophys.* **11**, 1239-60.

Sutherland, F. L. 1966. The Tertiary volcanics of the Tamar Valley, Northern Tasmania—a preliminary report. *Aust. J. Sci.* **29**, 114-15.

Tazieff, H. 1962. *Volcanoes.* Prentice-Hall International, London.

—— and Tonani, F. 1963. Fluctuations rapides et importantes de la phase gazeuse éruptive. *C.r. hebd. Séanc. Acad. Sci., Paris* **257**, 3985-7.

Thorarinsson, S. 1956. *Hekla on Fire.* Hanns Reich, Munich.

—— 1967. *The Eruption of Hekla, 1947-1948.* Vol. 1 of *The Eruptions of Hekla in Historical Times: a Tephrochronological Study.* Leiftur, Reykjavík.

Tricart, J. *et al.* 1962. Note sur quelques aspects géomorphologiques de la Fôret de Pierre de Huaron (Andes Centrales Péruviennes). *Revue Géomorph. dyn.* **13**, 125-9.

—— 1965. Geomorphology and underground water of the Santiago Basin, Chile. *Bull. Fac. Lettres Strasbourg.* TILAS, **43**, 605-74.

Tsuya, H. and Morimoto, R. 1963. Types of volcanic eruptions in Japan. *Bull. volcan.* **26**, 209-22.

Upton, B. G. J. and Wadsworth, W. J. 1966. The basalts of Réunion Island, Indian Ocean. *Bull. volcan.* **29**, 7-23.

Walker, F. 1958. Recent work on the form of dolerite intrusions in sedimentary terrains. *Dolerite Symposium*, University of Tasmania, Hobart, 88-92.

Warden, A. J. 1967. The 1963-65 eruption of Lopevi volcano (New Hebrides). *Bull. volcan.* **30**, 277-318.

Waring, G. A., Blankenship, R. R., and Bentall, R. 1965. Thermal springs of the United States and other countries of the world—a summary. *Prof. Pap. U.S. geol. Surv.* **492**, 1-383.

Wentworth, C. K. 1943. Soil avalanches on Oahu, Hawaii. *Bull. geol. Soc. Am.* **53**, 53-64.

—— 1954. The physical behaviour of basaltic lava flows. *J. Geol.* **62**, 425-38.

—— and Macdonald, G. A. 1953. Structures and forms of basaltic rocks in Hawaii. *Bull. U.S. geol. Surv.* **994**, 98.

Wilcoxson, K. 1967. *Volcanoes.* Cassell, London.

Williams, H. 1936. Pliocene volcanoes of the Navajo-Hopi country. *Bull. geol. Soc. Am.* **47**, 111-71.

—— 1941. Calderas and their origin. *Univ. Calif. Publs geol. Sci.* **25**, 239-346.

—— 1952. The great eruption of Coseguino, Nicaragua, in 1835. *Univ. Calif. Publs geol. Sci.* **29**, 21-46.

—— 1960. Volcanic collapse basins of Lakes Atitlan and Ayarza, Guatemala. *Int. geol. Congr. 21*, Part 21, 110-18.

—— and McBirney, A. R. 1964. Petrological and structural contrast of the Quaternary volcanoes of Guatemala. *Bull. volcan.* **27**, 61.

——, Turner, F. J., and Gilbert, C. M. 1954. *Petrography.* Freeman, San Francisco.

Wilshire, H. G. and Standard, J. C. 1963. The history of vulcanism in the Mullaley District, New South Wales. *J. Proc. R. Soc. N.S.W.* **96**, 123-8.

Wilson, J. T. 1963. Evidence from islands on the spreading of ocean floors. *Nature, Lond.* **197**, 536-8.

Wright, J. B. 1967. Contributions to the volcanic succession and petrology of the Auckland Islands. II. Upper parts of the Ross Volcano. *Trans. R. Soc. N.Z. (Geol.)* **5**, 71-87.

Zen, M. T. 1965. The future danger of Mt. Kelut. *Bull. volcan.* **28**, 275-82.

INDEX

(Bold figures indicate plate numbers)

171

ABOUT THE AUTHOR

Cliff Ollier is a graduate of Bristol University. After working as a soil scientist in Uganda and as a geomorphologist in the Geology Department, University of Melbourne, he became Senior Lecturer in Earth Science at the University of Papua and New Guinea. He is now Principal Lecturer in Geology at the Canberra College of Advanced Education. He has visited volcanoes, lava fields, and volcano observatories in Europe, U.S.A., East Africa, Madagascar and Mauritius, Australia, New Zealand, New Guinea and several other Pacific islands, and has worked on several aspects of volcanic geomorphology, especially maars, lava caves, and the weathering and erosion of volcanoes.

This book is set in 10/12 Times New Roman and printed on 85 gsm English Finish paper by Simmons Limited, Glebe, N.S.W., Australia